Choosing Canada's Capital: Jealousy and Friction in the Nineteenth Century

David B. Knight

The Carleton Library No. 105

Published by McClelland and Stewart Limited
in association with The Institute of
Canadian Studies, Carleton University

© *1977 McClelland and Stewart Limited*

ALL RIGHTS RESERVED.

ISBN: 0-7710-9803-0

The Canadian Publishers
McClelland and Stewart Limited
25 Hollinger Road, Toronto

Printed and bound in Canada

To
JANET
KAREN
and
ANDREW

TABLE OF CONTENTS

LIST OF MAPS

LIST OF TABLES

ABBREVIATIONS

LC   Lower Canada

UC   Upper Canada

CW   Canada West

CE   Canada East

RA   Royal Archives, Windsor Castle

PAC   Public Archives of Canada

PRO   Public Record Office

CO   Colonial Office

RG   Record Group

MG   Manuscript Group

EC   Executive Council

JLA   Journal of the Legislative Assembly

JLC   Journal of the Legislative Council

PREFACE

The purpose of this volume is to make readily available a selective compilation of materials relating to the seat of government issue as it developed in the Province of Canada, with special focus on the years 1840-1844, 1849-1859. Taken individually, many of the items incisively reveal something of the tensions that existed in the united Province. Taken as a whole, the documents reveal how these tensions came together on the divisive issue of capital city location.

An introduction preceeds the documents, which are arranged in chapters. The documents sections include exerpts from the official and private correspondence of Queen Victoria, her husband, and his secretary, Colonial authorities in London and Canada, and Canadians in private and public life. Some emphasis is given to the correspondence between the Colonial Secretaries and the Governors General. Several key documents that were privately published by the Colonial Office in 1857 are included, as are important Canadian Government documents that relate to earlier phases of the issue. Also included are excerpts from newspapers. Some of the newspaper materials included are informational, but most are illustrative of different kinds of biases that became entwined in the divisive issue. Many items are printed in full as they were in their original form. Other items are extracts from lengthier documents. For letters, formal introductions and conclusions ("Sir ... Yours very sincerely," etc.) have been omitted, as have sections not pertaining to the seat of government question.

Parliamentary proceedings are not given special emphasis in the document sections of this volume, even though the Legislative Assembly and the Legislative Council were important forums for discussion and decision making. A separate volume could be filled with just the numerous and often lengthy motions (and withdrawn motions) and amendments concerning the capital issue, and divisions on them. Also, if presented in full, speeches pertaining to the seat of government question that were made in the two Parliamentary chambers would fill several additional volumes. Consequently, only a few suggestive extracts have been culled from the hundreds of pages of speeches that were recorded by newspapers as there was no regular official "hansard''. Additional selections from the speeches would have been included in this volume if full renditions of them were not now becoming available in a huge reconstruction of the full proceedings of the Legislative Assembly, 1841-1866.[1]

Original maps are included in this volume. All but one of the maps show the areal patterns of voting by members of the Legislative Assembly on nineteen of the more than two hundred divisions that were taken from 1841 to 1859 on the seat of government issue. The information on divisions as recorded in the *Journals* of the Legislative Assembly gave only names by yea and nay groupings. To compile the maps the author had to associate the names with ridings. This process led to the plotting of data on the maps as shown. The key to each map shows the votes (yea and nay, the number of members absent, and totals) by Canada West and Canada East divisions. The reader will quickly recognize that the pattern of the votes is far more revealing than just the total yea-nay votes cast.

The collection brought together in this book is not an exhaustive one. A definite decision was made to omit many potential items—letters, petitions, motions, memoranda, despatches, etc. While the author's bias is that of a historical geographer with a special concern for cultural and political processes, the collection selected and printed here should have wide interest, both for scholars of many disciplines and general readers curious about an intriguing issue that developed during a critical, but understudied, period in Canadian history.

The general introduction and the brief chapter introductions by the author are based on a detailed and fully documented narrative and analysis of the seats of government issues, from 1791 to the 1830's for Upper Canada, and from 1840 to 1859 for the Province of Canada.[2] *A Capital for Canada* includes an analysis of the many votes that were cast in the Legislative Assembly. A measure of regional and sectional attachments in the Province of Canada is presented in that volume. Some of the materials cited in *A Capital for Canada* are printed in full in the present volume. The two books can be read as adjuncts to each other, but each can also be read by itself.

I am grateful for the generous assistance and support of many people during the several years spent in libraries and archives while gathering the materials from which have been culled the selection published in this volume. Foremost, Janet and our children, Karen and Andrew, have provided that intimate spark of life that can be gained from a close family relationship. I will always be indebted to them for their shared love and support. During the early phases of my research, Barbara Wilson (Public Archives of Canada) and historian Elizabeth Nish provided thoughtful guidance. Later, Robert Mackworth-Young (Librarian and Assistant Archivist to the Queen, Royal Archives, Windsor

Castle) gave me assistance in obtaining certain documents and in answering questions. On many occasions, I was aided by archivists and librarians (most of whose names I do not know) in the Public Archives of Canada, The Library of Parliament, The National Library of Canada, The Archives of Nova Scotia, The Archives of Ontario, Toronto Public Library (Baldwin Room), and the libraries of McGill University in Montreal, Queen's University in Kingston, and Carleton University in Ottawa. Moral support was given to me by several colleagues who have maintained an interest in my continuing research: historian John Taylor (Carleton University), and fellow geographers Duncan Anderson, David Bennett, and John Clarke (all of Carleton University), and especially Peter Goheen (Queen's University, Kingston). Practical support was provided by Donna Sally and, most particularly, Ann Saunders, who created typed versions of documents from my hand written transcriptions. Stefan Palko (Staff Cartographer, Department of Geography, Carleton University) expertly drafted the final maps for publication. Dean R.A. Wendt generously supported my work with two small but vital research grants. Mildred and Lewis Briner helped me in many indirect ways and to them I will always remain grateful.

I remain responsible for the materials selected for inclusion in this volume and for interpretations given in the general introduction, the chapter introductions, and the chapters dealing with "The Earlier Years" and "The Later Years".

David B. Knight
February 19, 1976
Carleton University
Ottawa, Ontario

Notes

[1]Elizabeth Nish, editor, *Legislative Assembly Debates of the Legislative Assembly of United Canada, 1841-1866* (Montreal: Presses de L'Ecole des hautes etudes commercials, 1970—).

[2]David B. Knight, *A Capital for Canada: Conflict and Compromise in the Nineteenth Century* (Chicago: The University of Chicago, Department of Geography, Research Series, 1977).

CHAPTER I

INTRODUCTION

An Overview

A capital city represents a primary nodal point in the mental maps of residents of a political unit. Clearly, a capital city becomes more than just any other city, for the seat of government for any political state acquires special attributes of power and prestige within the state. Since a capital city becomes an important central place, subjective measurements and expressions of attachments to place and territorial centrality may be developed, especially if a new site for the seat of government is being selected.

The selection of a site for the seat of government involves the resolution of conflict, for proponents of contending sites are generally vociferous and tenacious in their claims: "Capital cities . . . are [more] generally conceived in jealousy than in love."[1] Certainly, the Canadian experience in capital site selection is a good case in point, for local and regional conflicts of interest and outlook, motives and ambitions, all had to be dealt with within a political system that encouraged the expression of sectionalism before a site was finally selected. For the Province of Canada, the problem was difficult, as illustrated by the constantly moving governmental functions: Kingston in 1841, to Montreal 1844 until 1849 at which time a perambulating system was instituted between Toronto (1849-1851; 1855-1859) and Quebec (1851-1855; 1859-1865) before Ottawa finally became functional as legislative capital in 1866 (see Figure 1).

From the first session of the Parliament of the new Province in 1841, until 1859, the seat of government issue raged on and off, with continued and lively debates over the relative merits of various cities for housing the capital functions. Despite pleas for approaching the question objectively, local, regional, and sectional partiality was the order of the day. Indeed, because local, regional, and sectional frictions finally led to a legislative deadlock, the legislators in 1857 requested Queen Victoria to select one site from five possibilities submitted to her.[2] The choice of Governor General Sir Edmund Head, the Colonial Office, and the Queen was Ottawa, but the Canadian legislators rejected this decision in 1858 and then, early in 1859, finally accepted it, but only by a majority of 64 to 59.

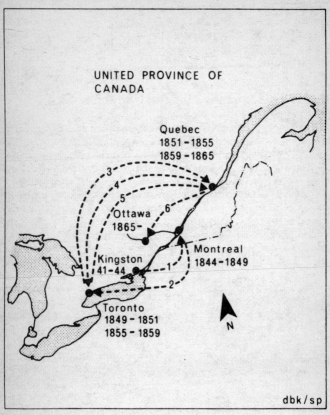

Figure 1.
Locations of the several seats of government for the Province of Canada.

This introductory chapter first briefly reviews the previous literature on the Canadian seat of government question. Thereafter selected aspects of the Province of Canada are highlighted before some broad issues relating to the problem of capital site selection in Canada are discussed.

Previous Literature on the Canadian Case

Even though geographers have a long standing interest in capital cities,[3] they have ignored the Canadian seat of government question, perhaps because, until recently, most of the work in the now rapidly developing field of Canadian historical geography has focused on patterns and processes of rural settlement and landscape change.[4] Canadian historians have neglected most of the details as well as the full sweep of the capital issue, even though the issue occupied public attention for many years and was extremely devisive for the body politic. This neglect is most surprising since the question was described in 1858 as "the most vexatious question which has yet arisen among us."[5] Most Canadian histories totally ignore the seat of government issue.

The author's book entitled *A Capital for Canada*, which is cited in the Preface, is the most complete examination of the Canadian seat of government question. The few researchers who have given more than cursory treatment to the capital question in the Province of Canada have limited their attention to an incomplete examination of some phase of the issue, as with L. Groulx's partial use of one series of letters in his brief overview of the 1841-1859 period,[6] D.J. Pierce and J.P. Pritchett's limited examination of Kingston's selection in 1841,[7] two brief initial "impact" evaluations,[8] J.E. Hodgett's highlighting of administrative problems caused by perambulating capitals,[9] or James Gibson who wrote two articles focussing on the 1857-1858 period, concentrating on only one document.[10] A former Mayor of Ottawa published a brief paper on aspects of the 1857 claims for capital honors made by six cities.[11]

Some participants in the legislative issue later wrote about their roles, but the evaluations are quite incomplete. One of the more valuable reminiscences was written by Sir Richard Scott. Scott presented an Ottawa-biased point of view and placed emphasis on his own actions.[12] An anonymous writer in Montreal in 1856 wrote a disjointed ramble in favour of Montreal and against the perambulatory system.[13] Dunbar Ross, a politician who strongly supported Quebec, wrote two booklets on the issue.[14] He claimed objectivity, but quite delightfully was subjective in his plea for Quebec as capital. Ross developed his own unique system of measuring objectively the advantages of the various sites under consideration. His technique for measuring centrality (and how he played with it to "prove" Quebec's centrality) has recently been reconstructed from the results he presented in writing as he included no methodology.[15]

There are also useful nineteenth and twentieth century evaluations of the period which include descriptions of isolated parts of the issue.[16] Some biographies also make reference to selected phases or events.[17] Other studies, histories of individual cities or regions, occasionally, refer to the places involved and to some of the events. These works commonly deal either with the well-known highlights and rely on secondary sources, or else they are local histories revealing little of the larger regional or national framework within which they are set.[18] Several general works exist which are incorrect in their facts.[19]

The Province of Canada

A persistent problem in British North America was how to reconcile the major cultural differences between the French who were dominant in Canada East (Lower Canada) and the English who were dominant in Canada West (Upper Canada).[20] Government policy recognized these cultural differences and attempted to manage the political problems arising from this condition in a series of decisions, first by dividing the region between the contending cultures in 1791 and then by uniting the colonies in 1841 after the passage of an act of union in 1840.

Canada West at the time of union in 1841, had a rapidly increasing, ethnically mixed population of 455,000 (Table I), over half of whom were immigrants from Britain. The majority of the 650,000 people in Canada East were, on the other hand, predominantly of French-Canadian origin. In 1841 there were approximately 160,000 English in Canada East and 14,000 French Canadians in Canada West.

Canada East had been long settled and was dominated by the two principal urban centers: the old capital, Quebec, with various military, religious, educational, and administrative institutions, as well as a shipbuilding industry and shipping facilities; and the commercially dominant, economically diversified city of Montreal. Three Rivers (Trois Rivières), the next ranked urban place, was small. The rural areas were largely French-Canadian, with the notable exceptions of the southern Gaspé and more especially the Eastern Townships (south of the St. Lawrence, along the United States border) which were heavily "English" (that is, 40,000 Scots, Irish, and New Englanders). Commerce in Canada East was controlled by English Canadians and the population in the centers of both Quebec and Montreal were largely

TABLE 1
POPULATION, PROVINCE OF CANADA.

	1841	1851	(% increase)	1861	(% increase)
CANADA	c.1,105,700	1,842,265	(67)	2,507,657	(36)
CANADA EAST	c. 650,000	890,261	(37)	1,111,566	(25)
Montreal	c. 40,000	57,715	(44)	90,323	(57)
Quebec	c. 35,000	42,052	(20)	59,990	(43)
Three Rivers	c. 3,000	4,936	(65)	6,068	(23)
CANADA WEST	455,688	952,004	(109)	1,396,091	(47)
Toronto	14,249	30,775	(116)	44,821	(46)
Kingston	6,292	11,697	(86)	13,743	(18)
Hamilton	c. 3,400	14,112	(315)	19,096	(35)
Bytown/Ottawa	3,122	7,760	(149)	14,669	(89)
London	c. 2,000	7,035	(252)	11,555	(64)

non-French in composition. The urban and rural landscapes of Canada East had a marked French flavour.

In Canada West the landscape was being vigorously remade, with a mixed American-British imprint. By the 1840's Toronto was well on its way to dominance of the urban hierarchy, but many other towns (including Kingston, Hamilton, and Bytown) also had grand dreams for a glorious future. The population of Canada West was ethnically mixed and largely Protestant, in contrast to predominantly Roman Catholic Canada East. Canada West was growing more rapidly than Canada East and by 1851 Canada West had the larger population.[21]

The union of the two Canadas eventually failed to accommodate regional attachments and sectional frictions, so a new system of government was proposed and eventually instituted—a federal union of the British North American colonies in 1867.[22] A principal reason for the failure of the 1841 union was that the Parliament was based on equal representations from the two sections. Union by this formula permitted the political recovery for French Canadians and, in Mason Wade's estimation, it also provided for French-Canadian cultural development.[23] However, in addition, sectional identities continued and indeed hardened.

One of the consequences of the dualism that was built into the political structure of the Province of Canada was the development of the concept of a double majority. The concept meant that the government would be based on a majority within each of the sections of the union. The application of the concept paved the way for the creation of dual premierships leading hyphenated ministries, in which one leader represented the majority party in Canada West and one that of Canada East. One politician later recalled that the dual premiership was "makeshift" and was reminiscent of "the old Roman custom of selecting two Consuls, each representing one of the great parties in the state."[24] The dual, or hyphenated, ministries were in direct response to the regionally based cultural dualism.

At times the union operated in a federal manner as the Canada West politician, John A. Macdonald, retrospectively noted:

in matters affecting Upper Canada solely, members from that section claimed and generally exercised the right of exclusive legislation, while members from Lower Canada legislated in matters affecting only their own section. We have had a Federal Union in fact, though a Legislative Union in name.[25]

There were also numerous times, however, when matters affecting Upper Canada were decided on by a Lower Canadian majority, and *vice versa*. Thus, equal representation for the two sections of the province and the double majority system were not enough to protect sectional interests and the recognition of these facts aroused further feelings of suspicion and ill will.

Ministerial government needs a clear-cut party system if it is to function effectively, but while there were political parties in the Canadas from 1841 to 1867, they were not parties in the modern sense.[26] Governments were formed on personal loyalties and cultural identities as much as on party affiliations. Political groupings during the period are difficult to identify, although P.G. Cornell has been able to find a measure of consistency in the political behaviour of most members of the Legislative Assembly.[27] The fascinating thing is that for the seat of government issue over the years, the alignment of members during the numerous divisions generally bore little relationship with their normal alignments, since city based regional attachments or sectional (Canada East versus Canada West) affiliations generally proved to have a greater pull.[28]

The Seat of Government Issue: Some Themes

In the Canadian seat of government case, of the numerous people involved, some acted independently and often privately, while others were openly public in their actions and reactions. It is not enough to say either that "Queen Victoria decided" or that the Legislative Assembly agreed. There were six levels of decision making. Theoretically, the Queen was at the top, then working down the hierarchy, there were the British Government (especially the Colonial Office), the Governors General, the Executive Council, the Legislative Council and the Legislative Assembly.[29] Conflict existed within and between the three latter bodies. Initially, the decision making lay in the hands of the Governor General, but this right was first tentatively challenged in 1841 and thereafter the Legislative Assembly came to initiate recommendations that went up the hierarchy. However, no matter at what level of the hierarchy a decision was made, ultimately final decisions were made by the Legislative Assembly and the Legislative Council because of their power to control supply. Even so, it is clear that these two legislative bodies would have been unable to conclude the question entirely by themselves since local, regional, sectional, and political party considerations intervened. Thus perhaps it was indeed necessary for a "third party" to make a recommendation to be accepted or rejected.[30] Since the third party called upon in 1857 was the Queen the acceptance of her "decision" thereafter was tied to loyalty and respect for the Monarch. Equally clear is that key individuals at the various levels of the decision making hierarchy formulated and guided decisions and responses.

Central to the seat of government issue for the Province of Canada were the Governors General, from Charles Poulett Thomson (Lord Sydenham; who selected Kingston), to Sir Charles Bagot and Sir Charles Metcalfe (both of whom were opposed to Kingston and who made recommendations to London in favour of Montreal), to Lord Elgin (who suffered insult in Montreal and thereafter helped guide the Government to its decision to relocate to Toronto with the initiation of an alternating system), to Sir Edmund Head (who privately favoured Ottawa and who was perhaps the single most important person in the process leading to the determination and acceptance of having Ottawa being chosen capital). Many of the frank thoughts these men had about Canada and the capital issue were shared only with the Colonial Secretaries over the years, but the Governors General often also privately brought pressure to bear on the Executive Council members. The Governors General were by no means simply figure heads.

Colonial Office personnel involved were few in number. Judging from the leading questions and suggestions posed for their political superiors by Arthur Blackwood and Herman Merivale, these two civil servants were most important in determining the way in which the Colonial Office responded to Canadian initiatives and requests. While the Colonial Secretaries and their fellow politician Undersecretaries played important roles too, in large measure they seem to have been guided to certain responses by Blackwood and Merivale. The Cabinet and the Queen also were guided, for recommended responses went from the Colonial Office to them. Queen Victoria was kept informed of proceedings and decisions were released from the Colonial Office in her name. In Canada, the symbolism of a Royal decision weighed heavily on the shoulders and perhaps consciences of many legislators, but there were also those who were angered by the referral to the Crown.

Little of the deliberations in the Canadian Executive Council and higher up in the Colonial-Imperial hierarchy were known to Canadians although on two occasions the public learned of dissension within the Council over the seat of government question. Openness of debate was experienced only within the Legislative Council and Legislative Assembly. The two Houses several times came into conflict, both in terms of recommendations regarding the seat of government as well as over supply for buildings.

Canadian newspapers carried detailed reports of the proceedings of both Houses, but particularly the Assembly,[31] and an interested and sometimes concerned public often reacted by holding public meetings about the seat of government question, informing legislators how they were expected to vote, sending many dozen petitions to all branches of government, and challenging candidates during election campaigns. Several members elected to the House lost their seats because of the way they voted on the seat of government issue. At least one member was burned in effigy by his constituents after one particular vote. On the other hand, some members were congratulated by their constituents after certain votes.

Public interest in the continuing question was fueled by the hundreds of columns of opinion and analysis that appeared in newspapers all over the country.[32] Newspaper partisanship, both in terms of political affiliation and allegiance to a particular city, was often blatant and sometimes outrageous. Indeed, so outrageously contentious did certain newspaper editorials become on occasion, that newspapers must be regarded as "participants" in the seat of government issue. The *Montreal Gazette* and the Toronto *Globe* were consistently aggressive participants, but many other papers also stirred public response.

The process involving the consideration of sites was restricted by an inertia of thought. Only five of the principal cities were given serious consideration. The competition between the four dominant urban places as well as their relative location within each section confined Governor Thomson's thinking in 1840 as he determined which place should be the capital of the new Province. Although he recognized Bytown's potential, he dismissed it from consideration. From 1841 onwards, Montreal was clearly recognized by most Lower Canadians as the best site. From 1849 on, members of the Legislature split into two camps, that is, the fixed site men (for Montreal, Kingston or Bytown/Ottawa) and the alternating men (for Toronto and Quebec). Kingston, after the 1844 relocation dropped out of serious contention in the minds of all but Kingston and district supporters. A similar filtering out process occurred for Montreal after 1849. Bytown/Ottawa supporters were the most persistent of any legislative group in presenting their city for consideration. Just as consistently, the House overwhelmingly rejected it. However, when referral was agreed to, the cities given consideration were Quebec, Montreal, Ottawa, Kingston and Toronto.

In the Legislative Assembly from 1841 to 1859 there were 218 votes that directly related to the seat of government question.[33] For the years 1841 to 1844 and 1849 to 1859 there were several votes during each session. There were clusters of votes in 1842 and 1843 before relocation from Kingston, in 1849 after the sacking of Parliament in Montreal, in 1853 when a bill was introduced to give money for new government buildings in Toronto, in 1855 shortly before relocation to Toronto occurred, in 1856 immediately following this move, in 1857 when there was a carryover from the 1856 session, and, finally, in 1859, as the issue was brought to a close. The Legislative Assembly formally approached the Governors General 10 times and Queen Victoria three times.

Cornwall and Hamilton both received one vote each but the first was in jest and the second was part of a strategy by Ottawa supporters and was not a vote for Hamilton as such. Most of the early votes for Kingston had a distinctively sectional character, and the town was not given serious consideration by House members following relocation. Thus, if we set aside Kingston, this leaves Toronto, Montreal, Quebec and, in the background, Ottawa. Montreal received eight direct votes over the years while Toronto received only four. However, with Toronto and Quebec, many of the fourteen direct votes for or against the alternating system after 1849 really were votes for one or both of those cities. Interestingly, Ottawa was the city to receive most direct votes, with eleven in total.

Canadians thus gave serious consideration only to pre-existing cities. A principal factor considered for each site was relative location, with especial attention being given to centrality. Centrality is a highly relative concept.[34] As an adjective, central means situated in the centre; as a noun it signifies the quality of being centre. The question is, of course, centre of what and in what sense?

For the Canadian case we can identify three principal levels of understanding. First there were the people in Britain who would have had the most abstract image of Canada. To the British politicians, civil servants, and the Queen, centrality in Canada likely was related to a geographic centre point on an east-west line. Such an opinion undoubtedly was supported by maps they would have seen, such as those prepared by Ottawa and the Colonial Office in 1857 in which Ottawa was roughly centred on an east-west axis. At the second level were the Governors General who had to balance Imperial policy directives, needs and views from London against political realities in the Canadas. A potent consideration for the Governors General is embodied in the clever use of distance data by a Canadian group (see selection no. 167) which typifies the third level of understanding of the concept, that is, local perception.

Every place in contention was said to be central and, of course, every place was—to the particular local observor! Centrality was claimed for the five main cities in their 1857 memorials, but it was also claimed for each city by newspaper writers, politicians, and other observors well before the institution of the 1841 union. After 1841, most stress on central location was given by spokesmen for Montreal, Kingston and Ottawa, but mention also was made of it by supporters of Toronto and Quebec. Torontonians rightly claimed centrality within Canada West, whereas Quebec claimed centrality in the event of a union of all the British North American colonies. This point was stressed in Quebec's 1857 memorial. However, Ottawa too claimed centrality in the event of such a union and received support for this claim from Torontonians (but only after the deciding vote in 1859) because of the likelihood of territorial expansion in the Northwest in the Hudson's Bay lands.

The concept of centrality was implicit in almost all that was written and said about the capital question. However, it was explicit in the Governors General evaluations in 1840, 1842 and 1843 and also in Edmund Head's 1857 memorandum, and in legislators speeches in 1842, 1843 and 1850-1856. A related concern that was discussed was whether the government should be in a large city or small town. Opinions differed, for some felt that it was better to be removed from large city influences while others felt that such influences were necessary. The city most referred to in this regard was Montreal. Those who favoured being in the large commercial centre referred to European experiences. The men who disagreed often referred to the United States decision to locate in Washington, D.C., rather than in New York or Philadelphia, or to the method used in many states of the United States, whereby a geographical central point was selected.

The presence of the United States influenced Canadians in other ways too. Initially there was the military concern and also a fear of "republican influences" which, it was perceived, would adversely affect Canadian society. Both of these factors were instrumental in the early identification of Bytown/Ottawa as a favoured interior location. Later, in the 1850's when there was renewed fear of the United States, the Governor General's conclusions, the military views sought by the Colonial Office, and the writers of the city memorials all explicitly mentioned defensive locations. Interestingly, while Colonial authorities always considered military matters, seldom was the defensiveness of the various sites discussed in the Legislative Assembly, perhaps because it was a given, but more likely regional and particularly local factors simply obscured any overriding defensive concerns.

A strong plus for Ottawa, in the minds of some French Canadians, was that it had a French-Canadian population. In addition, many men in Canada viewed Ottawa as a neutral location between Canada East and Canada West, thus neither section, it was said, would triumph if Ottawa were capital. In a sense, Ottawa was free of the ill feeling and jealousies felt between the other competing cities and the two regions, thus it was relatively neutral in regional politics and so it could serve as a uniting focal point for the political unit.[35]

The notion of neutrality proposed for Ottawa found meaning because of the bitter inter-sectional jealousies and suspicions that had particular focus in the four competing urban nodes of Quebec, Montreal, Kingston and Toronto. Ottawa thus was an alternative. It was the "forest city", the "city of the woods", with a small, rough but culturally mixed population in a relatively isolated region. It was linked by the Rideau Canal to Kingston, but economically and socially it was tied to

Montreal and Quebec. Ottawans were not tied to Toronto or *vice versa*.

When Ottawa was selected as the seat of government, one Torontonian wailed, as numerous Canadians have continued to do ever since, that

> Ottawa must not be like Toronto, or Hamilton, or Kingston, or Montreal, raised into importance by the industry and enterprise of their inhabitants; it must be fed with pap from the public kitchen, raised into independence by public money.[36]

Ottawa writers and politicians in their speeches always presented Ottawa's case in a good light. Boosterist speeches and articles were aimed at creating a positive image of the city in the minds of others, regardless of the complex truth. But the image so projected met with counter images based on other booster claims and on ignorance and partial information affected by attitudes. Richard Scott spoke much truth when he declared in the Legislative Assembly that he "was sorry to see that almost three-fourths of the members of this House were as ignorant of the Ottawa country as of Central Africa."[37]

Obviously, Canadians were "ignorant" about other places too, but ignorance is a relative concept, since ignorance is related to perception which is a personal process. Nevertheless, judging from speeches and editorials, certain images and attitudes were held about the other cities too. Toronto, a vigorously growing city, was called a Tory and Protestant place and was said to be influenced by the American press. Above all, Toronto, the "Queen City", symbolized the triumph of Canada West and especially the western parts of that section, and thus was viewed with dislike by Lower Canadians. Kingston also was Protestant, being a major stronghold of the Orange Order. It was a small place much disliked by French Canadians who claimed the air and water were unhealthy. Also, it was said that there was no agricultural hinterland. Memories of 1841-1844 remained and seem to have acted as a filter to serious consideration being given to new facts about Kingston. Montreal was acknowledged as the chief commercial center and so was viewed in a jealous vein. In addition, memories of the rebellion of 1837, the riots of 1849, and election days with radical crowds and bitter cultural conflict, later prevented its being viewed positively by many Canadians. Quebec, the "Garrison City", the "Ancient Capital", was the symbolic centre of Romanism in Canada and thus was utterly unacceptable to Canada West Protestants. Also, it was regarded as being so far to the east as to be neutral but quite inconvenient! In total, "Quebec, to an Upper Canadian, is about the most miserable place conceivable."[38]

Old inter-city jealousies, which section a city was in, dominant religious and ethnic characteristics, and relative location all influenced politicians and were used by them as they forged strategies and explanations. Political party affiliations sometimes temporarily modified some men's actions during the seat of government issue, but each man had his own "swan" and this fact led him to speak favourably of it and to condemn another man's "swan" as a "goose". This basic identification with place was a dominant factor in the seat of government question as it unfolded in the Province of Canada from 1841 to 1859.

The significance of a place becoming seat of government was great, judging from newspaper evaluations, for joy reigned when capital functions were moved in and grief was pronounced when they moved out. Interestingly, a city was said to become the capital (or metropolis) when the Governor General arrived, not when government departments moved in or when Parliament was opened. Likewise, a place was said to cease being capital when the Governor General left after the closing of Parliament, not when government departments relocated.

The impact of the changing seats of government is difficult to measure but at least three levels can be identified: the impact on the country, on the cities involved, and on individuals.

First, the full monetary consequences for the country cannot be measured. Only minimum costs can be cited. The relocation from Kingston to Montreal cost £9,187 and another £1,500 was spent on renovating the Montreal buildings in 1844. From 1849 to 1858 the expenses were great. Rents and repairs to the Public Buildings at the *existing* seat of government totalled £197,282, but because the buildings in the "other" place had to be kept up, rents and repairs to the Public Buildings *elsewhere* than at the existing seat of government totalled £51,062. In addition, there were removal costs. Allowances to clerks, ministers and others in consequence of removal totalled £7,613, while the actual expenses for removal of records and other materials amounted to £42,150. In total the country spent £298,107 from 1849 to 1858 for expenses connected with the several removals, but if we subtract the cost of rents and repairs at the existing seat of government from the total, then we can assume that the alternating system cost the country a minimum of £100,825. Additional amounts could be added to this if it were known how much Government departments and also individuals paid for lost or damaged documents and goods. The financial impact on the country of not having a fixed seat of government was great.

The second level of impact was on the different cities. This too is an illusive thing but clearly the impact was greater on the smaller centres of Kingston and Ottawa than on Toronto, Montreal and Quebec. In each of the five cities new buildings were constructed or converted for use by the Executive, Parliament, and government departments. The influx of government officials and legislators and their families had an inflationary effect on housing costs. The "necessaries of life" were said in 1856 to be higher in Toronto than in Quebec. Not only did housing and food costs increase as a result of moves, but the value of land rose. Profiteering occurred in each of the cities, but particularly in Kingston and Ottawa. For example, as soon as it was known that Ottawa had been fixed upon, land values advanced by fifty to one hundred per cent. Toronto, Quebec, and especially Montreal did not noticeably suffer when government relocated, but smaller Kingston received a critical blow from which it never recovered. If Quebec had been selected as the federal capital in the 1860's then Ottawa too undoubtedly would have suffered decline. Competing newspapers in the seat of government took on new importance as their column coverage of parliamentary proceedings expanded whenever their city was capital.

The third level directly affected individuals although once again it is difficult to be precise. Civil servants complained about the dreadful inconveniences of breaking up households and relocating families to a new city. Damages and losses to personal property occurred. Higher prices for food and rent invariably were encountered in the new capital. Also, during the alternating years, some civil servants suffered from having to pay double rents, that is, renting houses in both Toronto and Quebec because of the uncertainty of relocation dates. Frustration must have been great.

Expectations varied. In Toronto, Quebec, Kingston and Ottawa anticipation of a pending relocation was always great while in the commercial capital, Montreal, several writers and speakers over the years professed disinterest in having their city house the government. This feigned disdain was in marked contrast to the openly stated desire by supporters of Toronto, Kingston, Ottawa and Quebec for having the seat of government in their city. The use of the word metropolis, as meaning chief city, imparts something of the feelings held about the capital role. Montreal already was the commercial capital but the other cities desired the title and benefits of being political metropolis.

Anticipation was particularly great in Ottawa and the valley in 1858 and 1859, for Ottawans expected their town would reap benefits from having the capital functions relocated there. They also expected the surrounding countryside and the Ottawa Valley would too:

> all the unoccupied lands will speedily be settled by a sturdy and industrious people. Hamlets will spring, as if by magic, into villages, villages into towns, and towns into cities.[39]

Likewise Kingstonians believed that they would benefit from having

Ottawa capital since the "hitherto partly neglected townships lying between Kingston and Ottawa . . . will, in the course of a few years . . . be densely filled with an industrious population."[40] Such expectations never were realized, for in many ways the region has remained a blackwater, with the federal government's impact being focussed on Ottawa and, in very recent years, Hull.

Ottawa quickly became territorially eccentric, first as union with the Maritimes occurred and later as the Dominion of Canada spread westwards and northwards. Ottawa served well as capital during the 19th Century as expansionary forces based principally in Toronto and Montreal were balanced. Given the "French/English fact" in Canada's political and cultural life, Ottawa probably remains a good location for Canada's federal capital, although to many French Canadians today the "national" capital is Quebec city. On a different tack, given Canada's other powerful regionalisms it can be debated whether that the site remains the optimal location for the federal capital. To examine the implications of these thoughts would involve a major study.

Only in the mid-Twentieth Century did Ottawa become, to use geographer D. Whittlesey's term, the pet of government.[41] A symbolic landscape has emerged that is the result of federal action that has not always suited the needs of a city operating under Ontario Provincial authority. Competition and friction often seem to have been more prevalent than co-operation between the various levels of government. New conflict arose when the Trudeau Government expanded the concept of the capital to include Hull on the Quebec Province side of the Ottawa River. Such a symbolic link was suggested in the 1850's by a few people—but not by key decision makers nor indeed either in the December 31, 1857 official notification of Ottawa's selection or in the British North American Act.

Notes

[1] G.J.R. Linge, "Canberra After Fifty Years," *Geographical Review*, Vol. LI, no. 4 (October, 1961), p. 467.

[2] As will be seen later, six cities submitted memorials to London even though only five were invited. The sixth city, Hamilton, was not seriously considered and, indeed, harmed any chances it might have had by the tone of its submitted memorial.

[3] The literature is extensive. See the selective bibliography in Harm de Blij, *Systematic Political Geography* (New York: John Wiley and Sons, Inc., 1973), pp. 125-126.

[4] See R. Colebrook Harris, "Historical Geography in Canada," *Canadian Geographer*, Vol. XI, no. 4 (1967), pp. 235-250, and John U. Marshall,

"Geographer's Contribution to the Historical Study of Urban Canada," *Urban History Review*, no. 1-73 (May, 1973), pp. 15-24.

5(Montreal) *Pilot*, July 30, 1858.

6Lionel Groulx, "Le Choix de la Capitale au Canada," *Revue d'histoire de l'Amerique Francaise* (1951-52), pp. 521-530.

7D.J. Pierce and J.P. Pritchett, "The Choice of Kingston as the Capital of Canada," Canadian Historical Association, *Annual Report 1929*, pp. 57-63.

8J.E. Hodgetts, "The Civil Service when Kingston was the Capital of Canada," *Historic Kingston*, Vol. 5 (1956); C.C.J. Bond, "The Canadian Government Comes to Ottawa, 1865-1866," *Ontario History*, Vol. LV, no. 1 (1963), pp. 23-34.

9J.E. Hodgetts, *Pioneer Public Service: An Administrative History of the United Canadas, 1841-1867* (Toronto: University of Toronto Press, 1955), pp. 58-62.

10James A. Gibson, "The Choosing of the Capital of Canada," *British Columbia Historical Quarterly*, Vol. XVII, nos. 1 and 2 (1953), pp. 78-85, and *Idem*, "How Ottawa Became the Capital of Canada," *Ontario History*, Vol. XLVI, no. 4 (1954), pp. 213-222.

11Frederick Cook, *The Struggle for the Capital of Canada* (Ottawa: By the Author, 1938).

12R.W. Scott, *The Choice of the Capital: Reminiscences Revived on the Fiftieth Anniversary of the Selection of Ottawa as the Capital of Canada by Her Late Majesty* (Ottawa: The Mortimer Company, 1907).

13"Marullus", *Reflections on Itinerary Parliaments* (Montreal: B. Dawson, 1856).

14[Dunbar Ross], *Seat of Government (Canada)* (Quebec: T. Cary and Co., 1843). The manuscript was serialized, again with no reference to Ross as the author, in five January, 1844, issues of the *Quebec Mercury*. The second booklet was Dunbar Ross, *The Seat of Government of Canada . . .* (Quebec: E.R. Fréchette, 1856).

15David B. Knight and Susan Burrows, "Centrality By Degrees: A 19th Century Canadian's Measurement for Central Location," *The Canadian Cartographer*, Vol. 12, no. 2 (December, 1975), pp. 109-120.

16For instance, J.C. Dent, *The Last Forty Years: The Union of 1841 to Confederation*, 2 Vols. (Toronto: George Virtue, 1881; reprinted in the Carleton Library Series, No. 62, 1972); J.M. S. Careless, *The Union of the Canadas: The Growth of Canadian Institutions, 1841-1857* (Toronto: McClelland and Stewart, 1967); W.L. Morton, *The Critical Years: The Union of British North America 1857-1873* (Toronto: McClelland and Stewart, 1964); J. Monet, *The Last Cannon Shot: A Study of French-Canadian Nationalism, 1837-1850* (Toronto: University of Toronto Press, 1969).

17For example, D.G.C. Kerr, *Sir Edmund Head: A Scholarly Governor* (Toronto: University of Toronto Press, 1954); D.G. Creighton, *John A. Macdonald*, 2 volumes (Toronto: Macmillan Company of Canada, 1952, 1955); J.M.S. Careless *Brown of the Globe*, 2 volumes (Toronto: Macmillan Company of Canada, 1959, 1963).

18For example, selected items on Ottawa include: A.H.D. Ross, *Ottawa Past and Present* (Ottawa: Thornburn and Abbott, 1927); H. and O. Walker, *Carleton Saga* (Ottawa: Runge Press, 1968); Wilfred Eggleston, *The Queen's*

Choice (Ottawa: The Queen's Printer, 1961). The most informative book on Ottawa, and the one for which archival research on the capital question was completed, remains Lucien Brault, *Ottawa Old and New* (Ottawa: Ottawa Historical Institute, 1946).

19For example, Arnold Toynbee, *Cities on the Move* (London: Oxford University Press 1970), p. 108, is mistaken in twice claiming that Ottawa was an especially created capital city.

20Strictly speaking, Lower Canada and Upper Canada ceased to exist when, in 1841, they became, respectively, Canada East and Canada West. Both officially and unofficially, both terms continued in use after 1841.

21Many of the themes mentioned in the above three paragraphs are elaborated upon in R. Cole Harris and John Warkentin, *Canada Before Confederation: A Study in Historical Geography* (Toronto: Oxford University Press, 1974), especially chapters 3 and 4, and J. David Wood, ed., *Perspectives on Landscape and Settlement in Nineteenth Century Ontario* (Toronto: McClelland and Stewart, Carleton Library, No. 91, 1975). There is as yet no sound comprehensive historical geography of urban growth in Canada. See, however, G.A. Nader, *Cities of Canada*, Vol. I (Toronto: Macmillan, 1975), Jacob Spelt, *Urban Development in South-Central Ontario* (Toronto: McClelland and Stewart, Carleton Library, No. 57 [1955], 1972), and Leroy Stone, *Urban Development in Canada* (Ottawa: Queen's Printer, 1967). See also the germinal ideas of J.M.S. Careless, "Frontierism, Metropolitanism, and Canadian History," *Canadian Historical Review*, Vol. 35 (March, 1954), pp. 1-21 and the collection of articles in G. Stelter and A. Artibes, eds., *The Canadian City: Essays in Urban History* (Toronto: McClelland and Stewart, Carleton Library Series, No. 109, 1977).

22On the Province of Canada see Careless, *The Union of the Canadas. . . . op. cit.*, and Morton, *op. cit*.

23Mason Wade, *The French-Canadian Outlook* (Toronto: McClelland and Stewart, Carleton Library, No. 14 [1946], 1964), pp. 35-36.

24Richard Cartwright, *Reminiscences* (Toronto: William Briggs, 1912), p. 5.

25Province of Canada, *Parliamentary Debates on the Subject of the Confederation of the British North American Provinces* (Quebec, 1865), p. 30.

26Frank H. Underhill, "The Development of National Political Parties in Canada," *Canadian Historical Review*, Vol. XVI, no. 4 (December, 1935), pp. 367-387.

27Paul G. Cornell, *The Alignment of Political Groups in Canada 1841-1867* (Toronto: University of Toronto Press, Canadian Studies in History and Government No. 3, 1962).

28See Knight, *A Capital for Canada*, *op. cit*.

29In a sense we might add a seventh level since the members of the Legislative Assembly were elected "by the people".

30A similar situation existed in New Zealand in 1863-64 when an invited commission of three Australians examined potential sites for a new capital and then submitted their choice to the New Zealand House of Representatives for acceptance.

31The public demanded good parliamentary news coverage. Indeed, Mary McLean has observed that newspapers which failed to satisfy the desire for detailed reports on parliamentary proceedings were faced with financial ruin. Mary McLean, ''Early Parliamentary Reporting in Upper Canada,'' *Canadian Historical Review*, Vol. xx. no. 4 (1939), p. 382. See also W.H. Kesterton, *A History of Journalism in Canada* (Toronto: McClelland and Stewart, Carleton Library, No. 36, 1967).

32The aptness of the description of newspapers of the day as ''engines of opinion'' will soon become evident to the reader. The phrase is from P.B. Waite, *Confederation, 1854-1867* (Toronto: Holt, Rinehart and Winston of Canada, Ltd., Canadian History through the Press Series, 1972), p. 1.

33See Knight, *A Capital for Canada, op. cit.*, pp. 20-23

34See Knight and Burrows, *op. cit.*

35A central, neutral location that serves a linking function has been one of the dominant reasons for capital locations, although ''central'' has had several meanings. See, for example, O.H.K. Spate, ''Factors in the Development of Capital Cities,'' *Geographical Review*, Vol. xxxii, no. 4 (October, 1942), pp. 622-631; Vaughan Cornish, *The Great Capitals: An Historical Geography* (London: Methuen, 1923); H. Guthe, ''Jerusalem,'' *The New Schaff-Herzog Encyclopedia of Religious Knowledge*, S.M. Jackson, ed. (Grand Rapids, Michigan: Baker Book House, 1953), Vol. vi, pp. 130-137; David B. Knight, ''Gaberones: A Viable Proposition?'' *Professional Geographer*, Vol. 17, no. 6 (November, 1965), pp. 38-39; William Walton, *The Evidence of Washington* (New York: Harper and Row, 1966), pp. 6-11.

36Letter from ''An Onlooker'' to Editor of (Toronto) *Globe*, February 20, 1858.

37*Montreal Transcript*, February 10, 1859.

38(Toronto) *Leader*, April 2, 1855.

39*Ottawa Tribune*, January 30, 1858.

40(Kingston) *British Whig*, February 17, 1859.

41Derwent Whittlesey, *The Earth and the State* (New York: Henry Holt, 1939), p. 196. For a review of some literature which examines the relationships between political authority and the physical environment see David B. Knight, ''Impress of Authority and Ideology on Landscape: A Review of Some Unanswered Questions,'' *Tijdschrift voor Economische en Sociale Geografie*, Vol. LXII, no. 6 (November/December, 1971), pp. 383-387.

CHAPTER II

THE EARLIER YEARS

Prior to the creation of the Province of Canada, the political units of Lower Canada and Upper Canada each had their own seat of government. In the case of Lower Canada there had been but one capital, Québec, but in Upper Canada two places, Niagara and York (Toronto), had housed the government functions at different times.

This chapter offers a brief sketch of the pre-union period, focussing on the origins of the urban rivalry that was later to play such an important role in the seat of government issue.

The French Beginnings

Jacques Cartier's penetration of the St. Lawrence River in 1535[1] marked the beginning of official French interest in that region, although it was not until 1608 that a permanent settlement was founded. Henri IV's Royal Geographer, Samuel de Champlain, was to "search for a place suitable for our settlement, but I could find none more convenient or better suited than the point of Québec. . . ."[2] The settlement he founded eventually became the North American administrative centre for a vast domain, but the initial years for the colony were difficult.

As the highest point of navigation on the St. Lawrence, Québec became the link with France, with settlements upstream being administratively subservient to it. But other settlements were few for many years. Trois-Rivières[3] was not founded until 1634, and, as a trading place, represented the new colony's most advanced post upstream for the eight years until the religious settlement of Villé-Marie was founded on Montréal Island in 1642.[4] Communication between the settlements was made difficult by Indians, especially the Iroquois, in the Trois-Rivières to Montreal section of the river. The populations of the three settlements remained small and even as late as 1663 only Québec could really be called a town.[5] The principal purpose to the life of the colony was fur trading.[6]

In 1663 Canada, which was only a small area of New France, and which had been in the hands of the Company of New France, was made a royal province. As such, it became like any other province of France, so theoretically the government of Canada resided wherever King Louis XIV and his chief Minister, Colbert, happened to be.[7] However, in Canada there were governors, one each in Montréal and Trois-Rivières and, in Québec, their superior, who was the Governor of the Colony and also of the whole of New France.[8] Thus the higher authorities and the institutions for administering the people and territory of New France were in Québec and this in turn attracted others, including the Jesuits who founded a college there.[9] Also, the main office of the Compagnie des Indes, the only body permitted to export beaver fur, was located in Québec.[10] There was a cathedral in Québec —but only a parish church in Montréal—and there was a Bishop at Québec who was directly under the guidance of the Vatican. Such an arrangement was a source of friction between the French Crown and the Vatican until, in 1674, an independent diocese of Quebec was established.[11] As to the location of Quebec, Governor Frontenac, in a letter to France dated November 3, 1672, exclaimed:

> Never have I beheld anything so beautiful and magnificent as the site of the city of Québec; none better could have been chosen for that which it must one day become,—the capital of a great empire.[12]

The French were, of course, not alone on the continent: there was active competition between French and English traders, not only for furs but for the allegiance of the Indians.[13] In 1690, Governor Frontenac successfully repulsed a Boston fleet and army intent on capturing Québec[14] and then, in 1700-1703, peace was made with the Iroquois and other Indians: New France was at its zenith. Québec was not only the administrative, religious, and cultural capital, and military headquarters but was also the transhipment point for merchandise from France in exchange for furs.[15] The population of Québec was about 2,000. Upstream was Montréal with about 1000 people whose economic functions were even more closely dependent on the fur trade.[16]

By the Treaty of Utrecht of 1713, France lost Acadia, Newfoundland and Hudson Bay and although there was peace, the conditions of the Treaty favoured the British, for they were then in a position possibly to close New France's ''lifeline to the sea.''[17]. Also, because of ambiguous phrasing in the Treaty, the stage was set for British expansionism.[18] But at first there was peace and both Québec and Montréal began to grow rapidly and settlements slowly spread over the St. Lawrence lowlands.[19] Conflict between the English and the French broke out again in 1740, and, in North America, culminated in the defeat of the

French, first with the capture of Québec in 1759 and then, in 1760, Montréal, and the collapse of New France.[20]

Québec in Canada as "Québec"

With the conquest, the name Canada was replaced by the name, Province of Québec. The ceremonies inaugurating this event, and instituting civil government, took place in 1764 in the city of Québec,[21] which was to remain as capital. Following the precedent set by the French, the British had a governor of the colony in Québec and lieutenant-governors in Trois Rivières and Montréal.[22] In addition, Québec remained the ecclessiastical, judicial, military, and education center for the colony. Québec was likened to a French provincial capital and General Montcalm, who died on the Plains of Abraham when the British attacked Québec, is said to have considered Québec's society a more "fashionable" one than that of the frontier town of Montréal.[23]

The American Revolution led to an invasion of the Province of Québec. Montréal fell to the Americans, but the attempt to capture Québec failed.[24] The influx of many Loyalists after the American Revolution helped bring about a reorganization of the remaining British territories. In 1786 a new position of Governor General was created, the appointee being directed to take charge of "the empire in America."[25] Lord Dorchester thus became governor of Québec, governor of Nova Scotia and its dependencies, governor of New Brunswick, and commander-in-chief of all these provinces and Newfoundland.[26] The principal seat of government remained Québec city and, in fact, Dorchester stirred from his capital on only one occasion.[27]

With the decline of the fur trade, especially after the loss of the region south of the Great Lakes to the Americans, a new economy based on new staples (timber and then wheat) developed and Montréal and Québec continued to grow. However, by about the 1830's Montréal had usurped Quebec's role as the commercial "capital", although both cities still depended heavily on their trade connections outside the province.[28] Lord Dalhousie, Governor General in the 1820's, recognized Montréal as the logical centre of the new commercial system that developed, for Montréal was said to be the heart of the country and from it circulated the lifeblood of Canada.[29] With the influx of the new settlers the centre of population moved west. This fact, plus the commercial dominance of Montréal, threatened Québec. Yet Québec remained the administrative centre even while viewing Montréal with suspicion and remaining jealous of its own power and prestige. The jealousies and suspicions were later to find expression in the seat of government issue for the United Province of Canada.

Upper Canada[30]

Town and regionally based jealousies and suspicions also found expression in the Upper Canadian seat of government issue. In Upper Canada the choice of the site for the first capital was in the hands of a colonial administrator, Lieutenant Governor John Graves Simcoe, who gave thought to the problem early in 1791 even before he first set foot in the new province. Military considerations were to the fore in his mind but personal conflicts with his superior, Governor General Lord Dorchester, also played a role in his determinations not to locate in the largest "urban" place, Kingston, and instead to locate in Niagara, on the most active frontier zone in the province.[31] The same considerations prevailed again in 1793 when he decided to move the capital functions from Niagara.

Simcoe had dreams of having an inland capital[32]—at the site later called London—but the lakeside location of York (Toronto) was selected. York remained as the permanent capital of Upper Canada even as the small town struggled to compete with and eventually to surpass its rival, Kingston.[33]

During the period of earliest settlement there were local hopes expressed for having the capital in Kingston.[34] There also were continuing efforts made to have the government relocated from York to Kingston, especially following the War of 1812 during which York was twice captured by American raiders. Indeed, in 1815, the instruction was issued for such a relocation. Objections were voiced by the Lieutenant Governor[35] and also twenty-three officers of the Government[36]—who were threatened with financial loss— and the relocation did not occur. At various times suggestions also were made for changing the capital to other locations, but inertia prevailed. In 1830, however, these suggestions reached open public expression when debates occurred and votes were cast in the House of Assembly for Upper Canada.[37] The votes favoured either Kingston or York and although the majority wanted relocation to Kingston such a move did not happen.[38] In addition, the process of "boosterism"—the exagerated proclamation of worth of a particular place over all others—begun in Kingston during the late 1780's, continued to swell and develop in Kingston and York, but also in Bytown[39] and elsewhere. "Booster" activities grew with ever greater intensity as prospects for a union of the provinces increased during the 1830's.

Conclusion

Competition and jealousies existed between the two main urban centres and their supportive regions in each province. With the political union of the two political units in 1841, this city and regionally based competition was raised to a higher, sectionally based level, and was an important consideration in the continuing seat of government issue.

Notes

[1]H.P. Biggar, translator, *The Voyages of Jacques Cartier* (Ottawa: F.A. Acland, 1924).

[2]Quoted in N.E. Dionne, *Champlain* (Toronto: Morang and Co., Ltd., 1909), p. 41.

[3]A. Tessier, *Trois-Rivières* (Trois-Rivières: Le Nouvelliste, 1935).

[4]Gustave Lanctot, *Montreal sous Maisonneuve, 1642-1665* (Montréal: Beauchemin, 1966).

[5]Marcel Trudel, *The Beginnings of New France, 1524-1663* (Toronto: McClelland and Stewart, 1973), pp. 252-253. In 1629 the settlement at Québec was captured by the British but it was returned to the French in 1631.

[6]See H.P. Biggar, *The Early Trading Companies of New France* (Toronto: University of Toronto Library, 1901).

[7]W.J. Eccles, *Canada Under Louis XIV, 1663-1701* (Toronto: McClelland and Stewart, 1964), p. 10.

[8]There were other governors, also subservient to Quebec, in Acadia and, after 1698, Louisiana.

[9]On the administration see W.J. Eccles, *The Government of New France* (Ottawa: Canadian Historical Society, Historical Booklet No. 18, 1965), and Marcel Trudel, *Introduction to New France* (Toronto: Holt, Rinehart and Winston of Canada, Ltd., 1968), pp. 148-158.

[10]Trudel, *Introduction*, *op. cit.*, p. 121.

[11]Eccles, *Canada*, *op. cit.*, pp. 30, 71.

[12]Reprinted in *Quebec Mercury*, April 2, 1857.

[13]For a brilliant exploration of themes relating to this competition see W.J. Eccles, *The Canadian Frontier, 1534-1760* (New York: Holt, Rinehart and Winston, 1969).

[14]Frontenac mobilized the entire population of the colony and mustered it at Québec. See W.J. Eccles, *Frontenac: The Courtier Governor* (Toronto: McClelland and Stewart, Carleton Library, No. 24, 1959), especially pp. 230-243.

[15]Allana Reid, "The Development and Importance of the Town of Quebec, 1608-1760," unpublished dissertation, McGill University, 1950.

[16]E.R. Adair, "Evolution of Montreal Under the French Regime," Canadian Historical Association, *Annual Report* (1942), pp. 20-41; E.E. Rich,

Montreal and the Fur Trade (Montreal: McGill University Press, 1966).

17Yves F. Zoltvany, *Philippe de Rigaud de Vaudreuil: Governor of New France, 1703-1725* (Toronto: McClelland and Stewart, Carleton Library, No. 80, 1974), p. 130.

18For an exploration of this see *Ibid.*, pp. 131-132.

19R.C. Harris, "The French Impact in Canada and Acadia," in Harris and Warkentin, *op. cit.*, pp. 19-63; and R.C. Harris, *The Seigneurial System in Early Canada: A Geographical Study* (Madison: University of Wisconsin Press, 1966).

20George F.G. Stanley, *New France: The Last Phase, 1744-1760* (Toronto: McClelland and Stewart, 1968), especially pp. 242-258.

21A.L. Burt, *The Old Province of Quebec*, (Toronto: The Ryerson Press, 1933), pp. 74-101.

22The positions of Lieutenant Governors in Trois Rivières and Montreal were soon discontinued. *Ibid.*, p. 87.

23Harris, "The French Impact . . . ," *op. cit.*, p. 59.

24Burt, *op. cit.*, pp. 202-247.

25*Ibid.*, p. 427.

26A.L. Burt, *Guy Carleton, Lord Dorchester, 1724-1808* (Ottawa: Canadian Historical Association, Historical Booklet No. 5, revised edition, 1968), p. 13.

27Wade, *The French Canadians, op. cit.*, p. 82.

28R. Cole Harris, "Quebec in the Century After the Conquest," in Harris and Warkentin, *op. cit.*, p. 100.

29See Donald Creighton, *The Empire of the St. Lawrence* (Toronto: Macmillan Company of Canada [1937], 1970), p. 214.

30For a detailed expansion of the remainder of this chapter, based on original sources, see Knight, *A Capital for Canada*, *op.cit.*, pp. 24-41.

31On settlement spread in Upper Canada see R. Louis Gentilcore, "Settlement" in R. Louis Gentilcore, ed., *Ontario: Studies in Canadian Geography* (Toronto: University of Toronto Press, 1972), pp. 23-44, and Gentilcore and Wood, "A Military Colony in a Wilderness: The Upper Canada Frontier," in Wood, *op.cit.*, pp. 32-50.

32Simcoe mentioned the interior location in many letters and even visited the site in March, 1793. See the voluminous correspondence in E.A. Cruikshank, ed., *The Correspondence of Lieut. Governor John Graves Simcoe with Allied Documents Relating to His Administration of the Government of Upper Canada* (Toronto: Ontario Historical Society, 5 volumes, 1923-1931).

33Spelt, *op.cit.*, and Peter G. Goheen, *Victorian Toronto, 1850 to 1900: Pattern and Process of Growth* (Chicago: University of Chicago, Department of Geography, Research Paper No. 127, 1970). See also Edith Firth, ed., *The Town of York 1793-1815: A Collection of Documents* (Toronto: Champlain Society, 1962), and *Idem, The Town of York 1815-1834; A Further Collection of Documents of Early Toronto* (Toronto: Champlain Society, 1966).

34See R.A. Preston, *Kingston Before the War of 1812: A Collection of Documents* (Toronto: Champlain Society, 1959).

35Lieutenant Governor Francis Gore was not convinced that such a move was correct and so informed his superior. PAC, PRO, CO42, Vol. 356, pp. 111-112, Gore to Lord Bathurst, May 30, 1815.

36PAC, MG11, CO42, Vol. 319, pp. 152b-156.

[37](York) *Observor*, March 1, 1830, and Upper Canada, House of Assembly, *Journals*, 1830, pp. 44-45.

[38]For a map and discussion of the voting patterns see Knight, *A Capital for Canada*, *op.cit.*, pp. 35-37.

[39]The genesis in the 1820's of the idea to have Bytown (Ottawa) selected as capital, and its vigorous development to 1841, has been explored in David B. Knight, " 'Boosterism' and Locational Analysis, or One Man's Swan is Another Man's Goose," *Urban History Review*, Vol. 2, no. 3 (February, 1974), pp. 10-16.

CHAPTER III

THE FIRST COMPROMISE: KINGSTON

Introduction

Lord John Russell first introduced the Canadian union bill to the Parliament in Westminster in 1839. The draft of the bill declared that Montreal should be the capital of the proposed Canadian union. However, this was objected to by Governor General Charles Poulett Thomson (Lord Sydenham after late 1840) whose task it was to get Canadians to agree to the union. Thomson recognized the seat of government location to be one of the most sensitive and yet also "one of the most urgent"[1] issues he had to address. He further recognized that if one place was designated as capital prior to the acceptance of the union bill by Canadians then acceptance of union itself might be delayed or even prevented. The Imperial bill was withdrawn and only later resubmitted, but with no place identified as capital and with the provision that the matter should be left in the hands of the Crown's representative.

Thomson had to balance conflicting pressures. There were the sectional tensions between Canada East and Canada West. Upper Canadians stated flatly that it was "their right to have the seat of the Provincial Government within the[ir] Province"[2] while Lower Canadians were equally clear in their claim to the honour. These sectional claims in part reflected cultural jealousies and suspicions. At a different level, as anticipation of union grew, inter-city jealousies flourished while claims were made for this or that place to be the capital. Within Lower Canada, the long-standing rivalries between Quebec and Montreal was compounded by the meeting of Lower Canada's Special Council in Montreal rather than in Quebec. Within Upper Canada, supporters of both Kingston and Toronto were prominent in advancing the claims of their favoured city, but supporters of other places also spoke up. One of these other places was the small, rough and tumble lumber town called Bytown on the Ottawa River. Bytownians even privately approached Thomson (who by then had received the news of his lordship) with the idea of renaming their town Sydenham in his honour, but he was not swayed.[3] The Bytownians did not know that their Governor had already decided in favour of Kingston.[4]

The selection of Kingston as capital represented a compromise and it was hailed as an unpopular choice in almost all sections of the country. After the news of the selection was declared, efforts were made to have the decision altered. Pre-union talk of an alternating system between Toronto and Quebec was revived and the idea was accepted by the Legislative Assembly during its first session (Figure 2). The Queen, in council, rejected the request for change.[5]

In 1842, after the Queen's response to the 1841 Address was presented to the House, the Legislative Assembly debated the issue. While members claimed to recognize "the undoubted prerogative of the Crown" they felt free to discuss the merits of contending cities and to vote for them. In most of the divisions a strong areal association was shown between riding and place under consideration. However, when it came to a vote against Kingston, there was a sectional split (see Figure 3). Reaction to the vote against Kingston was swift within Canada as people in various places called for the retention of Kingston as capital,[6] for one of the other cities to be made capital,[7] or for the preservation of the rights of this section or that.

Governor General Sir Charles Bagot got the Executive Council privately to face the issue and, early in 1843, the Council recommended that Montreal should be made the capital. One of the members of the Council was from Kingston and he strongly objected to the report and he later resigned from office in protest. Of all this the general public were to learn nothing for almost seven months. Both Sir Charles Bagot and his successor, Sir Charles Metcalfe, wanted Montreal to be the capital although they both feared that the relocation of the seat of government to Canada East might lead Upper Canadians to seek dissolution. Of course, this threat always was to remain all through the life of the union.

As rumours spread, both of an impending move and of the belief that the Government would have Parliament debate the issue, the *Kingston Loyalist* raged that the Government was throwing "a new apple of fierce discord between contending parties" and that "if the capital of Canada be removed to the Lower section of the Province, there will be no censation of an agitation to repeal the Union so lately affected."[8]

Metcalfe opened Parliament on September 28, 1843, but made no mention of the seat of government question in his speech. Within a few days, however, members of the Assembly were angrily discussing the issue and they asked the Governor General for any correspondence he might have on the topic. He responded by declaring that "Her Majesty's Government declines coming to a determination in favor of any place" but then confined the choice of possible locations for capital to Kingston and Montreal. After a long and very heated debate, and several divisions, the Assembly finally agreed to recommend a relocation to Montreal. The vote was a sectional one for Canada East members, with some (but not all) Reformers from Canada West supporting them (Figure 4). The recommendation was accepted and relocation occurred in 1844.

Notes

[1]PAC, PRO, MG11, Vol. 705, p. 144, Thomson to Lord John Russell, May 22, 1840.

[2]Upper Canada, House of Assembly, *Journals, 1839-1840*, "Address to Her Majesty on Union of the Canadas," p. 93.

[3]See Knight, " 'Boosterism' and Locational Analysis . . . ," *op.cit.*, p. 13.

[4]Paul Knaplund, ed., *Letters from Lord Sydenham to Lord John Russell* (London: George Allen and Unwin Ltd., 1931), p. 90, Thomson to Russell, September 16, 1840, and *Ibid.*, p. 99, Sydenham to Russell, October 28, 1840.

[5]There are no papers in the Royal Archives relating to the 1841 Canadian seat of government issue.

[6]Kingston sent a memorial to London asking for Imperial support.

[7]Representations were made in London to Lord Stanley by Charles Shirreff of the Ottawa Valley, on behalf of Ottawa, using published reprints of newspaper articles stating Ottawa's case.

[8]*Kingston Loyalist*, cited in *Montreal Gazette*, August 30, 1843.

Documents

1. Charles Poulett Thomson (Governor General) to Lord John Russell (Colonial Secretary), March 13, 1840(PAC).

The choice of the Seat of Govt. must be left entirely to the Crown without giving the Parlt. any power to alter the Prerogative. I have left it so purposely, for no man can say where the first Parlt. ever ought to be held, and it is not unlikely that we must found a new capital. Kingston perhaps, for Bye Town [Bytown] is too cold and too far, tho' that wd. in other respects be the best place.

2. The Union Act, 1840.

XXX. And be it enacted that it shall be lawful for the Governor of the Province of Canada for the time being to fix such place or places within any part of the Province of Canada, and such times for holding the first and every other session of the Legislative Council and Assembly of the said Province as he may think fit, such times and places to be afterwards changed or varied as the Governor may judge advisable and most consistent with general convenience and the public welfare, giving sufficient notice thereof. . . .

3. Charles Poulett Thomson (Governor General) to Lord John Russell (Colonial Secretary), (Private and Confidential), May 22, 1840 (PAC).

Under the provisions of the Union Bill, should they receive the sanction of Parliament, there will remain so little time for carrying into effect the objects contemplated, and for making preparations to meet an United Legislature, that I am compelled, with a view to prevent difficulties arising too late to enable me satisfactorily to overcome them, to consider most attentively & maturely some points upon which a decision of Her Majesty's Government is required to enable me satisfactorily to fulfill my duty.

One of the most urgent, & one which has engaged my most serious attention is the question of the future seat of Government, and of the means which I shall have to adopt for satisfactorily assembling the first United Legislature, which I presume must be called together early next year.

I have given to this subject the best consideration in my power, and altho' I am not at all prepared to offer any definite recommendation upon it, or entirely decided in my own mind upon the course to be followed, as it will be too late for correspondence with references to the first meeting at least to wait until then, I can only state my present views & solicit from Her Majesty's Government discretionary powers to carry them into effect as shall hereafter appear most advisable.

There are four, if not five, possible situations for the seat of Government of the new Province of Canada; Quebec-Montreal-Kingston-Toronto-and Bytown.

The last I will dismiss at once however. Altho' presenting considerable advantages from its position away from the Frontier, or at the mouth of the Rideau, it is so very small a place, would require such vast increase of Buildings, & is altogether so remote from thickly settled Districts, that I cannot consider it as fit for the purpose at present.

Of the four others, Quebec & Toronto enjoy in point of convenience of accommodation & the necessary Buildings, considerable advantages. At Quebec there is a Building for the House of Assembly & Legislative Council, and Public Buildings for the different offices—No Government House.—At Toronto, there are all these Establishments on a moderate scale, which might without much difficulty or expense be increased.

But both these places are unfortunately utterly unfit from their position & other circumstances for being made the permanent seat of Government, nor are they suited even for the place in which the first Legislature should hold its sittings.—Quebec, situated at the extreme East of the Province, nearly 1000 miles from the Western position of the country, surrounded by a French Population, and removed at a Great distance from communication thro' the states with Great Britain, would be unsuited to the wants of a Government constituted as this is.—Toronto is on the other hand too far to the west for affording the means of guiding affairs in Lower Canada. It is a Town altogether undefended & indefensible—a bad Port—an unhealthy District. The communication thro' the states must in the winter be carried on thro' Hamilton & Niagara round the Lake, a tedious circuit, & its extreme distance from the Eastern Provinces renders communication with England by Halifax open to great delay. There are many political reasons too which would make this city an extremely unfit place for the seat of Government, & even undesirable as the place where the first Assembly should be holden.

I cannot therefore entertain the idea of fixing the seat of Government at either Quebec or Toronto, & altho' it might be possible under an emergency to hold the first Parliament at Toronto, I should regret being obliged to do so. Quebec is out of the question even for that purpose.

There remains Montreal & Kingston.

With respect to accommodation at present existing for the Legislature, the Governor & the Government offices both stand much upon a par.—There is little or none in either.

At Montreal there is one Building only belonging to the Civil Government—the old Government House, of one story only and of moderate size, affording partial accommodation for the Civil Secretary's office & a Room for myself in which the special Council assemble. There is no Government House or Residence for the Governor. I occupy a House hired by the year of W. Bingham. There are no offices whatever for the different Departments of Government. Rooms have been engaged for this purpose for short periods as best can be done, and the different officers of Government receive large additional Pay for quitting Quebec, and establishing themselves here. There is no Parliament House.

At Kingston there is of course nothing of the kind either.

On the score of defence Kingston enjoys a great superiority over Montreal. It is defensible & may be rendered still more so.—The Public Archives could be in safety there, which they would not here.

In respect to any communication with England they are about on a par.—Kingston affords greater facilities at all times of the year thro' the States than does Montreal—the latter place enjoys about 24 hours advantage over the other thro' Halifax.—Montreal is at the head of the

Atlantic navigation—Kingston at the outlet of the Lake navigation & the head of the Rideau. The first is about 180 miles from Quebec, which may be considered the extreme East of the Province requiring attention, and upwards of 600 from Sandwich the extreme West.—Kingston is about 360 from Quebec & about 450 from Sandwich.—Montreal is the older & more populous City of the two.

So far then the matter would stand thus between the two cities.

Montreal is the most populous & extensive of the two.—It is a greater commercial place.—Kingston is more central to the whole Province. It is more easily defensible & more secure even at present. Neither have any Public Buildings, & they must be erected whichever be chosen. Both afford about equal facilities of communication with Europe.

But with a view to the future Government of the Province, Kingston possesses Great advantages over Montreal—and with regard merely to the expense to be incurred in preparation it seems to me to enjoy also a Superiority, altho' for mere temporary purposes the other City, owing to its greater population & extent, would afford perhaps more immediate facilities.

I am strongly of opinion that the most important portion of the Canadas is the Upper Province. The fertility of its soil—the character of it's people, the nature of Settlement, the direction which it has taken Westward—the Capabilities for improvement, the room afforded for Emigration, make Upper Canada even now an object demanding the utmost care & attention from the Government, and will render it if properly governed hereafter the source of our wealth & greatness on this Continent.

Lower Canada has, it is true, a numerical majority of population but of what does it consist?—Of a vast body of French Canadian Peasantry cultivating in the most barbarous way a soil of far less fertility—a people not incapable of improvement, but still only to be very slowly and gradually improved in the Habits & Education—and of an English or Scotch Town population in the cities engaged chiefly in forwarding the products of Upper Canada. The Eastern Townships indeed exhibit a healthy & thriving population of British & American Settlers, but the want of water communication & the rigor of the climate as compared with the other Province will make their growth slow and set limits to their improvement.

These are the general features of the two Provinces, & from their consideration I infer that it is most important that the government should be pleased as far as possible in a situation to superintend & give close attention to the affairs of that which demands it most, namely Upper Canada, rather than in such a position as would render its control less effective, its means of communication with that Province more difficult, & place it in immediate contract only with that portion of the Country where direct superintendence will be less useful.

Next it seems to me very desirable that the seat of Government & above all the sittings of the Legislature should be removed from the presence of a large French Population. Montreal is it's centre. To bring the French members to the middle of English Population would instil English ideas into their minds, destroy the immediate influence upon their actions of the host of little Lawyers, Notaries & Doctors—the pest of Lower Canada, who swarm in the District—and shew them the advantages of practical improvements & the working of English habits.

In regard to the expense which must attend the Establishments required for Government & Parliamentary purposes, Kingston would likewise probably possess an advantage to a considerable extent over Montreal. At the last mentioned City there is no land belonging to the Crown, at the other there is a great deal, which might be taken advantage of. The expense of erecting Buildings would be less too, at Kingston than here. For a permanent Establishment therefore that City would possess superior advantages to the other in every respect. For a mere makeshift for a year or two a moderate Expenditure would probably suffice to erect a place for the first meetings of the Legislature at Montreal. Buildings might be hired there for the Public Officers, & less difficulty would be found for the servants of the government & others attending on Business in procuring for themselves the accommodation which is necessary to them. But this expense would of course be so much lost.

Of the two therefore as the permanent seat of Government I give the preference decidedly to Kingston, & it would be extremely desirable if possible that, if intended as such, it should also be the place for the meeting of the first Legislature.

My stay in that City was not however sufficiently long to enable me to examine the locality so much as I would desire to do—nor have my enquiries enabled me to ascertain the extent of accommodation which might be obtained there, or the time which would be required to prepare what may be wanted, sufficiently to form an opinion whether it would be possible to have the means of meeting the Legislature there next year. These enquiries however I have ordered to be made, & upon my journey to the Upper Province in July, or August I shall examine more closely into the matter in order to come to a determination.

As however it may be necessary to make immediate preparations either at Montreal or Kingston, with a view to a place for the Legislature to meet in & for the Government Offices, even tho' they should be of a temporary character, I would solicit your Lordship's authority to act at once in the manner which may seem best, with reference to the whole subject, as soon as I have the necessary data upon which to come to a determination, either by preparing temporary Buildings, if I find it impossible to have permanent ones ready in time, or by making arrangements for permanent Buildings if I find that possible.

Should further examination of Kingston confirm me in my opinion, I shall endeavour of course to make arrangements if possible for meeting the Legislature there next year—at all events with a view to the Government being fixed there hereafter. Should the first not be possible, I must then consider whether temporary arrangements can be made here, or whether under all the circumstances I may not meet the first Parliament at Toronto—it being clearly understood that Kingston was the seat of Government, that the buildings were in preparation, & that the arrangement was purely temporary.

The expense must I presume be ultimately borne by the Province, but there are no funds at present applicable to the purpose & it may be necessary therefore in the first instance to draw upon the military chest and arrangement can afterwards easily be made when a financial settlement for the United Province comes to be effected.—My utmost endeavours will of course be to observe the strictest economy.

Before closing this Dispatch I may as well with reference to this subject remark that there cannot be a greater fallacy than the notion which I have sometimes heard, that it would be expedient to allow the Legislature to meet alternately in different Cities of the Province.—It would not only be inexpedient, but it would be utterly impossible to conduct the Business of the Government under such a system.—Here everything centres in the Government. The most trifling affairs are matter of reference from all parts of the country, and the most constant and immediate reference is daily required to the Public Departments and the Documents preserved in them. The utmost inconvenience is even now felt from the circumstance of the Government Departments for this Province being divided between Quebec and Montreal. The offices and Archives there—the officers themselves here and I assure you that the difficulty of conducting affairs satisfactorily is in no small degree increased by this circumstance. It would be next to impossible to conduct the Business of the United Province upon such a system, still less with an ambulatory Executive.

4. Lord John Russell (Colonial Secretary) to Charles Poulett Thomson (Governor General), June 22, 1840 (PAC).

I received by the British Queen your despatch of the 22nd of May, marked private, and confidential, on the question of the future Seat of Government in Canada.

I beg you to accept my thanks for the very clear and useful information which you have communicated to me on this subject. My own opinion is strongly in favour of Kingston as the seat of Govt. and the permanent place of meeting for the Legislature. With respect to the first Assembly so many local circumstances of convenience must be considered, that I leave it entirely to your discretion, only desiring that you will consult persons of all parties before your decision is formed.

The distance of Toronto from Quebec wd. I should imagine, make a journey to that place from Quebec very burthensome.

5. (Kingston) *Upper Canada Herald*, February 2, 1841.

We are happy to be able to inform our readers that the secret is at last out. Kingston is to be the Seat of Government.

6. (Kingston) *Chronicle and Gazette*, February 6, 1841.

. . . the Public Records will now be placed in a situation equally secure from foreign invasion on the one hand and from internal insurrection on the other.

7. Lord Sydenham (Charles Poulett Thomson; Governor General) to Sir George Arthur (former Lieutenant Governor of Upper Canada), February 10, 1841.

I expected that there would be a breeze at Toronto about the Seat of Government, but it can't be helped, and I am satisfied that the rest of the Province will not sympathize with the Toronto-ites. *All* that the [Upper Canada] House of Assembly asked in their 'recommendations' has been conceded to them by taking Kingston, and Upper Canada therefore ought to be very well pleased. As a set off, I have at least as great a row from Quebec, whose claims are about the same as Toronto's. Montreal on the contrary, which really might have expected to see the Government established there, is quite quiet and does not repine.

8. (Toronto) *Examiner*, February 10, 1841.

The good people of Toronto without distinction of party, have been astounded at the intelligence that the first meeting of the United Legislature is to be held at Kingston.

9. (Montreal) *Morning Courier*, February 10, 1841.

Notes of wailing and wrath have already reached us from Toronto upon the selection of Kingston for the first Session of the Legislature. As for Montreal, we hear not her lament upon the subject. The independent citizens feel that they are to acquire greatness without artificial aids, by the advantage of position and their own energies.

10. *Quebec Mercury*, March 6, 1841.

The Toronto papers in general are much incensed at the removal of the seat of Government from their city. Many of them indulge in wild assertions of promises implied and violent invective against the Governor General; others, again, sit down despondingly and weep over what they consider an irremediable evil.

11. *Kingston Herald*, May 18, 1841.

The time approaches when the Governor General will enter Kingston, to open the first Parliament of Canada. It is an event important in itself; but it has additional interest in this Town, owing to it being the place chosen for the sitting of Parliament, by which the metropolitan dignity is conferred on Kingston.

12. (Montreal) *Le Canadien*, July 7, 1841.

[Kingston is] a town without local colour, without character.

13. Legislative Assembly, September 16, 1841.

Three identical votes on alternating the capital between Toronto and Quebec or for compensation, and for sending an Address to the Queen on this topic: Yeas 26, Nays 21; Figure 2 and also next selection.

14. Address of the Legislative Assembly to Queen Victoria, September 16, 1841. (JLA)

MOST GRACIOUS SOVEREIGN:
We, Your Majesty's most dutiful and loyal subjects, the Legislative Assembly, of Canada, in Parliament assembled, humbly beg leave to approach Your Majesty with renewed expressions of our devoted attachment to Your Royal Person and Government.
We would, most respectfully, beg leave to represent to Your Majesty, that the Inhabitants of the, now, Province of Canada, having never been expressly called upon to offer an opinion upon the Union of the Provinces of Upper and Lower Canada, do not presume, on the present occasion, to obtrude upon Your Majesty our views and opin-

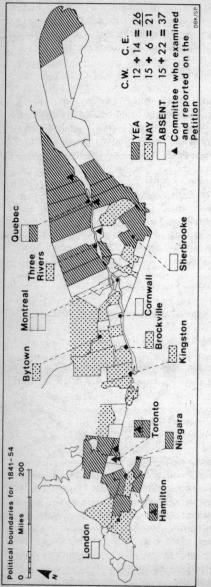

YEA

NAY

ABSENT

▲ Committee who examined and reported on the Petition

	C.W.	C.E.	
YEA	12	+ 14	= 26
NAY	15	+ 6	= 21
ABSENT	15	+ 22	= 37

Quebec

Three Rivers

Montreal

Bytown

Sherbrooke

Cornwall

Brockville

Kingston

Toronto

Niagara

Hamilton

London

Political boundaries for 1841-54

0 Miles 200

N

DBK/SP

Figure 2. For alternating system (Quebec and Toronto) or for compensation; September 16, 1841. (See selection 13)

ions on that measure; but content ourselves, now that it has taken place, with expressing our fervent wishes that every advantage, contemplated by its promoters, may be fully realized.

That the Inhabitants of these Provinces did not anticipate, from the adoption of the union, that the vital interests of any portion were likely to be jeopardized, as recent events seem to threaten, because there is no principle in Legislation more fully established than that when a Law, though necessary for the good of the Community, bears severely on particular Sections, and causes serious loss and inconvenience, such loss and inconvenience should be as fully remunerated as possible, at the expense of the public, for whose benefit it is sustained.

That, in considering the union of the Province, the Inhabitants of the Cities of *Quebec* and *Toronto* did not conceal from themselves the possibility of being called upon to make greater sacrifices than the Inhabitants of any other part of the Province; but they did not anticipate any greater disadvantage than what might arise from holding the Provincial Parliament alternately at *Toronto* and *Quebec*; for they assured themselves that their Most Gracious Sovereign, the Queen, in the exercise of Her just prerogative, would be entirely directed, in selecting the place for convening the Legislature, by a due regard to existing claims, and interests, as well as the general convenience of the Province.

That, while the question of the Union was under discussion, only two places seemed to offer any just Claims to become the seat of Government—*Quebec* and *Toronto*—both had been the Capitals of their respective Provinces, from the very first; they possessed all the necessary convenience, and the great interests which had grown up in each respectively, from the fact of their being the seat of Government, required favourable consideration.

That the vast extent of the United Province, (sufficient, in the practice of our neighbours, to constitute six or seven Sovereign States) seems to render any position, however near the centre, undesirable as the permanent place for the meeting of Parliament for the following, among other reasons:

The great object of the Union is to amalgamate, as soon as possible into one people, the population of both Provinces; gradually but gently to assimilate their laws and customs, their hopes and interests. We respectfully beg leave to express our sincere conviction that no measure can, with equal facility, quicken such happy results as causing the Legislature to meet four years in the midst of one population, and four years in the midst of the other.

The Representatives of Eastern and Western Canada would thus become acquainted with the respective Inhabitants; their habits and views; their wants and expectations, and become able to meet their just desires; and to adopt such measures as will, without violence to any feelings, or even prejudices, transform them, in a reasonable time, into one people.

That the measure of alternate Parliaments, in like circumstances, is not without many precedents, and in the present case will be attended with many essential and paramount advantages. The only objection that can be raised must be confined to a small matter of expense which will bear no proportion to the interest of the very large sums required for erecting such buildings to accommodate the Legislature, and the several Public Departments, as already exist at *Toronto* and *Quebec*.

That although these may be deemed among the leading points in favour of alternate Parliaments at *Quebec* and *Toronto*, there are other reasons, to which, though somewhat of a local nature, we would respectfully pray Your Majesty's consideration. *Toronto* from the change of the Seat of Government is threatened with even greater loss than *Quebec*, from the removal of the Superior Courts. Now such removal would be of great and serious disadvantages to Western Canada. *Toronto* is very nearly in its centre, being about 280 miles from the Point au Baudet, the Eastern extremity and 270 miles from Amherstburg, the Western; and therefore convenient, beyond all other places, for transacting the public business of the Province.

It has all the public buildings required, and as the Laws, Customs, and habits, of the two Provinces, differ essentially, at present, many years may elapse before they can be assimilated so as to unite the Judiciary.

Add to all this the fact that seven-tenths of the population of Western Canada must always be found west of the *Bay of Quinté*, and to them the loss and inconvenience of managing their business will be greatly increased should the Courts be removed from *Toronto*; and all this without the slightest equivalent.

That many of the inhabitants of the late Provinces of *Lower and Upper Canada*, relying on the emphatic language of His late Majesty, King William the fourth, "that a Union of the Provinces of *Upper* and *Lower Canada* was not a measure fit to be recommended to Parliament" and therefore not anticipating any such enactment did, under the conviction that *Toronto* and *Quebec* would continue the seat of Government in their respective Provinces, expend the greater part of their means on fixed property, and will therefore, be impoverished, and many of them exposed to the greatest sacrifices should the seat of Government be wholly removed.

Indeed the loss to merchants and tradesmen begins already to be felt, and to some it will prove utter ruin, all must suffer should there be no remedy; for the depreciation of real property, cannot under such a disastrous event, be less than several hundred thousand pounds.

Wherefore we most earnestly entreat that Your Majesty, in the exercise of Your Royal prerogative, will be pleased to order that the Parliament of Canada, hereafter, assemble alternately at *Quebec* and *Toronto*, the respective capitals of the late Provinces of *Upper* and *Lower* Canada, or should such prayer be thought unadvisable, and any other measure be adopted, that adequate and just renumeration be granted for the loss sustained by the inhabitants of *Toronto* and *Quebec*.

15. Sir Richard D. Jackson (Administrator of the Province of Canada) to Lord Stanley (Colonial Secretary), September 28, 1841 (PAC).

I have the honour to transmit to you herewith in order that it may be laid at the foot of the Throne, an Address to the Queen from the Legislative Assembly of this Province, on the subject of the Seat of Government.

Two similar Addresses had been previously presented to the Governor General, by the Inhabitants of Toronto, and in forwarding the present Address, which was adopted in the last few days of the Session, after a large proportion of the Members had left Kingston, and then only by a small majority, it is my duty to state to your Lordship that, as far as I can learn, this question excites but little interest in any place besides Toronto. The Inhabitants of Quebec, though naturally regretting the removal of the Seat of Government from their City, have apparently acquiesced in the reasonableness of that measure; at any rate they have taken no active steps to urge the matter on the consideration of the Government.

The prayer of the present Petition is, that the Parliament should be summoned for alternate periods of four years at Toronto and Quebec; an arrangement which would of course involve a quadrennial removal of the Executive Departments. The impracticability of such an arrangement, from the expense attending it, must be evident to every one—and of the inconvenience and interruption to business which it must create, we have had sufficient experience in the removal during last spring from Montreal to this place. This inconvenience too would be annually increasing as the Records of the Departments grew in bulk, until even if there were no other difficulty, this alone would render the proposed scheme impossible.

There are many other objections to the proposal, which it seems scarcely necessary to point out, considering that the single advantage which it is proposed to obtain at so great a sacrifice , is an indemnity for their supposed loss to the Inhabitants of Toronto and Quebec. But I would observe that the Petition of the House of Assembly of Upper Canada to the Crown, which accompanied the Resolutions on the

Union of the Provinces, merely prayed that the Seat of Government should be within the limits of the Upper Province, a prayer that has been fully complied with; the present demand is altogether of a different character, and supported on different and more questionable arguments.

I cannot therefore recommend that Her Majesty should be advised to comply with the prayer of this Address.

16.   Lord Stanley (Colonial Secretary) to Sir Charles Bagot (Governor General), November 2, 1841 (PAC).

I have received Sir Richard Jackson's Despatch of the 28th of September, forwarding an Address to the Queen from the Legislative Assembly of the Province of Canada, praying Her Majesty to order the Provincial Parliament to be held alternately at the Cities of Quebec and Toronto.

I have had the honour to lay that Address before the Queen, and I have received Her Majesty's commands to instruct you to acquaint the House of Assembly, that Her Majesty is always desirous, so far as may be possible, of consulting the wishes of Her Loyal Subjects in Canada, deliberately entertained and constitutionally expressed through their Representatives in the House of Assembly; but that the establishment of Kingston as the Seat of the United Legislature was not adopted without full consideration, and that a change involving among other consequences largely increased expenditure, ought not to be sanctioned, except upon the clearest necessity, and the general sense of the Province unequivocally expressed in its favor. Many and serious objections attach to the proposal for holding Sessions for alternate periods of four years each at distinct and distant places, which, upon reconsideration, Her Majesty can hardly doubt will induce the House of Assembly to take a different view from that which is expressed in the Address now submitted to Her Majesty.

17.   Sir Charles Bagot (Governor General) to Lord Stanley (Colonial Secretary), (Confidential), January 19, 1842 (PAC).

In my despatch of the 17th Instant, I have alluded to the final decision as to the Seat of Govt. of this Province as a question which has given rise to a great deal of excitement, and one on which it would be desirable to avoid discussion in the Legislature until the Govt. should be prepared to take a decided course. I now proceed to explain more at length the views which I [have] been led to form respecting it and the decision to which I think H.M. Govt. should come.

Lord Sydenham's Private and Confidential despatch of the 22 May,

1840, the advantages of the several places in which the Seat of Government might be fixed and more especially those of Montreal and Kingston are discussed at considerable length and the preference given to the latter. No doubt much weight is due to Lord Sydenham's opinion, and in many of his arguments I entirely concur. In his view for instance as to the expediency of removing the first meeting of the Legislature from the midst of a French population and thus of opening the eyes of the French Members to their real position in the midst of a people of English descent and feelings, I quite agree, and have reason to believe that the proposed effect was produced during the last Session.

But the time which has since elapsed, and more especially the experience of the last nine months give us more ample means of judging of the capabilities and fitness of Kingston than Lord Sydenham possessed, and have produced a very general impression that it is not the most convenient place for the Seat of Government. The town is small and poor; and the Country around it unproductive. There is no accommodation for the Members of the Legislative when the Session is in progress nor even at other times for those Strangers who may be compelled to resort to the Seat of Govt. on business. And although it might no doubt be so fortified as to make if difficult for an enemy to hold the Town, it would be impossible to secure it from attack and insult and even from danger of being destroyed should its destruction as the depository of the public archives be of sufficient importance. Situated on the border of the Lake to which it is perfectly open—within twelve miles of the American Shore and within fifteen miles of their principal naval station on Lake Ontario, it is evident that its security must depend on the enemy never being able, even for a few hours to obtain the superiority on this end of the Lake. This however is a contingency on which in the event of a war it would of course be impossible to reckon.

Still Kingston has so many advantages from its central position and it is so important to avoid the expense and inconvenience of moving the Government Offices that I should not think of a change did I suppose that the permanent settlement of the Government here would be not unacceptable to the great body of the people. But I have every reason to believe the contrary. The utter want of accommodation, and, I regret to say, the extortion which has been practised by the Inhabitants on those who have been compelled to come here, have produced a universal dislike to the place; and I have not met with a single person unconnected with the Town or its immediate vicinity who does not deprecate its selection as the permanent Seat of Government. It would therefore, I apprehend be a matter of extreme difficulty if not of absolute impossibility, to persuade the Legislature to vote the necessary Funds for Public Buildings in this Town, or even for the continuance of the present arrangement, except on the understanding that it is altogether temporary.

The H.M. Government can of course have no interest in the locality of the Govt. of Canada, provided it be in a position where the Records and Officers will be secure, and which may be acceptable to the great bulk of the population. There is no fear that the proposition of last Session for alternate Parliaments at Quebec and Toronto should be renewed: indeed had any other proposal by which to get away from Kingston been brought forward, that proposition would probably not have been carried. But there appears to be an increasing desire that the permanent Seat of Government should be fixed at Montreal or Quebec—the former as the most central, the most populous and the most accessible Town in the Province—the latter as the strongest, and as already possessing a great portion of the necessary buildings.

Montreal has undoubtedly many advantages. It is a very large and growing city containing from 45,000 to 50,000 inhabitants—and capable therefore of accommodating any number of strangers who might resort to it. It is at the head of the Sea Navigation, and is accessible from the Sea for about three weeks later than Kingston is by the Rideau Canal; and it is removed from the Frontier, and therefore, although not defensible in itself, perfectly secure from a coup de main—and within less than 12 hours of Quebec to which in case of necessity the Government and the Public Archives could be removed. All the members from Lower Canada would naturally prefer Montreal to Kingston, and so also would the members from the Eastern part of Upper Canada. The members from Toronto and its vicinity would likewise prefer Montreal from feelings of jealousy towards this Town—leaving those only who either have property here or who come from the Western District, to support its pretensions. Quebec also would as compared with Kingston and even perhaps as compared with Montreal have a majority of Lower Canadian Members in its favor; also one strong argument for it would be the saving of expense in the erection of the public buildings; but I apprehend that the Western Members would be indisposed to vote for a situation so distant from them, and with which they have not the same commercial relations as with Montreal.

The arrangement which now subsists for the Parliament buildings, the Public Offices and the Government House will expire in May 1844, and it is indispensable that before that time permanent accommodation should be provided for the Government. It is also highly desirable that an end should be put to the uncertainty and excitement now existing on the subject, and with this view that it should be brought forward and decided at the next meeting of the Legislature—should that meeting not take place till the summer.

But this [is] a question on which it would be neither prudent nor becoming in the Government to leave the initiative to an individual member, or to appear to be without any definitive views of its own. Still less would it be becoming that the Government should find itself in opposition to a majority of the House of Assembly and should be compelled either to abandon it's proposed vote, or to adopt whatever decision the House might come to. There appears but one way to avoid the risk of such a dilemma. There is little fear that opinions will be so balanced as to leave a doubt respecting the wishes of the Legislature; and I shall have an opportunity during the coming Summer and more especially when the Legislature shall be called together of ascertaining exactly the nature of those wishes. I would propose to determine my course according to the result of these enquiries. If, as I expect a decided preponderance should appear in favor of Quebec or Montreal, it should I think be the policy of the Government to adopt either of those Cities as might appear most desirable, and to bring the matter forward as a Government measure. If the House should appear to be nearly balanced, or even to incline a little in favor of Kingston, the Government might then by throwing its weight into the Scale decide the question and fix the Seat of Government where it is. But it is indispensable that whatever is to be carried should be carried by the Government and not by individual members.

I would therefore solicit your Lordship's authority to frame my course on this subject as I shall on enquiry find to be most agreeable to the People of the Province, and as may appear most advantageous to the public service. Your Lordship may be assured that I shall use this discretion solely with a view to public considerations, and without any personal predilections in favor of any place. Whatever decision may be come to it will be impossible to remove from Kingston for the next two years, and for that time the existing arrangements must be continued; but there will I apprehend be no difficulty in obtaining the sanction of the Legislature to that course provided their wishes in regard to the permanent Seat of Government be not thwarted.

18. *Quebec Mercury*, September 29, 1842.

The despatch [of November 2, 1841] of the Colonial Minister respecting the future Seat of Government has been communicated to the Legislative Assembly; it is completely on the non-committal principle and leaves the choice in the hands of that body. The great contest will be between Montreal and this city, and the advantages and disadvantages of both are so nearly balanced that it is probable the convenience of the public buildings already in existence, will, on the score of expense, restore this city to its former rank as the true Metropolis of British North America. . . .

. . . . It appears however pretty certain that whatever place may be ultimately chosen as the Seat of Government the sessions of the Legislature will, for the next two years, be held in this city.

19. Legislative Assembly as House in Committee, October 5, 1842 (JLA)

Resolved, That it is the opinion of this Committee, that it is the undoubted prerogative of the Crown, and conformable to the positive enactment of the Statute of the Imperial Parliament of the United Kingdom, under which this House is constituted and assembled, that "The place or places, within any part of the Province of Canada, for holding each and every Session of the Legislative Council and Assembly," should be fixed under the authority of the Crown. (accepted)

Resolved, That it is the opinion of this Committee, that the building in which the Legislative Assembly is now held, and which was erected several years ago, for a different purpose, does not afford sufficient accommodation to enable the Members to discharge their duty to their Constituents with due enquiry, and sufficient deliberation, and that the locality of Kingston is not central to the majority of the population, and is badly provided with accommodation for the residence of the Members, particularly during Winter, which is the Season in which they can attend to their Legislative duties, with the smallest sacrifice to their general interests. (Yeas 40, Nays 20; see Figure 3)

20. Sir Charles Bagot (Governor General) to Lord Stanley (Colonial Secretary), October 8, 1842 (PAC).

I have the honor to inform your Lordship that on the 28th ultimo I transmitted, in a Message to the House of Assembly, Her Majesty's Answer to the Address of that House, adopted last Session, relative to the Seat of Government, as communicated in your Lordship's Despatch of the 2nd November last.

The result was that on the 5th instant a motion was made in the form of two Resolutions, brought forward by an independent British Member, to the effect, first—of declaring the undoubted prerogative of Her Majesty to fix the said Seat, and secondly, of condemning Kingston as the locality for it, and the present Parliament Buildings as insufficient and incommodious.

. . . . The first Resolution was carried in the affirmative. Before passing the second, propositions were made and divisions were taken upon the propriety of expressing a preference in favor of the Towns

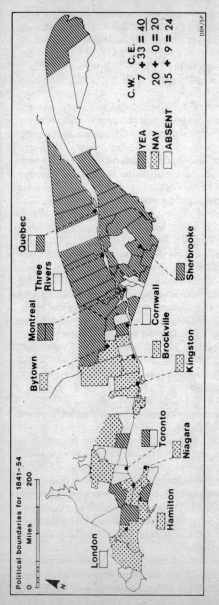

Political boundaries for 1841–54

0 Miles 200

	C.W.		C.E.	
YEA	7	+	33	= 40
NAY	20	+	0	= 20
ABSENT	15	+	9	= 24

Bytown Montreal Three Rivers Quebec

Sherbrooke

Cornwall

Brockville

Kingston

Toronto

Niagara

Hamilton

London

DBK/SP

Figure 3. Against Kingston; October 5, 1842. (See selection 19)

of Toronto, Quebec, Montreal, and Bytown, but the motions were negatived on the double ground that their adoption would stultify the first Resolution, and that it was impossible to induce the House so far to agree upon the choice of a substitute for Kingston as to furnish a majority large enough to mark the feeling of the public upon the subject, and to have an influence upon Her Majesty's determination.

The division on the several Resolutions finally took a sectional character. Twenty Members, all belonging to Upper Canada, opposed it, and forty Members, of whom seven were Upper Canadians, supported it.

The question, thus your Lordship will perceive, is left in the same position as before; and it is not my intention to recommend to Her Majesty to take any steps in the matter, until some strong sense of public convenience or public policy, or some more definite expression of the general feeling of the Province shall lead me to pronounce an opinion upon the subject.

21. Lord Stanley (Colonial Secretary) to Sir Charles Bagot (Governor General), November 11, 1842 (PAC).

I have received your correspondence relative to the removal of the Seat of Government in Canada, From Kingston to some other Town.

I think that you have acted wisely in abstaining from any public step on this subject; but as the question must be definitely settled at no very distant period, I would suggest to you the propriety of making up your mind, with the aid of your Executive Council, on the point, in order that you may be prepared to guide public opinion whenever the measure may be brought into discussion.

22. Sir Charles Bagot (Governor General) to Lord Stanley (Colonial Secretary), October 28, 1842 (PAC).

[The] very difficult [question should] remain in status quo—which at present may be the best state in which it can be left—all parties acknowledge the absolute prerogative of the Crown to decide it—but the question of the money is unfortunately their own.

23. Sir Charles Bagot (Governor General) to Lord Stanley (Colonial Secretary), (confidential), November 11, 1842 (PAC).

. . . it is very desirable to keep the question of the Metropole in abeyance at this moment if it should be found possible.

24. Sir Charles Bagot (Governor General) to Lord Stanley (Colonial Secretary), December 11, 1842 (PAC).

. . . eventually, and if things hold, there is no doubt that Montreal is the proper place. . . . The question virtually must be in the hands of the Assembly which holds the purse strings. . . .

25. Report of a Committee of the Executive Council to Sir Charles Bagot (Governor General), March 16, 1843 (EC).

May it please your Excellency,

The important question respecting the locality of the seat of Provincial Government of Canada, upon which your Excellency is desired by Her Majesty's Secretary of State for the Colonies to form an opinion with the assistance of the Executive Council, has engaged the anxious attention of the Committee of the whole of that body, and the Committee, fully sensible of the difficulties attending such a subject of inquiry, and aware of the impossibility of reconciling local interests in favour of any decision which may be pronounced, respectfully offer their advice, the result of much deliberation, and which, though not in accordance with the first impression on the mind of the late Governor-General, or with the policy which directed the assemblage of the Legislature at Kingston, and the removal of the public departments to that place, they believe, nevertheless, to be most conducive to the public welfare, and most likely to meet with the general approbation of the people of the Province.

As might naturally be expected, the popular opinions most strongly expressed are either openly based upon the claims of the inhabitants of certain localities to have the seat of Government in their own city or neighbourhood, or they are traceable to local pecuniary interest, though assuming the appearance of taking public and general ground. Thus, for example, the citizens of the ancient capitals of Upper and Lower Canada complain of depreciation in the value of property, consequent upon the removal of the Government from these cities. The inhabitants of Kingston set up a like claim because of their late investment of capital in building, and in the purchase of building-ground, under an expectation formed by them that Kingston was to be the permanent capital. Then on behalf of Quebec, its military strength and its possession of buildings for the use of the Legislature are said to give that city the preference, on the arguments of security and economy. The existence of public buildings in Toronto, the rapidly increasing population and wealth of that city and the neighbouring districts, are urged as public grounds of economy and future convenience in its favour; while in Kingston its central position and defences, and the expenditure, that lately took place under the authority of Lord Sydenham, in the purchase of lands for the erection of public buildings, are brought forward, not only as inducements for making Kingston the provincial capital, but as in a manner binding Her Majesty's Government to fulfil expectations to which the acts of Government gave rise. Then in favour of Bytown, its inland position on the boundary river between the late provinces, and at the mouth of the great military canal of the Rideau, are said to give it claims to consideration above other places, because it is comparatively safe in case of war, and convenient alike for Upper and Lower Canadians.

The Committee look upon the selection of a locality for the Government and Legislature as far too important to the public generally, to permit of much consideration of the local interests of the inhabitants of the places claiming to be chosen. The convenience and advantage of the whole community are mainly to be sought, and it may be said that these are the sole objects to be served in the selection of a capital in a country like Canada, where as yet no great local interests are created of sufficient importance to entitle them to regard in a national point of view. The removal of a Government is unquestionably a great calamity to the possessors of property in the place from which the removal is made and measures of change in this respect should never be lightly adopted; but these facts only make it more imperatively the duty of the Government to be careful of the choice, and at the earliest possible period to fix the capital at a place from which the future condition of the country will not require a removal. To continue for a time any seat of Government injudiciously chosen, exposes the place to the aggravated but certain future evil of abandonment when the interest involved would be vastly greater than at present; and therefore while the Government is bound to avoid as much as possible changes in the location of a capital, this desirable object can only be attained by a correct selection made in contemplation, not of local or temporary, but of general and abiding interests.

The union of the provinces of Canada brings together in one legislature and in one city those interested with the management of the public affairs of a people scattered over an extensive region, and differing in language, in laws, and, in many respects, in local interests. It also brings to the seat of the Provincial Government a continual concourse of persons having private or public matters to solicit. To cause this assemblage in any portion of one section of the province, which, from its position, would place the legislature and suitors from the other section at once out of view of everything connected with their own race and country, and at a distance from those whose interests they are bound to represent, and whose confidence it is essential to them to continue, would, in the opinion of the Committee of Council, prove a never-ceasing source of discontent, and would promote a sense of banishment and abandonment which no arguments could overcome, or no advantages counterbalance; some of this feeling is unavoidable, from the fact that any capital in Canada must be a great distance from the extremities of the province, and those at a distance from the scene of legislative deliberation and executive action will always imagine their interests more or less overlooked or their opinions slighted; but dissatisfaction of this nature must be very much aggravated if legislation be carried on in a locality where neither the language, laws, or manners of a large portion of the community prevail, or are known, and where the actual condition and requirements of that part of the population cannot be observed, and can only be learned upon statements liable to be denied or controverted. Could no common locality be found on ground equal, or nearly so, to both parties, a great obstacle would be offered to the success of the measure of the union, for the Committee think that one or the other party would continue discontented, and would suffer under a sense of injustice and oppression most injurious to the Government, and inimical to the tranquillity of the province. To find the place which leaves the least foundation for complaint on any side, has therefore been the object of the Committee of Council in the present inquiry, and it is one which they think ought to be paramount to all others.

Quebec, it is true, has its fortifications; it is the mart of the timber-trade, in which a portion of the people of Upper Canada are concerned; it has Houses of Parliament already constructed, which might temporarily answer for the meeting of the Legislature, and part of which would serve the same purpose in future; and it is not materially different in climate from most other parts of the Province. But its distance from Upper Canada; its want of equal commercial connection with the Upper Province, except as regards one branch of trade; the little personal common intercourse between its inhabitants and people from the western portion of the Colony, form, in the opinion of the Committee, strong objections to its being chosen as the seat of Government. Upper Canadians having business to transact with Government, or who are engaged in public affairs, would feel themselves forced to go to a distance from their country to a place where everything would appear strange, and where even the distance from, and expense of communication with, their own section of the Province would be considered unnecessary inflictions. Toronto, though a flourishing and rapidly-rising city, situated in a fertile country, and having a large extent of territory in its rear, peopled and in the course of settlement, has, nevertheless, little interests in common with the Lower Province, unless as a place through which its commerce must pass. And its strangeness to Lower Canadians would ever be greater than would be felt in Quebec by people from Upper Canada, whilst its distance from Eastern Canada would cause many and constant inconveniences, too great to admit the continuance of the capital there. Kingston, it is true, is somewhat nearer to a centrical position, but its importance, except as a military post, depends mainly upon the forwarding trade; and not having an improved back country, its progress has not been rapid, notwithstanding its being one of the most ancient towns in the Province, and favoured by the presence of large naval and military establishments. The coming of the Government caused improvements, which, however, must be limited to the wants of the influx of population consequent upon that occasion. It is close upon the American frontier; many of its supplies are taken from the United States; and the inhabitant of Lower Canada feels himself alienated from his own people as much in this city as he could well be anywhere in Canada; while it is not a place in which any considerable number of the inhabitants of Upper Canada, besides its own citizens and the country in the neighbourhood, have any interest. It is not surprising, therefore, that when the question was discussed in the last two sessions in the Legislative Assembly, a very large majority of members declared decidedly against Kingston. Of Bytown, it may be said that it is comparatively safe from attack in the interior; that when the country of the Ottawa comes to be settled, it promises to rise into importance; and that it is situate on the Provincial Boundary. But then its position makes it inconvenient both for Upper or Lower Canadians; it is, in fact, out of the way of both; and thus possessing disadvantages which would be equally felt by both divisions of the Province, it would probably unite both in one feeling, and that not in its favour.

The Island of Montreal was chosen as the site of a great city, by the French Government, in the early times of the Colony. In making this choice, the acknowledged sagacity and foresight displayed by the officers of that nation in their selection of positions, for either civil or military occupation, along the course of the St. Lawrence and down the Mississippi in a country then a forest wilderness, was scarcely required when Montreal was designated as a future city. No discoveries of localities claiming to be equal; no development of the vast resources of later times; no improvement in canal navigation and not even the discovery and use of steam, which in other instances have set at nought the calculations of the wisest and most profound of early politicians, have made any change in the prospects of importance to Montreal, except as they have confirmed and advanced all prognostications of its future greatness. Situated at the head of navigation from the sea, and at the foot of the river and canal navigation, not only of Canada, but of North Western America, Montreal has long been the commercial capital of the Province, and bids fair to be the mart of commerce of a larger portion of the vast north-western country of the American States. It is not merely a city through or by which the commerce of the country passes, but it is the depot and place of exchange of that commerce, and consequently it is, beyond all comparison, the centre of the wealth of Canada; a wealth not derived from any partial or changeable source, but flowing to it alike from the Atlantic, from the distant Western Lakes, and even from waters whose natural outlet is to be found at New Orleans, but which, by means of canals, have been made to communicate with the Canadian lakes, and to bring contributions to the favoured city of Canada. Ships from the ocean and vessels from the interior lie together in the port, and men from all quarters meet there in the ordinary course of business. Montreal has no concern in the sectional jealousies of the different positions in the western country; but it is impossible to imagine an improvement in the condition of that country by which that city is not benefited; while, on the other hand, the Upper Canadians, having little to do with the affairs of the other ports of Lower Canada, have a deep interest in Montreal, as their own seaport and their own market. Montreal is, therefore, essentially a city of both the late Provinces, one in which each claims an interest, and is, moreover, a city familiar to Upper Canadians as it is to the inhabitants of the section of which it forms a part; it is the place of all others in which to study the statistics and politics of the whole of Canada, in which there is the least chance of partial legislation, or of the interests of any part of the people of the Province being overlooked or disregarded. There can be no stronger proof of the correctness of these opinions, than the claim set up by the inhabitants of the western country, long before the Union, to the city of Montreal, as a place built up with the result of their industry, and sustained by their commerce, but of the resources arising from the wealth of which they were deprived, in consequence of that city forming part of a different Province. That the Lower Canadians resented and resisted a proposition for the dismemberment of their country, and the loss of their chief city, is undoubted; and surely this contest for a place in which both claimed a deep and obvious interest, shared by no other locality, ought to be conclusive evidence in favour of the disputed position, when the inquiry is made, where shall be the United Capital of these contending Provinces? That the capital of the United Provinces ought to be placed in the position which would enable Upper Canadians most effectually to look after the concerns of their own seaborne and outward trade, and in the place in which Lower Canadians can most effectually investigate and control the internal management of communications, of which they share the expense, and in the advantages of which they expect to share, appears to the Committee of Council almost an indisputable proposition. That Montreal possesses these advantages is not to be disputed; and that there are facilities afforded to a Government Resident in Montreal of closely and constantly ascertaining what is for the public advantage of the whole community, and what is the true bent of public opinion, superior to any offered by rival cities claiming the choice of the Government, the Committee think is equally apparent. All the advantages of common and universal interest in one locality are, in the opinion of the Committee, found in Montreal in a superior degree to those existing in most capital cities and therefore they feel bound, without giving much weight to local claims, or to desires naturally entertained of political preponderance in either section of the Province, to tender to your Excellency their respectful advice to recommend to the Queen the choice of Montreal as Her Majesty's Canadian capital.

The Committee further beg leave to suggest that although it is for Her Majesty to declare her gracious pleasure upon this subject, yet in whatever place the seat of Government shall be fixed, heavy expenses will attend its establishment, which have come through the vote of the Legislature, and they have no doubt but that it would be gratifying to Her Majesty, as it would to your Excellency and Council, to see the necessary expenditure cheerfully and cordially undertaken and borne by the Provincial Parliament. And the Committee need not say how much it would mortify them to see any serious difference of opinion in the Legislature on such a point. The proceedings in the two last sessions of Parliament would, the Committee apprehend, indicate such a difficulty, to an extent which would make an application to Parliament almost hopeless were Kingston to be continued, or any of the places which put forward their own claims, chosen, and they are of opinion that although the citizens of Montreal appear to take little interest in the question, as they might be personally affected by its decision, and although, in fact, that city is so full of other resources as to account for the indifference of its inhabitants to the acquisition of the character of a political capital, yet the advantages to the public generally appear so plain, and the general objects in view in the choice so defensible, that they have the strongest hope of a concurrence in the selection by the Legislature, and of the avoidance of the difficulties which any other would probably occasion. In favour of whichsoever place Her Majesty may be pleased to decide, the Committee of Council would respectfully suggest that the interests of individuals are suffering, and will continue to suffer, by any delay in the final decision. The popular mind is also kept more or less unsettled and agitated on the question, so as to affect other politics injuriously. When once the provincial capital is definitively chosen, bad feeling on the subject will cease, and common favourable interests will be awakened. The more quickly the intention of Her Majesty shall be carried into execution, the sooner will its beneficial objects be understood and admitted. And should your Excellency be pleased to agree in the recommendation of the Committee, and should Her Majesty be advised to concur in the measure of fixing the capital at Montreal, the Committee think that facilities for a very early removal of the Government thither can be found in that city, and the accommodation offered by its extent and position, as well as by the possession of public property there, available for the use of the Government.

The urgent necessity for an immediate decision, and for early action thereupon, is further shown by the approaching want of funds to pay the rents of the public buildings and Government House occupied in Kingston. As application to Parliament for those funds would bring on the question respecting the seat of Government in its most embarrassing shape. The buildings occupied for public offices and for public offices and for Parliament in Kingston, are, moreover, totally unfit for the purpose to which they are temporarily turned. The members of the Legislature have been put to the greatest inconvenience for the want of a tolerable building in which to hold their sessions, and the facilities for the erection of buildings in Montreal, and the superior cheapness of their construction at that place, give it advantages in an economical point of view, which would more than counterbalance the value of any public edifices that exist either in Quebec or Toronto.

26. Protest dated March 20, 1843, by Mr. Harrison, to the Executive Council's Committee Report of March 16, 1843 (EC).

Mr. Harrison, as a Member of the Executive Council of Canada, present on the 16th instant, in a Committee of Council, when a minute was agreed upon, by which the Committee advise the transfer of the Seat of Government of Canada from Kingston to Montreal, feels it to be his duty to communicate to His Excellency, the Governor General, that he has not concurred in the Minute of Council above referred to.

Anxious to avoid every possible cause of embarrassment, and feeling satisfied that all the political arguments upon every view that can be taken of the subject have been fully exhausted, Mr. Harrison refrains from entering into any statement of the process of reasoning by which he has been led to the conclusion at which he has arrived, and therefore contents himself with making this communication to His Excellency.

27. *Montreal Gazette*, May 22, 1843.

[The Governor General's] reply to [an] Address from the Municipal Council of the Prince Edward District, stated that 'the question as to the permanent seat of Government has always been, and still remains unsettled,' the matter is revived as briskly as ever. When will this vexed question be settled? The Home Government, if they wish a grant for the public buildings, will never find a more pliant House of Assembly to vote it, for the thirty-eight office holders, and as many more office expectants, would vote, if need be, for the seat of Government to be at Penetanguishine.

28. Lord Stanley (Colonial Secretary) to Queen Victoria, August 17, 1843 (RA).

. . . . Lord Stanley is humbly of opinion, after a very careful consideration of the case, that there is no ground for regretting, or departing from, the Instructions which he has already sent out under Your Majesty's sanction; and with regard to the solution of the Seat of Government which Sir Charles Metcalfe fears may lead to a general desire for a dissolution of the Legislative Union, the course adopted appears . . . the one obviously required by a due regard to Your Majesty's name and station. That instruction, in substance, left to the Members of the Canadian Government the duty, and the responsibility of recommending to Your Majesty the solution of the seat of Government and of obtaining the assent of the Legislature to the measure necessary for giving effect to Your Majesty's Orders. In any case, it would appear, that the solution will give great offence, and cause great exasperation, in one of the two portions of the Province; and if Montreal be selected, as Sir Charles Metcalfe upon the whole recommends, it will be in violation of an 'assurance alledged to amount to a promise,' made in Your Majesty's name, and on which, in great measure, the assent of the Upper Province to the Union was originally founded. While Lord Stanley fully admits that such an engagement cannot be binding against the expressed wish of the majority of the Colonial Legislature, he continues of opinion, that it should be strictly observed in the absence of such an expression; and he cannot regret that by refusing to permit a Message to be sent down in Your Majesty's name, or any practical step to be taken on Your Majesty's behalf, he has precluded the possibility of a charge of bad faith being brought against Your Majesty's Government, and has left the responsibility of proposing the change, where he conceives it ought properly to rest, with the local advisers of the Governor General. Lord Stanley trusts that Sir Charles Metcalfe will have seen the extreme inconvenience of making such a question the subject of a direct appeal to the people by the dissolution and General Election.

29. *Montreal Gazette*, August 28, 1843.

Having made careful enquiry in well informed quarters, we believe the following may be taken as the exact state at present of the question

as to the seat of Government. Five towns have been named as eligible—
Quebec, Montreal, Bytown, Kingston and Toronto. The last three all
urge their claims very strongly, but the Colonial Office positively
declines to sanction the removal of the seat of Government to either
Toronto or Quebec, both being too far from the centre of the Province.
With respect to the other three, it is understood that the wishes of the
majority of the Legislature will be the guide of the Executive. The party
at present in the majority have always complained very bitterly of the
holding the sittings of the Legislature so far West as Kingston. We are
not aware that they have expressed any predilections in favour of
Bytown, and we apprehend that there can be little doubt that this
Parliament will be the last that will ever assemble at Kingston, and that
the removal to Montreal will be effected at as early a period as possible.
It is much to be regretted, we think, that the Act of Union did not
specifically fix the seat of Government, and equally so, that the Governor General is not instructed to exercise the Royal prerogative on his
own responsibility, and prevent the reopening of a vexatious and
irritating question.

30. *Kingston Herald*, September 12, 1843.

We have hithertoo refrained from noticing the rumors set afloat
lately respecting the Seat of Government, but shall now make a few
remarks thereon. . . .

It was said in the Montreal papers that when His Excellency the
Governor General was in that city, he intimated that the Seat of
Government question would be left to the disposal of the Legislature, or
the Assembly, and that the decision would probably be between
Montreal and Kingston. Thereupon the Montrealers [declare it] as
being settled in their favor and tell us that the Legislature will meet no
more in Kingston; and the Toronto people are also in ecstacies, thinking that if Kingston lose the Seat of Government, they will keep the
Courts of Law at Toronto, and may obtain something more beside, as a
deputy land office &c.

We shall say nothing on the probability of all this, but come to the
point at once, by declaring, that to remove the Seat of Government
from Kingston would be a breach of faith on the part of the Government
with the people of Kingston and to remove it from Kingston to Montreal
would be a breach of faith with the people of Upper Canada. . . .

. . . The people of Kingston did not seek to have the Capital of the
Province fixed here. It was done by the Governor alone, without
consulting them; and having been done, they naturally concluded that it
was intended to remain here for, if otherwise, the Governor should
have said so. But there was not the least hint give of this being still an

'unsettled' question; nor was it so considered by the Governor then, as is seen by Lord Sydenham's private correspondence.

. . . if we move the Seat of Government to the east, we shall move against the current of population, and away from where its growing numbers will mostly congregate, requiring supervision and control. In fact, to move the Seat of Government to Montreal will, in a few years, render a dissolution of the Union necessary.

And then the amalgamation of the two sections of the Province will be much more effectively carried on if the Capital of the United Province remains here, because the members from the east on coming to the west have to fall in with the language, manners, and customs of the west; but if they remain in the east, they will retain their own.

31. (Montreal) *Le Canadien*, September 30, 1843.

We forsee that the discussions on the question of the Seat of Government will be of the most animated character. The result of the deliberations of the Assembly on this question will be the touchstone for the recognition of the true friends of 'equal justice' in Upper Canada. Lower Canada cannot be on a footing of equality with Upper Canada so long as the Seat of Government shall be in the Upper Province, which does not contain a single town in which the two populations are to be found in any considerable proportions, as in our two great towns of Quebec and Montreal . . . in one word, every one will find himself at home, while, so long as the gentlemen from Lower Canada who are called by the business of the Government or the Legislature to Kingston, are detained there, they feel themselves as it were exiles in a foreign land.

32. *Montreal Gazette*, September 30, 1843.

The selection of the future Seat of Government of the United Canadas, is destined to create much agitation and contention, both within the walls of Parliament and without, until the matter has been finally decided. . . .

Many of the most influential inhabitants of Montreal, indeed, entertain strong doubts if the establishment of the Seat of Government in our great commercial city would not prove prejudicial rather than advantageous to its real interests and prosperity. The luxury, the glitter, the expensive habits which always, more or less, prevail in capitals, are calculated to interfere, injuriously, with the industry, order, and sobriety which are so necessary in a commercial community; and for our own part, we feel persuaded that neither our morals nor our manners will be benefited by the establishment among us of the Vice-regal

Court, and its often showry, idle, and luxurious train of officials and other satelites. Man is naturally an imitative animal; and we would shortly see our sober citizens, their dames and children, vying with Honourables, Colonels, and office holders in luxury, fashion, and expense. This was, in formerdays, the case in Quebec; and clearly have the merchants and other inhabitants of that city paid for their folly in that respect. But, still, this must be decided on broader grounds than these; and the main point is, where does the general welfare demand that the Seat of Government should be placed, so as to secure the greatest good of the greatest number. . . . If it come to Montreal, it shall be welcome; if it do not, we will bear the blow with philosophical coolness.

33. Legislative Assembly, October 3, 1843 (JLA).

Resolved, That an humble Address be presented to His Excellency the Governor General, praying that His Excellency will be pleased to cause to be laid before this House, copies of all communications between the Executive Government of this Colony, and Her Majesty's Government, relative to the subject, as His Excellency may feel himself at liberty to communicate to this House.

Ordered, That the said Address be presented to His Excellency, the Governor General, by such Members of this House as are of the Honourable the Executive Council of this Province.

34. Sir Charles Metcalfe (Governor General) to Legislative Assembly, October 6, 1843 (JLA).

The Governor General informs the House of Assembly, in reply to their Address on the subject of the Seat of Government, that he does not consider himself at liberty to lay before the House copies of the communications which have passed between Her Majesty's Government and the Governor of this Colony, relative to that subject; but that the substance of the instructions issued to him is to the effect, that Her Majesty's Government decline coming to a determination in favor of any place as the future Seat of Government, without the advice of the Provincial Legislature; and that Her Majesty's Ministers will be prepared to submit favourably to Her Majesty such Addresses on this subject as may be presented by either, or both, of the Legislative House, in recommendation of either *Kingston* or *Montreal*; provided, that in any Address for this purpose from the House of Assembly, the House shall pledge itself to provide the necessary supply for the expenditure which may be expected to attend the permanent location of the Seat of Government at the place that they may recommend; it being understood that the selection is now neccessarily limited to one of those places; the former Capitals; *Quebec* and *Toronto*, being alike too remote from the centre of the Province, and the plan of alternate Sessions at one or the other of these last mentioned, or any other places being deemed objectionable and impracticable, on account of its manifest and extreme inconvenience; as connected with this subject, the Governor General transmits a copy of a Report from the Committee of the Executive Council, and a copy of a Protest from one of its Members on the subject thereof, which were submitted for the consideration of Her Majesty's Ministers.

35.   *Cornwall Observer*, October 12, 1843.

The business of the country—the business which more peculiarly affects the community, is deferred, until such subjects as the seat of government question be first settled.

36.   *Kingston Herald*, October 17, 1843.

It will be observed that in the Report of the Executive Council the subject is discussed as if nothing had been done on it—as if no selection of a Seat of Government for United Canada had been made, but the question was now brought up for the first time. Had this been the case, we should have said only little about it, but might have acquiesed, without remark, in whatever the Legislature decided. But action has been taken on this question previously, and the Executive, having the sole right and authority to decide it, has decided it, and selected Kingston as the Seat of Government; and so far from giving any intimation of the selection being only temporary, gave the opposite, by making extensive purchases of land for government buildings, to the amount of about £70,000, thus declaring in the most expression manner, that the selection was of a *permanent* Seat of Government. On the faith of this selection, confirmed by this vast expenditure on the part of the Government, the people of Kingston have made extraordinary exertions to meet the wants of the Town, and have expanded, according to the Mayor's calculations, £300,000 in the erection of buildings, etc. We contend then, that their expenditure on this account, warranted as it was by the actions and expenditure of the Government, has given them a claim to retain the Seat of Government, which cannot be set aside without injustice. If it be said that they were hasty in the matter, and should have waited until the question was placed beyond a cavil or dispute, it may be replied, that they concluded, and had right to conclude, that the question was settled beyond dispute, and if they had not done what they did to provide accommodations in the town, it would have been argued that they did not deserve to keep the Seat of Government, because they would not do any thing to be worthy of it. Their exertions to supply all that was wanted for the Seat of Government prove that they are worthy of keeping it among them.

37. Legislative Assembly, November 3, 1843 (JLA).

That it is the opinion of this House, that it is expedient that the Seat of Government for this Province, should be at the City of Montreal (see Figure 4).

38. Sir Charles Metcalfe (Governor General) to Lord Stanley (Colonial Secretary), November 4, 1843 (JLC).

[Regarding the actions] of the Legislative Assembly of Canada, on the question of the permanent location of the Seat of Government. . . . The largest Majority, i.e., 29 to 50, was on an Amendment moved to refer the question to be decided by Her Majesty's Government. After Divisions on several Amendments, one in favor of Kingston, one for Upper Canada, and one for an appeal to the sense of the people, the motion in favor of Montreal was carried, by 51 to 27. A second Resolution pledging the House to provide the requisite expense of the removal, was carried by 55 to 22.

39. R.E. Caron (Speaker of the Legislative Council) to Sir Charles Metcalfe (Governor General), November 8, 1843 (JLC)

May it please Your Excellency.
    We, Her Majesty's dutiful and loyal subjects, the Legislative Council and Assembly of Canada, in Provincial Parliament assembled, beg leave to approach Your Excellency with our respectful request, that you will be pleased to transmit our Joint Address on the subject of the future Seat of Her Majesty's Provincial Government for this Province, in such way as Your Excellency may deem fit, in order that the same may be laid at the foot of the Throne.

40. Joint Address of the Legislative Council and the Legislative Assembly to Queen Victoria, November 8, 1843 (JLA).

Most Gracious Sovereign:
    We, Your Majesty's dutiful and loyal Subjects, the Legislative Assembly of Canada, in Provincial Parliament assembled most humbly beg leave to approach Your Majesty with renewed expressions of a devoted attachment to Your Majesty's Royal Person and Government.

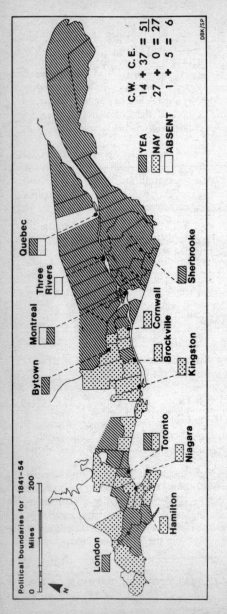

Figure 4. Expedient to move to Montreal; November 3, 1843. (See selection 37)

During the present Session of Your Majesty's Provincial Parliament, Your Majesty's Governor General of this Province has, by Message communicated to us, that Your Majesty's Imperial Government decline coming to a decision in favor of any place as the future Seat of Government for this Province, without the advice of the Provincial Legislature; and that Your Majesty's Ministers will be prepared to submit favourably to Your Majesty such Addresses on this subject, as may be presented by either or both of the Legislative Houses, in recommendation should be accompanied by a Parliamentary pledge to provide the necessary supply.

We assure Your Majesty, that we most deeply feel this additional proof of Your Majesty's Gracious desire to consult the wishes of your Canadian people. And we most respectfully beg leave to submit to Your Majesty, that we have in compliance with the gracious wish thus expressed, taken this most important subject into our most careful and deliberate consideration—and that in our opinion it is expedient that the Seat of Your Majesty's Provincial Government, for this Province, should be at the City of Montreal.

We further beg leave most respectfully to assure Your Majesty that upon Your Majesty, in the Gracious exercise of Your Royal Prerogative, giving directions for the location of it at that place, we pledge ourselves to provide the necessary supply for the expenditure which may be expected to attend upon the establishment of the Seat of Government at that City.

41. Sir Charles Metcalfe (Governor General) to Lord Stanley (Colonial Secretary), November 9, 1843 (JLC).

I have already reported the Resolutions of the Legislative Assembly, in favor of the location of the Seat of Government at Montreal.

2. The Assembly subsequently sent a Message to the Legislative Council, inviting them to concur in an Address to Her Majesty to the same effect.

3. When it was determined by a majority of the Legislative Council to take this Message into consideration. The Votes being 18 to 13, the minority protested against that Resolution as a violation of Parliamentary usage, the question having been disposed of by a previous Address, and withdrew from the House, with the avowed intention of seceding at least during the agitation of the Seat of Government question.

4. The Speaker was among the seceders, and as he persevered in his determination, I was under the necessity of appointing a new Speaker. . . .

5. The Legislative Council having resumed its proceedings, after the nomination of a Speaker, concurred with the Legislative Assembly in the proposed measure, and I am to receive both Houses to-morrow with their Joint Address.

6. . . . I regret the conduct of the minority in deserting their posts. That of the Speaker especially was calculated to produce considerable embarrassment. They could not reasonably have expected that the real majority of their body would allow the stratagem to succeed by which the minority had obtained a momentary superiority. I hope that the seceders will return to the exercise of their functions when they see that the question so warmly disputed has been settled. Several, however, have quitted Kingston, and returned to their homes at a distance. If they persist in abandoning the field to their adversaries, they will have themselves to blame for the consequences of such neglect of their duty to their County.

42. Sir Charles Metcalfe (Governor General) to Lord Stanley (Colonial Secretary), November 10, 1843 (JLC)

I have the honor to submit a Joint Address from the Legislative Council and Legislative Assembly of Canada to Her Majesty, recommending that the Seat of Government of the Province be established at Montreal, and engaging to supply the sums required for the necessary expenditure, if Her Majesty should be pleased to order that arrangement to be carried into effect.

43. Sir Charles Metcalfe (Governor General) to Lord Stanley (Colonial Secretary), November 11, 1843 (JLC).

I learn from public report that a meeting held at this place [Kingston] has been resolved to send Delegates to England with a view to endeavour to prevent the removal of the Seat of Government from Kingston to Montreal. . . .

44. Lord Stanley (Colonial Secretary) to Queen Victoria, November 17, 1843 (RA).

Lord Stanley, with his humble duty, submits to Your Majesty copies of several Dispatches arrived by the last mail from Sir Charles Metcalfe on the subject of proceedings in Canada in reference to the Seat of Government. Your Majesty will not fail to perceive that the Inhabitants of Upper Canada lay great stress upon the engagement entered with previously to the Union that the Seat of Government should be within the limits of that Province; and notwithstanding the excitement which has been caused by the reference of the question to the Legislature, Lord Stanley sees in these documents reason to rejoice that Your Majesty was not advised to interpose Your Royal Prerogative for the settlement of this question in a sense which it is evident that a large body of the people of Canada would have considered to involve a breach of faith.

45. Lord Stanley (Colonial Secretary) to Queen Victoria, December [2?], 1843 (RA).

Lord Stanley, with his humble duty, submits to Your Majesty . . . the Draft of a Despatch which, subject to Your Majesty's pleasure, Lord Stanley proposed to send out by the Mail of Monday the 4th Inst. It would seem desirable that the final decision of this question should not be longer delayed, and as Your Majesty had already signified Your intention of being guided by the opinion of the local Legislature, and that opinion has been unquestionably declared, no object would be gained by awaiting the arrival of the Delegates whom Sir Charles Metcalfe announces to be about to proceed to this Country to demonstrate against the decision.

46. Queen Victoria to Lord Stanley (Colonial Secretary), December 3, 1843 (RA).

The Queen approves of Ld. Stanley's proposed Draft to Sir Ch[arles] M[etcalfe]. This question can in no way be settled without giving offence to one part of the Country; the Queen however hopes that the fixing upon Montreal as the Seat of Govt. will hereafter be considered as fair by impartial minds. Sir Ch[arles] continues to show great discretion & firmness in his most arduous & unsatisfactory situation & deserves much praise & encouragement.

47. Lord Stanley (Colonial Secretary) to Sir Charles Metcalfe (Governor General), December 2, 1843 (PAC).

I have laid before the Queen, the joint Address of the Legislative Council and the Legislative Assembly of Canada . . . in which the Houses of the Provincial Parliament submit to the Queen their opinion, that it is expedient that the Seat of Her Majesty's Provincial Government for Canada should be at the City of Montreal, and assure Her Majesty that upon Her Majesty, in the gracious exercise of Her Royal Prerogative, giving directions for the location of it at that place, the Houses pledge themselves to provide the necessary supply for the expenditure which may be expected to attend the Establishment of the Seat of Government at that City.

The Queen having taken this Address into Her consideration, and adverting to the terms of the Act of the Imperial Parliament for reuniting the Provinces of Upper and Lower Canada, and for the Government of Canada, has been pleased to command me to instruct you, to acquaint the Legislative Council and the Legislative Assembly of Canada, that, in compilance with their expressed wish and opinion, it is Her Majesty's pleasure that the City of Montreal be henceforth the place of the habitual residence of yourself and your successors in the Government of Canada; and that it is Her Majesty's further pleasure, that the future Sessions of the Legislative Council and Assembly of the Province, be holden at Montreal, subject of course to the strict observance of the provisions of the Statute already mentioned, respecting the selection of the proper place for that purpose.

The Queen is further pleased to direct you to acquaint the Legislative Council and the Legislative Assembly, that Her Majesty accepts their offer of providing the necessary supplies for the expenditure which may be attendant on this measure, and will give the necessary orders for ensuring the effective and economical application of any such funds, in executing the service for which they may be so appropriated.

48. [Dunbar Ross], *Seat of Government (Canada)* (Quebec: November 20, 1843).

It will be necessary to combat this new feature of the case, which would seem to [have] excluded the Gibralter of the American continent, from any consideration whatever in the choice of the future Capital of the Canadas. . . . Quebec outstrips the boasted advantages of its pigmy rivals. . . . Quebec is decidedly the most central point for the Seat of the Provincial Government, upon the only true and rational grounds by which centrality can be tested. . . . It is in vain to defend the propriety of choosing Montreal as the Seat of Government, by reason of its greater territorial centrality . . . it is but twelve hours stream distant from [Quebec]. Centrality!—what particular evil or inconvenience has resulted to the many great Capitals of representative Europe, which are situate on the confines of their respective States and Kingdoms, from the want of centrality? Has there ever been a hue and cry raised in those countries upon such a ground? Who ever heard of such a thing, except amidst a few of the mushroom capitals, of the mushroom states, of the neighbouring Union.

49. *Kingston Herald*, January 9, 1844.

The Seat of Government question is still the engrossing topic of conversation in Kingston, and amidst the universal expression of the injustice done to us by the change is mingled a general opinion that, after all, the town is not ruined, but that a strenuous improvement of the advantages we still possess will overcome this treacherous blow. Treacherous it is most certainly, for the mayor was encouraged by Lord Stanley to proceed with borrowing money for the market buildings.

50. James Hopkirk to Sir George Arthur, January 17, 1844.

. . . all the Kingston people are in a fever about the removal of the Seat of Govt. to L[ower] C[anada] and I must say their case is a hard one, after the exertions they made and the money they have laid out to accommodate the Public. Two thirds of them will be ruined.

51. (Toronto) *Patriot*, cited in *Quebec Gazette*, May 10, 1844.

Toronto has, in our humble judgement at least, quite as much cause of complaint as Kingston.

52. (Kingston) *British Whig*, June 21, 1844.

. . . The inhabitants did not muster strongly, and of those present a general air of gloom and discontent was on each countenance. Shortly after twelve o'clock a salute of nineteen guns commenced firing, and His Excellency moved towards the steamer, accompained by his staff, and followed by his guests. During his progress to the Ottawa and Rideau Wharf, no cheer greeted his ear, no single hat was lifted to do him reverence—he passed to his boat amid the most profound and ominous silence.

. . . Thus did the Governor General leave Kingston the chosen capital of Canada, 'after mature deliberation', and with him departed the pledged faith of the Imperial Government!

53. (Montreal) *Morning Courier*, June 25, 1844.

. . . The streets [of Montreal] were thronged to excess, as the Governor passed along, he was greeted with the most hearty cheering we ever heard. We think he must be very popular amongst the ladies, for the windows were full of them, and the enthusiastic manner in which they waved their handkerchiefs, showed pretty plainly the way their little hearts were inclined. . . .

54. *Quebec Gazette*, June 26, 1844.

We hope that His Excellency's residence in the new capital, may allay at least, the wretched personal, national origin, and factious feelings, which at various times have brought discredit on Montreal, and so much injured the rest of the Province.

CHAPTER IV
MONTREAL: THE PARIS OF CANADA

Introduction

Montreal may have remained as Canada's capital until the present day had it not been for cultural and political passions which burst forth in violence in 1849. Because of the burning of the Parliament buildings, the physical abuse of the Governor General and several politicians by roving mobs, and newspaper tirades against the Governor, there followed the implementation of a system of a perambulating seats of government. A principal ideal to be achieved by the system was better understanding between peoples. In reality, the alternating system was a compromise arranged by supporters of two cities, Toronto and Quebec (see Figure 5), each group of whom later sought to have their city named permanent capital.

The causes of the outburst of violence were many. The country was feeling the ever worsening effects of world depression, with exports dropping, unemployment critical, the Montreal business community facing ruin, and revolutionary thoughts rampant. Lord Elgin, Governor General since 1847, was deeply concerned over "the generally uneasy and diseased condition of the public mind."[1] Dreams of a great, expanded Montreal-based commercial empire were rapidly collapsing.[2] In 1846 the British Parliament had repealed the Corn Laws and imperial preference soon came to an end. Montreal Tories, shocked and dismayed at the depression which followed and at the bad treatment they had received from the British, turned their thoughts to annexation with the United States. The Tories, who had for so long controlled the government, were further crushed when the Reformers swept the country in the 1848 election. The Montreal and Eastern Townships English Canadian minority feared French-Canadian domination. When their deteriorated economic situation and their disgust at the actions of the British Government were added to these fears they found themselves in an extremely frustrating position. The accumulated frustrations were vented on April 25, 1849. The trigger for releasing the explosive tensions was the Rebellion Losses Bill.

The bill was a legacy from the 1837-38 troubles. Compensation for property losses during the Upper Canada rebellion had been granted earlier but similar payments in Lower Canada had not been issued. The

French-Canadian members were determined that the redress should be made, and the Canada West Reformers generally supported them as part of a cross-sectional political alliance that had been forged. Resolutions were introduced to the Legislative Assembly on February 13, 1849, and, in the days that followed the "debates were the most exciting in our Parliamentary annals."[3] A British newspaper wrote of the situation in Canada at that time as being

> even more critical and dangerous than we originally supposed. . . . The [introduction of] the 'Rebellion Losses' Bill. . . . has acted as a match laid to a train of gunpowder; and there is too much reason to fear that the explosion will shatter the existing political and social system of Canada to atoms.[4]

The issue was of symbolic importance: to the French Canadians it meant, among other things, the test of equality and also of the newly achieved responsible government. But to the Tories it meant rewarding rebels for treason.[5] The debate was extremely heated, but finally the bill was passed. The big question then became, would Lord Elgin sign the bill?

In accordance to the concept of responsible government, Elgin was determined to "stand apart from any appearance of favouring one side in the country, and to accept any measure which was suggested by his ministers."[6] Elgin thus decided to accept the bill and so he went to the House for the ceremony for accepting a number of bills. It was shortly after 5 p.m. on April 25, 1849, and before a packed House that the Governor General's decision was made public with the reading of the title of the bill. At mention of Royal assent for the bill a tumolt arose in the galleries. After the proceedings, as Elgin left for his residence, he was pelted with eggs and other missiles. Meanwhile, with the Assembly still in session, word quickly spread through the city. At 8 p.m. a large crowd of "loyal British" assembled in the Champ de Mars and, after hearing inflammatory orations on French domination and British rights, the crowd moved off. Smashing windows all the way, they surged on toward the Parliament building which they then attacked, forcing the members of the House to flee. The building was burned to the ground. Over the next few weeks there were pro- and anti-Elgin demonstrations all across the Province and Montreal remained an extremely tense place. Fear of annexation remained high.

The Legislative Assembly and Council came into disagreement, for the Assembly recommended that a perambulatory system for capital be instituted, whereas the Council felt that such a measure would prove "injurious to the best interests of the whole Province."[7] Elgin clearly favoured a removal from Montreal, and the Executive Council agreed.

It was accepted that Toronto would house the government for the final sessions of the Third Parliament and then Quebec would have the honours for the following four years.

Notes

1Arthur Doughty, ed., *The Elgin-Grey Papers 1846-1852*, 4 Volumes (Ottawa: King's Printer, 1937), Vol. I, p. 280, Elgin to Earl Grey, January 4, 1849.

2See Creighton, *The Empire of the St. Lawrence*, *op.cit.*, pp. 349-385.

3Dent, *op.cit.*, p. 200.

4(British) *London Morning Chronicle*, cited in *Montreal Gazette*, May 5, 1849.

5On the symbolism of the bill see Careless, *The Union of the Canadas*, *op.cit.*, p. 124.

6Arthur Keith, *Responsible Government in the Dominions*, 3 Volumes (Oxford: Clarendon Press, 1912), Vol. I, p. 18.

7(Montreal) *Pilot*, May 29, 1849.

Documents

55. Lord Elgin (Governor General) to Earl Grey (Colonial Secretary), May 7, 1847 (PAC).

. . . as respects a Union of the [British North American] Provinces— My impression is that there is little feeling here in favour of the project. The French dislike a measure which has, they feel, a tendency to increase British Influence. The inhabitants of Montreal dread it, because they fancy that it will lead to the removal of the seat of Govt. to Quebec.

56. Statement in *Journal* of the Legislative Assembly, April 25, 1849.

The Proceedings of the [House in] Committee were interrupted by continued volleys of stones and other missiles thrown from the streets, through the windows, into the Legislative Assembly Hall, which caused the Committee to rise, and the Members to withdraw into the adjoining passages for safety, from whence Mr. Speaker and the other Members were almost immediately compelled to retire and leave the Building which had been set fire to on the outside.

57. Henry Rose to William Manson, May 7, 1849 (PAC).

I never saw anything like the fire;—so awfully grand—the whole scene is indescribable. . . .

58. (Toronto) *Globe*, April 28, 1849.

The Tories of Canada have at length unmasked themselves before the world. The garment of loyalty under which they have concealed their deformity, has been cast off by their own hands, and they stand revealed as the enemies of British Connexion—the enemies of the constitutional liberty—the abettors of mobs, and the destroyers of property.

59. (Kingston) *British Whig*, May 4, 1849

[We are] not among those who feel pleased that a British Mob has herded a French House of Assembly. We deplore the act. . . . had Lord Elgin refused the Royal Assent to the Act, it would have satisfied the loyal population of Canada.

60. (British) *London Morning Chronicle*, reprinted in *Montreal Gazette*, May 5, 1849.

We are sorry to find that the letters and newspapers brought by the mail steamer from Canada, represent the state of public feeling in that province to be even more critical and dangerous than we originally supposed. The discontent and disaffection are more deep seated; the chances of reconciliation are fainter, and the sympathy with the United States more openly pronounced. The "Rebellion Losses" Bill, which Lord Elgin has suffered his Ministers to introduce, without any remonstrance on his part, has acted as a match laid to a train of gunpowder; and there is too much reason to fear that the explosion will shatter the existing political and social system of Canada to atoms. A war of races has been again proclaimed—a war which, during the past ten years, has been slumbering, and, by judicious management might have been extinguished altogether, but which must now run its course, and will only end with the complete subjugation of the one or the other nationality.

61. (Kingston) *British Whig*, May 11, 1849.

The first fruits of the removal of the seat of government from Upper to Lower Canada, are only beginning to develop themselves. . . . On the heads of those who are responsible for placing and retaining it in Montreal, all those evils and consequences, and bloodshed, and probably a civil war—a war of races—must rest.

62. (Bytown) *Packet*, May 19, 1849.

. . . Bytown received pretty fair attention [in the Legislative Assembly], having received fourteen votes, while Kingston—once the Capital—received but ten. Should the removal take place as now suggested by the House,—which one very much doubts,—we foretell that eight years will not pass ere Bytown will have a majority in its favour, and before ten we the inhabitants of the City of Ottawa will bask in the sunshine of Governmental patronage.

63. Legislative Assembly, May 19, 1849 (JLA).

See selection 65 and Figure 5.

64. Comments by members of the Legislative Assembly, May 19, 1849.

Supporters of alternate system:
   (a) . . . nothing could be better calculated to carry out the Union than placing the seat of Government alternately in Upper and Lower Canada, for periods not exceeding 4 years. Nothing could be more fair and equitable.
   (b) it is imprudent to have the seat of government in the very vortex of sedition. [Montreal] is the Paris of Canada, where a mob could be at any time collected at the tinkling of a bell.
   (c) in great commercial cities it is impossible to prevent a mob rising, in a short time without notice, and destroying property: in the United States, great commercial cities were not chosen for the seats of Government.

Opponents of alternate system:
   (a) the effect of adopting the scheme . . . would be to throw both sections of the Province into confusion, and to lead to the dissolution of the Union.
   (b) the disturbances have been magnified by the personal apprehension of hon. gentlemen . . . Montreal [is] the best place for the amalgamation of the two races, and the best place to keep the Government to carry out the working of the Union.
   (c) . . . the late disturbances [were] disreputable and blackguardly, but [I] could not consider them the acts of the whole, nor the majority of the population of Montreal, who ought not to be punished for the acts of

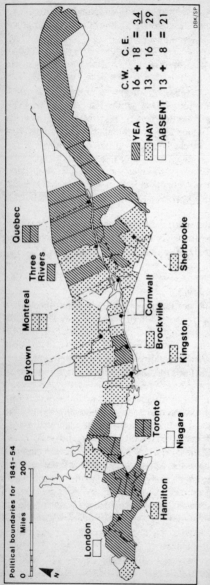

Figure 5. For alternating between Quebec and Toronto; May 19, 1849. (See selection 63)

a few blackguards . . . it would be an evidence of weakness to remove the seat of Government now. [I] would never consent to be driven from [my] position, by a lawless mob.

(d) one member ridiculed the idea of a perambulatory Government as being absurd, and advocated the removal of Government to some central part of the Province, near to the division line of the two sections of the Province, and spoke strongly in favour of removing the Government to Bytown, as being well adapted for the seat of Government.

65. Address from Legislative Assembly to Lord Elgin (Governor General), May 19, 1849 (JLA).

We, Her Majesty's dutiful and loyal subjects, the Legislative Assembly of the Province of Canada, in Provincial Parliament assembled, humbly beg leave to approach your Excellency with feelings of respect, and to represent—

That the time has arrived when a different and much more satisfactory arrangement may be made as regards the place of convening Parliament than at present exists.

That it was the cause of complaints on the part of many of the inhabitants of Upper Canada, that the Parliament was, in 1843, removed altogether from within the limits of their province.

That it was suggested at that time, as each province had enjoyed the advantage of having a separate legislature within its limits, from the first establishment of its representative form of government down to the time of the union, that after the union it would be an act of common justice only for the representative of the Sovereign to convene Parliament alternately at Toronto, in Upper Canada, and at Quebec, in Lower Canada; but the Legislature to whom the subject was submitted thought otherwise, and advised Montreal as the place to be selected, which advice was received and acted on. Within a very short period of time, however, we have seen the building in Montreal occupied by the Legislative Council and Legislative Assembly, rented and fitted up as it was, at a great expense to the country, wilfully burnt before our eyes, and the libraries belonging to the respective houses, and their records and proceedings consumed with it.

That such then, being the state of the case, and with the view of removing every obstacle that may have a tendency to hinder, or in any way interfere with the well working of the union, we most respectfully beg leave to recommend to your Excellency to adopt the suggestion referred to, that after the present session, your Excellency will be pleased to convene the Parliament alternately at Toronto and Quebec, during periods not exceeding four years at each place. The first sitting under this arrangement to be held at such of the two places mentioned as your Excellency in your discretion may deem most advisable for the general good. That the plan now submitted to your Excellency is not without precedents in other countries, and that it can now more easily than at any antecedent period be carried out, inasmuch as all former records and proceedings in Parliament have been destroyed.

That each branch of the legislature will now have to commence anew again, and with a view to alternate sittings as herein recommended, their records and proceedings ought henceforward to made out in duplicate, so that one copy may be deposited in the vaults of the Parliament House at Toronto, and the other within the walls of the Citadel of Quebec, where they will be secure from the ravages of fire, and from the attacks of external and internal foes.

That the Parliament buildings at each of the cities of Toronto and Quebec are the property of the province; that they are commodious and comfortable, and can be made ready for the reception of the legislature at comparatively small expense. That under this arrangement the members of the legislature will have a better opportunity of ascertaining and understanding by personal observation, the condition, the wants, and the wishes of the whole people, instead of being confined, as they now necessarily are, in their knowledge of public affairs, to the narrow limits of their respective sections of the province.

66. Lord Elgin (Governor General) to Legislative Assembly, May 22, 1849 (JLA)

. . . in my opinion so serious a change in [public] policy ought not to be lightly adventured upon, and that above all the pressure of an apparent temporary necessity for that change, must not be allowed to exercise an undue influence upon the adoption of it.

67. (Montreal) *Pilot*, May 22, 1849

Another of the consequences of Tory outrage develops itself in the vote to which the Legislative Assembly on Friday last [May 19] came, with reference to the Seat of Government. We cannot wonder at that vote, however we may reject it.

68. Resolution accepted by Legislative Council, May 25, 1849 (JLC).

That is the opinion of this House that it would be extremely inconvenient and expensive to hold alternate Parliaments at Quebec and Toronto inasmuch as such an arrangement would keep the public mind unsettled and uneasy under the constant influence of local and personal feeling; and therefore this House cannot withhold its opinion that any such measures would prove injurious to the best interests of the whole Province.

69. (Toronto) *Globe*, May 30, 1849.

Our own feeling used to be that the seat of government should be located either at Montreal, as the most westerly city of Lower Canada, or at Kingston, as the most easterly of Upper Canada; when it was resolved to give the preference to Montreal, while we felt Kingston was deeply injured by it, we justified the choice on grounds of high public expediency. In common with others, we felt the advantage of having the government in a large city, where public feeling might naturally have been expected to be more enlarged than in a small community, and we anticipated great benefit from the free social intercourse, which the selection of Montreal promised, between Canadians of British and French origin.

Experience has in our opinion shows conclusively that the benefits expected from the selection of Montreal have not arisen; but, on the contrary, that such a bitter hostility exists on the part of the Anglo-Saxons (as they love to describe themselves) of Montreal, towards their French Canadian fellow-subjects, as to forbid the hope that any fruit but violence and bloodshed can grow from continuing the seat of government longer where it is now.

Adhering to our principles, we are therefore of opinion that the seat of government should be removed back to Kingston. . . . Failing this, and we fear the yeas and nays on the several divisions in the house, and the known sentiments of the leading public men of the country forbid the hope, we conceive that to call parliament at Quebec and Toronto alternately would be a wise and beneficial measure. . . .

There are two strong arguments in favour of alternate meetings at Quebec and Toronto. The first is that Quebec being very much a French city, and Toronto being entirely British, the visits of persons of one race to the city of the other will enable each to appreciate the other better, and draw closer the bonds of friendship. There is no jealousy of race between Upper and Lower Canadians—it exists solely between the Montreal Anglo-Saxon and the Montreal French Canadian. There is no city in the Province where such bitter internal dissension exists as in Montreal.

The second argument is that the alternate system will enable the feelings of the people of both sections to tell more directly on the administration of public affairs. Out of sight out of mind, is an old and truthful adage. It matters not how honest a man is—how anxious he may be to do right—he will always do your work better if you are standing beside him, than if you are six or eight hundred miles off. By the time an Upper Canada Cabinet minister resides in Montreal a year—aye, by the time an Upper Canada member of Parliament stays there three or four months—he begins to exhibit, unknown to himself, symptoms of local influence. . . .

The moral influence of society at or near the seat of Government is very great; a more pernicious influence than that of Montreal could not exist; it is not desirable to have it all Lower Canadian nor all upper Canadian—and the only way to do justice to both divisions is the alternate system. . . .

Should Quebec and Toronto be fixed upon, we think it quite obvious that Toronto should have the first visit. Upper Canada had the seat first, for between two and three years—Lower Canada has now had it between five and six years—and surely it cannot be doubted that the Upper Province should have it next. The Ministry will do justice and in our opinion show sound policy by throwing their weight into the scale in favour of Toronto.

70. Kingston City Council to Queen Victoria, June 1, 1849 (PAC).

MAY IT PLEASE YOUR MAJESTY,

We, Your Majesty's most dutiful and loyal subjects, the City Council of the city of Kingston, in that part of the province of Canada known as Upper Canada, having learned that it is in contemplation to remove the seat of Government of Canada from Montreal, in consequence of the insults to Your Majesty's representative, and the violent disturbances and destruction of property, so much to be deprecated, which have recently occurred, consider it a duty which they owe to the inhabitants of Upper Canada, as well as to their fellow-citizens, to set forth the claims of this city to be restored as the capital of Canada.

We humbly beg to assure Your Majesty, that the union of the Canadas was effected with a distinct expression of opinion on the part of the Legislature of Upper Canada, that the seat of the united Government should be placed wintin the limits of that province, and their assent was undoubtedly given upon that understanding; accordingly, the seat of the Canadian Government was fixed at Kingston by the late Lord Sydenham after the "most mature deliberation" (as stated in the Despatch of the Colonial Secretary, Lord Stanley, dated February, 1842), and where it remained for three years until removed to Montreal.

We further beg humbly to inform Your Majesty, that a large and valuable tract of land in this city, now lying vacant, was procured by Lord Sydenham in order to erect thereon the necessary provincial buildings, which tract still remains public property, and is now available for the purpose for which it was purchased: That the inhabitants and Corporation of Kingston, under the assurance that the town was permanently fixed upon as the seat of Government, expended large sums of money in erecting public and private buildings to provide for the increased population, which expenditure, upon the removal to Montreal, occasioned serious and ruinous losses to many citizens, and has ever since caused great embarrassment to the Corporation.

This Council humbly express to Your Majesty their opinion, that had the seat of Government been allowed to remain at Kingston, a far better opportunity would have been afforded for carrying out the main objects of the Union, which are understood to have been gradually to remove sectional interests, to amalgamate the population, and make the united province one people, "British in fact as well as in name:" That one branch of the Provincial Legislature having recently expressed an opinion in favour of alternate seats of Government at Quebec and Toronto (a scheme which has since been unanimously condemned by the other branch of Parliament), we humbly crave Your Majesty's attention to a message from Sir Charles Metcalfe to the Legislative Assembly of Canada, dated the 6th day of October, 1843, when that nobleman communicated the instruction of Your Majesty's Government in these words:—"The former capitals, Quebec and Toronto, being alike too remote from the centre of the province, and the plan of alternate sessions at one or the other of these last mentioned, or any other places, being deemed objectionable and impractable, on account of its manifest and extreme inconvenience."

We most humbly beg to state to Your Majesty, that the rapidly increasing population of Canada tends almost entirely to the west, which circumstances will, in a short period, cause the census of Upper Canada to be equal to, if not greater than that of Lower Canada, and that Kingston, from its central situation at the junction of the great chain of lakes with the River St. Lawrence; at the head of the communication with the River Ottawa by the Rideau Canal; its accessibility at all seasons of the year; the great strength of its position and fortifications, with its public buildings, superior to any in the province for Government purposes, recently offered by your petitioners to his Excellency Lord Elgin for such purposes, and immediately available, is peculiarly eligible for the seat of the Canadian Government.

Your petitioners, therefore, humbly beg, in view of these various circumstances, most strongly, but most respectfully to urge upon the attention of Your Majesty, that the loyal and peaceable inhabitants represented by your petitioners have strong and undeniable claims for a restoration to Kingston of the seat of Government, and which they humbly solicit may be restored accordingly.

And that heaven may bless Your Majesty, long to rule over an united empire, your petitioners will ever humbly pray.

71. Lord Elgin (Governor General) to Earl Grey (Colonial Secretary), (private), June 3, 1849 (PAC).

I have sent you the copy of the address of the Assembly recommending that the seat of Govt. should be changed and that it should be fixed every four years alternately at Toronto and Quebec. I confess I think if this Union is to work at all a great deal may be said in favour of the plan.—Nothing however should be done hastily in the matter,—and if we move from this place I am decidely of opinion that the first move should be towards U. Canada. Meanwhile Sherwood who proposed the plan in Part* has been obliged to fly the Town—He received some very significant hint of the fate which awaited him if he remained in Montreal after having slandered the mob who had done so much for him and his party.

72. Earl Grey (Colonial Secretary) to Lord Elgin (Governor General), (private), June 22, 1849 (PAC).

The change of the seat of Govnt is a very important and difficult question—I see many strong reasons for moving it from Montreal but there wd be great difficulty and expense in having it alternately in the Upper and Lower Provinces for periods of 4 years—I see by the votes that it was suggested that Kingston or Bytown shd be chosen and if this cd be managed I am inclined to believe that it wd be an improvement expecially if it were part of the arrangement that the favored Town shd provide the necessary buildings.

73. Lord Elgin (Governor General) to Earl Grey (Colonial Secretary), (private), August 20, 1849 (PAC).

We are again in some excitement here. La Fontaine's House was attacked by a mob (for the second time) two nights ago. . . . The most atrocious articles issue from the Tory Press—and there is room to fear that mischief may ensue.

The immediate cause of this excitement is the arrest of certain persons who were implicated in the destruction of the Part Building in April last.—All this . . . affords the occasion for a fresh exhibition of

*From documents 71 to 92, for Part or Parts *read* Parliament.

the recklessness of the Montreal mob, and the demoralization of all other classes in the community.

Nevertheless I am not altogether without hope that better times may be at hand.—The Montreal rioters cannot now raise themselves to the dignity of revolutionists for it is clear that annexation is dead for the moment. They must be rioters and nothing more. I cannot but think that the tradesmen in the city will begin to feel that even constitutional Govt is more tolerable than the continuance of a system which must lead if persevered in t[o] the removal of the seat of Govt and their own ruin.

74. Earl Grey (Colonial Secretary) to Lord Elgin (Governor General), (private), September 12, 1849 (PAC).

. . . . Your account of the state of feeling in Montreal is far from a pleasant one, but I trust this spirit is local and confined chiefly to that place, if so its existence seems to me to afford a conclusive reason for changing the Seat of Government, and I have directed a Despatch to be prepared expressing that opinion officially; if it is not a local feeling our chances of keeping Canada would seem to be but small.

75. Earl Grey (Colonial Secretary) to Lord Elgin (Governor General), September 14, 1849 (PAC).

I have had the honour to receive your Lordship's Despatch of the 20th of August, transmitting the copy of a letter addressed to the Provincial Secretary of Canada by the police magistrates of Montreal, reporting the occurrence of disturbances on the occasion of the arrest of certain persons charged with having destroyed the Parliament House in April last.

I have received with great regret, the intelligence of these fresh interruptions of the public peace in Montreal, and I cannot withhold the expression of my opinion, that the existence of such a spirit of insubordination in that city would appear to render it a very unfit place for the seat of the Provincial Government, and for the meeting of the Legislature.

76. Lord Elgin (Governor General) to Earl Grey (Colonial Secretary), (private), August 27, 1849 (PAC).

I begin to hope that there may be some return to common sense in Montreal.

My advisers however who are somewhat *impressionable* have been horrified beyond measure by what has occurred here lately and loudly protest that it will be impossible to maintain the seat of Govt here.—We had a long discussion on this point yesterday.—All seem to be agreed that if a removal from this town takes place it must be on the condition prescribed in the address of the Assembly presented to me last Session, (viz) that there shall henceforth be Parts held alternately in the Upper and Lower Provinces. A removal from hence to any other fixed point, would be the certain ruin of the Party making it.—Therefore removal from Montreal implies the adoption of the system which although it has a great deal to recommend it is certainly open to great objections, of alternating Parliaments. But this is not the only difficulty. The French Members of the administration declare that they cannot keep their section of the Party together unless Quebec is the point to which the first move is made. They are willing to go to Toronto for 4 years at the close of the present Part, but they give many reasons, which it were tedious to enumerate, and which appear to have in a great measure satisfied their U. Canada colleagues, for insisting on Quebec as the first point to be made. Now I have great objection to going to Quebec at present because I fear that it will be considered both here and in England as an admission that the Govt is under French Canadian influence, and that it cannot maintain itself in Upper Canada. I therefore concluded in favor of a few days more being given in order to see whether or not the movement now in progress in Montreal may be so directed as to render it possible to retain the seat of Govt here.

77. Lord Elgin (Governor General) to Earl Grey (Colonial Secretary), (private), September 3, 1849 (PAC).

. . . I regret to say that I discover as yet nothing in it [the comparative quiet of the last few days] to warrant the belief that the seat of Govt can properly remain at Montreal. The existence of a perfect understanding between the more outrageous and respectable fractions of the Tory party in the town is rendered even more manifest by the readiness with which the former through their organs have yielded to the latter when they preached moderation in good earnest. Additional proof is thus furnished of the extent to which the blame of the disgraceful transactions of the past four months falls on all. Even now every effort is made to make it appear that the present tranquility is rather a triumph over the Govt than submission to law—All attempts, and several have been made, to induce the Conservatives to unite in an address inviting me to return to the Town have failed—which is the more significant because it is well known & (indeed it is so stated in their own Press) that the removal of the seat of Govt is under consideration, and that I have deprecated the abandonment of Montreal. I do not think that the indisposition to sign this address arises so much from personal hostility to myself as from a determination not to admit that the Party were not justified in resorting to the acts of violence which caused me to avoid the city. You may imagine how dogged is the resolution to refuse to acquiesce in the conditions of constitutional Govt when the acknowledgement that it is improper to pelt the Queen's representative with brickbats cannot be extorted even by the dread of Montreal's ceasing to be the metropolis of Canada. The existence of a Party animated by such sentiments,—powerful in numbers and organization, and in the station of some who more or less openly join it,—owning a qualified allegiance to the constitution of the Province,—professing to regard the Part and the Govt as nuisances to be tolerated within certain limits only,—raising itself, whenever the fancy seizes it, or the crisis in its judgment demands it, not an imperium in imperio-renders it I fear extremely doubtful whether the functions of Legislative or of Govt can be carried on to advantage in this city. 'Shew vigor and put it down,' say some.—You *may* and *must* put down those who resist the law, when overt acts are committed—But the Party is unfortunately a national as well as political one—After each defeat it resumes its attitude of defiance, and whenever it comes into collision with the authorities there is the risk of a frightful race feud being provoked. All these dangers are vastly encreased by Montreal's being the seat of Govt.—

There are other arguments of no small force in favor of removal—I am assured that a good many of the members have declared that nothing will induce them to come again to Montreal—We shall lose one of our regiments, for you have determined (very properly I think) not to build a new Barrack, and it is believed that so far from voting money for this purpose there is very little probability that the Assembly could be induced to make provision for a building for the Part itself—As to the corporate authorities, they are without funds—and the city council consists of an utterly inefficient Mayor who is attached to Papineau in Politics, and of councillors, for the most part equally inefficient, who may be generally classed as Papineauistes, repeal Irish, and British Ultras—Nothing is to be hoped for from such a body, until the seat of Govt is removed and the citizens feel that they have nothing to rely on but themselves.

In addition to the reasons which I have given, there is one argument in favor of leaving Montreal which struck me forcibly even before the recent disturbances occurred. You find in this city I believe the most Anti-British specimens of each class of which our community consists—The Montreal French are the most Yankeefied French in the Province—the British, though furiously anti-Gallican, are, with some exceptions, the least loyal—and the commercial men the most zealous annexationists which Canada furnishes—It must I think do great mischief to the members who come from other parts of the Province to pass some months of each year in this hot bed of prejudice and disaffection—

These being among the reasons for removal from this place which, although not new, have been pressed upon me with renewed force lately. I have to add that Mr Baldwin who has just returned from the U. Province & with whom I have had a good deal of conversation on this subject, is entirely in favor of going to Western Canada. He does not think that the arguments for a first move to Quebec can stand for a moment against the consideration of the moral effect which will be produced both here and in England by a move on the part of the Govt to Kingston or Toronto in the face of the taunt that it is Anti British and subject entirely to French influence. On this point I am altogether of his opinion and I only hope that when La Fontaine returns from Halifax and Hincks from England he may be able to make his views prevail.—It is fair too that I should say that I believe the council are quite ready to go to either section of the Province that I indicate, if I make a point of it.—on a subject however involving such serious consequences—it would be more agreable to me that difficulties should be solved by discussion than by an arbitrary edict proceeding from myself.

78. (Kingston) *British Whig*, September 21, 1849.

MADAME LaFONTAINE'S POODLE

Among the numerous arguments which are daily made use of in favor of the Seat of Government's returning to Kingston, one trifling, though not unimportant matter has been lost sight of. It will be recollected by all the constant readers of the *British Whig*, that the ill health of Madame Lafontaine's poodle was the originating cause of the loss to Kingston of the Seat of Government. The air of our good old city did not agree with this interesting animal, which panted for the balmy breezes of Montreal—hence the fatal removal. Now, from some inquiries made, and information received (private of course,) we learn that the sanatory condition of the sweet poodle still remains precarious —that the affection which Madame retains for her canine favorite will not allow her to risk any further derangement of its health, and consequently, that any Removal of the Seat of Government is wholly out of the question. The condition of the poodle will not allow Madame Lafontaine to leave it—Madame Lafontaine will not allow Mons. Lafontaine to quit her—Mons. Lafontaine will not allow the Governor General to go without him; and therefore it follows that the Seat of Government remains at Montreal.

79. Extract from a Report of a Committee of the Executive Council,
     October 18, 1849 (EC).

The Committee of the Executive Council have had under consideration upon your Excellency's reference, the Resolution of the Honourable the Legislative Council, and also the Address of the Honourable
the Legislative Assembly of last Session, on the subject of the place at
which the future Sessions of the Provincial Parliament should be
holden, together with your Excellency's answer to the latter; and the
Committee most respectfully beg leave to report, that after the best
consideration that they have been able to give the matter, they see no
sufficient grounds arising out of anything that has transpired since the
prorogation of Parliament, to lead them to a different conclusion upon
this question from that arrived at by the popular branch of the Legislature in their Address. The Committee therefore respectfully advise your
Excellency that the recommendation of the House of Assembly, that
Parliament be in future convened alternately at Toronto and Quebec
during periods not exceeding four years at each place, be adopted and
acted upon.

As it would be manifestly most inconvenient to have the public
archives and the departments of the State at a different place from that at
which the Parliament is to sit, the Committee conceive that the adoption
of the views of the House of Assembly in this particular, leads of
necessity to the removal of those archives and departments to the place
at which Parliament is to be assembled. They therefore conceive it to be
expedient that the place where it may be your Excellency's pleasure to
summon Parliament for the next session should be decided upon, and
the necessary steps taken for the removal of the public departments
thither with as little delay as possible. And they are respectfully of
opinion that, under all circumstances it will be most expedient that such
removal should in the first instance be to the city of Toronto, for the
period of the constitutional duration of the present Parliament, and that
the quadrennial periods of alternation be commenced with the removal
to Quebec, at the expiration of that time.

The Committee would also recommend that, in order to prevent any
misapprehension as to the full intention of the Government and Parliament to carry out strictly the principle of an alternate periodical residence in each section of the Province, estimates be prepared and
submitted to Parliament at the next session, for making such alterations
and additions in and to the public buildings, both at Toronto and
Quebec, as may be necessary for the accommodation of the Representative of the Soveriegn, the departments of State, and both houses of
Parliament in each of those cities.

80. Lord Elgin (Governor General), to Earl Grey (Colonial Secretary), November 18, 1849.

1. With reference to your Lordship's Despatch, of the 14th September, in which you express the opinion, that the spirit of insubordination existing in the city of Montreal, would appear to render it a very unfit place for the seat of the Provincial Government, and for the meeting of the Legislature, I have the honour to report, that I have resolved on the advice of my Council, and after full and anxious deliberation, to act on the recommendation of the House of Assembly, conveyed in the address of which a copy was transmitted to your Lordship . . . and with that view to summon the Provincial Parliament for the next session at Toronto.

2. Exception is taken to the system of alternating Parliaments on various grounds, chiefly on that of its alleged inconvenience and expense. It is to be observed, however, on this head, that buildings which with moderate additions and repairs may be fitted for the uses of Parliament and of the departments of State, exist both at Toronto and Quebec, while the St. Lawrence and its canals afford the greatest facilities for the cheap and expeditious conveyance of the records of Government between these two points. Looking at these facts and to the considerations of public policy advanced in the address of the Assembly, I am disposed to believe that the advantages attending this arrangement will be found in practice to outweigh its inconveniences.

81. Lord Elgin (Governor General) to Earl Grey (Colonial Secretary), (confidential), October 19, 1849 (PAC).

. . . We have decided on leaving Montreal and summoning the Legislature at Toronto. LaFontaine is much against the plan—but except a sort of vague idea that by means of a great fight we might subdue the faction and restore order in Montreal he seems to me to have nothing to offer to justify remaining there. My own conviction is that our return to Montreal at present would give a great impulse to the annexation movement in U. Canada, and that the Members could not pass a Session there in the present temper of men's minds without being themselves to a great extent corrupted. At the same time I am quite aware that the removal will do some mischief among the French who are Narrow Minded and bigotted on all these points beyond belief—

In order to meet this difficulty as we best may we have determined to act on the suggestion of the Assembly itself—and to adopt the principle of alternate Parliaments—The plan of leaving Montreal for a Session with the view of obtaining additional powers did not obtain much support. We all feel that the evil is of a moral and chronic character, that it is intensely aggravated by the presence of the seat of Govt, and that it cannot be eradicated by force. When I say all I mean the English councillors for perhaps some of the French think differently—The truth is the French would like nothing better than to see the power of England employed to break down the party which has so long domineered over them—The Military! The Military! is their everlasting cry—It is most extraordinary to me to observe that persons who have such a pious horror of shedding blood that they never will consent to the execution of a criminal who has been convicted by the tribunals of the most atrocious murder are the first to grumble if the troops do not find occasions to fire upon the multitude—

The crisis is certainly a very serious one—It may lead not improbably to a break up of parties—If it splits the French it will be a consummation devoutly to be wished. Toronto is the most Tory place in Canada—it contains 25,000 people and I am assured that in the Town and neighbourhood there are not less than 25, orange Lodges. I am confident however that the respectable classes are averse to rioting and violence—That they will not stand by as the respectabilities of Montreal of all politics have done while riot and arson have their swing.—And if the worst comes to the worst you have there a homogenous population and you may call out the supporters of Govt and order without risking a war of race.—I think too that the orangemen in U. Canada are generally attached to the connexion.

82. (Toronto) *Globe*, October 23, 1849.

IMPORTANT ANNOUNCEMENT!
TORONTO SEAT OF GOVERNMENT!!

We have great pleasure in congratulating our fellow citizens that the Seat of Government will in a few days be in Toronto once more. How much it will add to the value of property, and the business of our rising city, it is impossible to estimate, but it must be considerable. . . . The Telegraph announces that the Provincial Secretary has issued a general order to the different departments (excepting the Educational department) directing preparations to be made for removal to Toronto, with all possible despatch.

83. Lord Elgin (Governor General) to Earl Grey (Colonial Secretary), (private), October 25, 1849 (PAC).

I believe that if we had returned [to Montreal] this complex iniquity would have worked the desired result—and that the Annexation mania would have spread rapidly through U.C.—what can you do with such a set?

. . . Everything depends on this section [Canada West] of the Province and the removal of the seat of Govt was absolutely necessary to keep it right.—Even the bugbear of French domination is made less frightful by our coming to the most British and Tory Town in N. America.

84. (Kingston) *British Whig*, October 26, 1849

The Montreal papers, as might be expected, are raising a mighty howl at the loss of the Seat of Government. Nobody in Western Canada cares one jot about their howling so they may as well keep their breath to cool their porridge. It was the wretched selfishness of the Montrealers which caused the removal of the Seat of Government from Western Canada; from amid an Anglo-Saxon race, to place it within the control of French Oligarchists and their Helots. Had the Government remained at Kingston, or at any place within the limits of the upper province, the Franco-Canadians never would have attained and exercised that arbitrary power which has been the exciting cause of all the late political riots and troubles. A war of races might have existed, as it now does, but it would have been a defensive war on the part of the Eastern Canadians, who would have had their hands full in making laws for themselves, instead of inflicting upon their neighbors the ills of an oppressive statute book.—From such evils the province, in future, will be protected, while legislation takes place in an educated land, and among free men. The Radicals may rule over us, and they will, but our rulers will be Anglo-Saxon Radicals, and not aliens to us in blood, language, and religion.

85. Lord Elgin (Governor General) to Earl Grey (Colonial Secretary), (private), October 28, 1849 (PAC).

The Montrealers are very angry about the removal of the seat of Govt but hitherto there have been more symptoms of confusion and stupor among them than of any other emotion—I had a message from a very high Tory a resident in Montreal only this morning who shews that feelings are divided even there—'Tell Lord Elgin' he said to my correspondent 'that he has saved Canada by this removal'—I have no doubt that I have done so at least for the time—The annexation movement has received no support from the Press out of Montreal—but of course so long as it had the prestige of being the metropolis its press had a great influence in the Province and was regarded beyond it as the exponent of the sentiments of the Community at large.

86. Lord Elgin (Governor General) to Earl Grey (Colonial Secretary), (private), November 1, 1849 (PAC).

It is hardly possible to determine how far the return of the Govt to Montreal would have been expedient without taking into consideration the peculiar condition of the Press in that city.

87. Earl Grey (Colonial Secretary) to Lord Elgin (Governor General), (private), November 16, 1849 (PAC).

I presume for the reasons you have the removal of the seat of Govnt was indispensable & I hope it will work well, but this arrangement of alternate Parlts in the two Capitals has not an air of permanence & I shd think it wd be very difficult t[o] manage.

88. Lord Elgin (Governor General) to Earl Grey (Colonial Secretary), (private), November 15, 1849 (PAC).

. . . it was hopeless to expect that the truth respecting Public opinion in this Province ever could reach England, so long as the Montreal Press had the prestige of being Metropolitan.—
Meanwhile it is satisfactory to see that the removal of the seat of Govt has had an excellent effect on the tone of the Montreal Press itself— . . .

89. Earl Grey (Colonial Secretary) to Lord Elgin (Governor General), December 13, 1849 (PAC).

I am glad to hear that your removal of the seat of Govnt has answered your expectations & promises to be useful, but this reminds me that you have never yet reported to me that measure officially.—this is an omission that may prove inconvenient when Parlt meets [in London] & considering how much we are to be the object of attack I cannot impress upon you too strongly the importance of writing to me safe producible despatches reporting to me all facts of importance on wh. it will not do for me to be without official information.

90. Earl Grey (Colonial Secretary) to Lord Elgin (Governor General), January 1, 1850 (PAC).

I have had the honour to receive your Lordship's Despatch and its Enclosure of the 18th November, reporting that you had resolved, on the advice of your Council, and after full and anxious deliberation, to act on the recommendation of the House of Assembly on the subject of the place at which the future sessions of the Provincial Parliament should be held, and summon the next Parliament to meet at Toronto.

As the Assembly in their Address proposed this arrangement, I have only to express my hope that it may prove successful, and my approbation of your Lordship's determination to act upon the opinion expressed to you by the representatives of the people of Canada.

91. Lord Elgin (Governor General) to Earl Grey (Colonial Secretary), (private), December 2, 1849 (PAC).

I see by the English Papers that I am well abused on all hands for the change of the seat of Govt—I have the consolation of knowing that I would have been quite as much abused if I had done anything else —Meanwhile the measure is producing the important and valuable fruit which I expected—Annexation is arrested, and stigmatised as a merely local movement. The movement is a disappointed self seeking fraction—If Montreal had continued to be the Metropolis it would have spread and become, I do not say triumphant, but certainly Provincial.

. . . As respects Montreal itself the effect of this measure has been just what I expected.—Having no Govt to fight on the spot the inhabitants are taking to their business—Even the Press is comparatively mild only indulging once or twice a week in some violent abuse of the Govr. Genl . . .

P.S. . . .

I intended to have said at an earlier part of this letter that the conduct of the French in reference to the seat of Govt has been excellent. The annexation movement does not appear to have made any head among them.

92. Lord Elgin (Governor General) to Earl Grey (Colonial Secretary), (private), January 14, 1850 (PAC).

Before your next letters will have been despatched you will probably have received from me something official both with respect to the annexation movement and to the removal of the seat of Govt—I am most anxious, I can assure you, to give you despatches for Parliament-.—But while I maintain my constitutional position here, acting as I believe you agree with me in thinking I ought to act, *on & through my Ministry*, you must feel how difficult it is for me to discuss my own name and person, in documents which are sure to be published, acts of the administration which may at a later period be the subject of controversy in the local Parliament, perhaps the ground work of new ministerial arrangements. I do not think that there is any class of duties more difficult to define even theoretically than those which devolve upon a Governor under our newly adtoped system of constitutional Govt towards the colonists on the one hand, and the Imperial Govt and Part on the other.—and what it is so difficult to define in theory it is not easier to work out in practice. As respects the seat of Govt question I would respectfully suggest that you should throw the whole responsibility of the change on the local Govt & Part—But if you want a case made out I can do it easily enough.

CHAPTER V
PERAMBULATION AND REFERRAL

Introduction

The system of alternating the capital between Toronto and Quebec seems to have been beneficial, in the minds of some Canadians of the day, in terms of better acquainting politicians and civil servants with other regions, places and peoples. However, the system was also very expensive, it caused great administrative inefficiences, important public records were damaged or lost during moves, and civil servants and others were frustrated by the many inconveniences caused by the several relocations.

Following the implementation of the system, members of the Legislative Assembly split into two groups: the coalition of "central" Canada members (that is, supporters of Montreal, Kingston, or Bytown/Ottawa) who were the "fixed-site men", and the "log-rolling compact" or "alternating men" who were supporters of Toronto and Quebec. Frustrations mounted and deadlock developed between the two groups. Some of the "alternating men" did accept the wisdom of having a permanent seat of government, but "on principle" they felt that the alternating system had to continue, and thus it was twice ratified (in 1851 and 1853; see Figure 6). On these and other occasions the point was forced either by supporters of the city (Toronto or Quebec) about to receive the capital functions or by the "fixed-site men" who sought to disrupt the system in favour of one of the three more centrally located cities. The latter men could not muster enough votes to force a change, so the costly and inefficient system continued.

One body of the Parliament, the Legislative Council, did get a majority to agree in 1855 that the alternating system should cease. When the Council approached the Assembly for their concurrence the Assembly refused. This conflict, coupled with many earlier votes for particular places by the Legislative Assembly, and also the Assembly's reaffirmation of the alternating system (Figure 7), led many people to conclude that the whole issue had either to be taken out of the hands of the legislature or else made a ministerial question (whereby members would be forced to consider political party affiliations). The *Montreal Gazette* correctly observed, however, that the question would remain a complex one:

... the final decision rests with the Governor General or the Colonial Office, that being a part of the absolute prerogative of the Crown. The exercise of that prerogative, however, may be checked by either House. The Lower may refuse to vote the necessary supplies; the Upper may refuse to sanction them. The question in its present shape is beset with difficulties for the Governor General.[1]

The Government relocated from Quebec to Toronto in 1855. The 1856 session of Parliament was marked by great bitterness, some of which arose because of the seat of government issue. The capital issue was much discussed. One observor said of the Assembly debaters that they showed "the same narrow-mindedness, the same local selfishness"[2] as in previous years. William Lyon Mackenzie, member for Haldimand, C.W., jested in the House that "the children of Israel travelled 1750 miles in 40 years, and the children of Canada had beat[en] them in a fifteen years pilgrimage."[3] Another member of the Assembly denounced the "nomadic system" and claimed that there was "no such system found in any country having any aspirations after nationality."[4] Some speakers, but most notably reform leader George Brown from Toronto, stressed cultural differences and also called for a new system of representation that would reflect what the 1851 census had revealed—Upper Canadians' numerical superiority (see selection 123).

On April 10, 1856, a report by the Department of Public works was laid before the Assembly. It indicated that over £300,000 would be needed for the construction of new government buildings and associated seat of government facilities. This estimated cost surprised the members, for it was higher than previous estimates. Four days later it was moved in the House that the system (of alternating capitals) should be discontinued. This was accepted (Figure 8) and an address to this effect was then presented to the Governor General.

Following the Governor General's response, a series of motions and amendments were made in the Assembly and the divisions which followed were fascinating, since the voting patterns reflected a series of city-based alliances and or sectional attachments (see Figures 9-14). Old strategies suddenly and unexpectedly failed that night, and Quebec was accepted by a slim majority as the site for the permanent seat of government.[5] Joy in Quebec was soon crushed when the decision was rejected by the Legislative Council and renewed stalemate threatened the Legislative Assembly.

Encouraged by Governor General Sir Edmund Head, and desirous of ridding itself of a political nightmare, the Government in 1857 was able to achieve an essentially party-based majority in Parliament in support of referring the highly contentious issue to the Queen (see Figure 16).

The referral was itself a contentious act, for many Canadians (but notably Opposition members and their supporters) claimed that the Government was irresponsible because it was referring a local issue. A Government newspaper, however, later declared that

> we might have gone on fighting about localities until doomsday had not the happy expedient been hit upon of referring the question to the Queen, as the person most likely to give it a calm, impartial and unbiased decision.[6]

Remembering that Ottawa was later to be declared ''the Queen's choice'' it is important to note that Ottawa's supporters were few in number before that city's fortunes came to be entwined with the Royal name (see Figure 15).

Notes

[1]*Montreal Gazette*, April 27, 1855.
[2]*Montreal Gazette*, March 26, 1856.
[3](Toronto) *Leader*, March 18, 1856.
[4]*Ibid*.
[5]Considerable attention is payed to the alliances and strategies as they formed and reformed during the night of April 16, 1856, in Knight, *A Capital for Canada*, *op.cit.*, pp. 159-169.
[6](Montreal) *Pilot*, January 28, 1858.

Documents

93. *Times* of London, January 10, 1850.

Toronto is now basking in the sunshine of the increased business and high house rents caused by the influx of Government employees . . . . Lord Elgin is now residing with his family at Toronto, where he appears to be generally popular, as it is certain he is throughout Upper Canada.

94. (Kingston) *British Whig*, May 10, 1850.

In the course of a few days the Provincial Legislature will have assembled. Some predict a stormy Session; but our opinion is the Session will be a remarkably quiet one. There is nothing political to quarrel about. . . .

The Lower Canadians may probably kick up a dust about the Seat of

Government, as doubtless, a pretty good intimation will be given to them that the Upper Canadians will never peaceably consent to Quebec's being made, even for four years only, the metropolis of Canada, being so wholly out of the way. But in all probability, the Ministers may bluff off the matter for the present time. While Lord Elgin remains in the province, he will never consent to dwell again in Montreal; but should he return home, it is not at all unlikely, that under other auspices, Montreal will be made the permanent Seat of Government.

95. (Toronto) *British Colonist*, August 13, 1850.

In this matter-of-fact age—this age of wonders—an age of big events . . . who could have forseen . . . that the Seat of Government of United Canada would, in the short space of nine years, be seen moving to and fro, like a city shaken by an earthquake, having neither stability nor security?

96. (Bytown) *Statesman*, reprinted in [Kingston] *British Whig*, May 16, 1851.

The perambulating Seat of Government scheme, we look upon as a monster humbug—too absurd to be reasoned upon, and too dear to be laughed at. We trust Bytown will be the place ultimately chosen. It is central in [its] situation—removed from the frontier—would give a triumph to neither section of the Province—the French could reside in Hull, the British in Bytown—a Railroad to Montreal and Prescott, would bring Quebec, Boston and Toronto, within a day's journey of it—it would be secure in time of war—central in time of peace; and taking all circumstances into consideration, is we believe, the true position for the permanent Seat of Government. We think Bytown only requires some few men of talent and influence in the Councils of the Country, to ensure its success. Should Bytown not be able to succeed, we should then go for Kingston, being the next best place.

97. (Toronto) *British Colonist*, September 2, 1851.

The melancholy event took place on, Saturday last [August 30]. The room of the Legislative Council was crowded almost to an inconvenience, by those who were anxious to see the close of what many supposed to be the last Parliament in Upper Canada.

After the prorogation, His Excellency . . . took his departure, and proceeded by the steamer City of Toronto, to Niagara Falls . . . there was not the slightest manifestation of popular rejoicing either as his

Excellency entered or left the House, with the exception of a sickly cheer, given by some of the assembly messengers as the carriage rolled off.

98. William Stewart, "To the Electors of Bytown," October 1851 (PAC).

With regard to the Seat of Government, the idea of perambulating from City to City, with a Political Menagerie yclept "a Government," has become a subject of derision to every sensible man in the Province; apart from every other consideration connected with so important a subject, I hold the enormous wasteful expenditure to be nothing less than a plunder of the public monies of this country.—One with 'half an eye in his head,' can easily discern where the most central and suitable place for the Seat of Government is; but as I presume the settlement of that important question would not yield that amount of servile Ministerial support which is desirable, it is probable that public rights, and public justice, will be violated for some time longer.

99. W.L. Mackenzie in (Dunnville, C.W.) *Haldimand Independent*, October 11, 1851.

Bytown and its environs astonishes me; I have walked ten miles to view the river scenery, and, though much fatigued, am highly gratified. This place has a large trade, and will increase with the prosperity of the country around it; nature seems to have destined it for the site of a great city, and I suppose it would have been chosen for the capital of United Canada had it not been located above tide-water, or had not some plan for consolidating the colonies, or creating a Northern federation, been in the minds of men in power in England.

100. *Quebec Mercury*, October 18, 1851.

We, in Quebec, are on the eve of a pleasing and important event in the advent of Her Majesty's Representative to the Ancient Seat of the Government of this Province, both under the French and English rule, and the restoration of our metropolitan position.

The seat of Government returns to Quebec, after a long hegira, occasioned by a shallow and time-serving policy here, and a mistaken concession on the part of the Crown of the right of naming and definitely fixing the Capital of the Colony; a course which threw local and sectional jealousies, and partizan interests into the question, which never ought to have been permitted to influence it, as it should have been decided on the mere ground of local fitness; and would, without doubt, have been so decided, had it been left for decision where the above named minor considerations did not prevail.

The remarkable salubrity, picturesque beauty and historical reminiscences of Quebec render it no less eminently fit for a Vice Regal residence, than the important political advantages of its position, its security, and its comparative proximity to the ocean and the Seat of Empire, render it the fitting resting place of the Executive and Legislative powers.

101. *Quebec Mercury*, October 21, 1851.

RESTORATION OF THE SEAT OF GOVERNMENT—ARRIVAL OF THE GOVERNOR GENERAL

Quebec is once more the Capital of the Canadas, the forerunner, as we trust, of a still prouder position for her among the cities of British North America.

102. *Quebec Mercury*, May 26, 1853.

A UNION OF ALL THE PROVINCES TO BE DESIRED

We perceive that the people of Montreal are far from resigned to their fate, in being excluded from a return to their former glory as the seat of the Provincial Government. We cannot, for our part, discover what claim Montreal has or ever had to be the Metropolis of Canada. The capital of the country ought to be a fortress as well as a seaport— Quebec is both: and the jargon talked about centralism is pure "bunkum" and nonsense. In these days of steam and electricity, locality does not constitute centralism in the political import of the word, a day's difference by river navigation, six hours by a railway, and a few minutes by telegraph, are scarcely advantages sufficient to compensate the many defects of Montreal.

We not only regard Quebec as the most elegible metropolis for Canada, but as the only capital for British America, which is, without doubt, destined to be before many years are over, but one country. Everything tends to this result; everywhere at the present moment the centralising principle is at work, bringing large masses of the human race into compact communities, and drawing as it were vast tracts of country within the boundary of single states—the Union, perhaps, may, in the opinion of some, be at present excepted. . . .

103. Legislative Assembly, June 3, 1853 (JLA).

It is expedient to discontinue the present system of Parliament sitting alternately at two places. (See Figure 6)

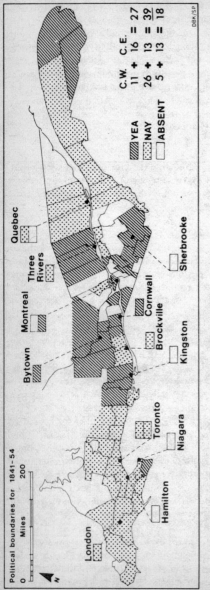

Political boundaries for 1841–54

0   200
Miles

N

London

Bytown   Montreal   Three Rivers   Quebec

Toronto   Kingston   Brockville   Cornwall   Sherbrooke

Niagara   Hamilton

	C.W.		C.E.	
YEA	11	+	16	= 27
NAY	26	+	13	= 39
ABSENT	5	+	13	= 18

YEA
NAY
ABSENT

DBK/SP

Figure 6. Expedient to discontinue alternating system; June 3, 1853. (See selection 103)

104. G.B. Lyon, member for Russell, C.W., on the Ottawa River, speaking in the Legislative Assembly, June 3, 1853.

[Since] the majority of the people were in favour of the union there should be a permanent seat of government for the United Province. There was a place that neither section of the country could complain of—a sort of District of Columbia, on the borders of both. He was not so wedded, however, to Bytown, but that if he could not get the best place he would like Montreal as the next.

105. *Quebec Mercury*, June 4, 1853.

[There is a] union between the advocates for Quebec and Toronto upon the principle that half a loaf is better than no bread.

106. (Bytown) *Ottawa Citizen*, June 11, 1853.

Some [of the leading men] are interested in Quebec, others in Toronto, and as both could not have their purposes served they have made a compact with each other and agreed to devour the alternately. School boys sometimes eat an apple by taking a bite turn about;—it is thus our great men [who] eat up the people's money.

107. *Quebec Mercury*, February 11, 1854.

The present moment is one at which the question of a permanent seat of government must necessarily occupy a large share of public attention. There can be no doubt, but that Quebec is the only fit place in Canada for a Provincial Metropolis, in the opinion of any impartial reasoner. On the ground of centralism (so much spoken of during some years past) Quebec possesses immense advantages. IT IS IN REALITY THE MOST CENTRAL CITY IN CANADA, *the nearest to the sea-board, the nearest to the seat of empire*, most directly in the track of trans-marine commerce in peace, and the natural and necessary basis of military operations in war. These things form the elements of centralism; they are the advantages it holds out, and they are to be found to an equal extent only in the City of Quebec. Nations have in all times selected their capitals chiefly for their capabilities of defence, security against aggression, and convenience as emporiums of trade. These are the grounds on which the site was selected. Such reasons have prevailed since builders were, from Nineveh to Rome, from Rome to London, from London to St. Petersburgh; and when in Quebec, salubrity of climate, and beauty of scenery, is added to these eminent advantages, prejudice alone can question the eligibility of the situation.

As for the rest, telegraph, steamboat, and railway are appliances of the age which devour space and leave little to be said on the subject of speedly transit from the western extremity of the province.

108. *Quebec Mercury*, November 9, 1854.

The House will very likely decide tonight on the question of the seat of government, probably the perambulatory principle will prevail. For the present the legislature will adjudge this question: in a little time the mob will settle it for them; all the facts of history in Canada shew that in its present state of society the Assembly never can be safe unless protected by walls, batteries, and troops. They were driven out of Montreal, and in Toronto many of their members were considered unsafe in the streets at noon-day, and to cap the climax one of their members, Mr. Brown, would last year have been murdered on the floor of the House by a mob on their road from sacking a church, had it not been that Quebec is a fortified town, and one wing of the parliament buildings happened to abut on a guard house.

109. *Montreal Gazette*. November 11, 1854.

The really important question of the Seat of Government, is at length, I am sorry to write it, reduced to the magnificent proportions of a game of grab. Members from different sections of the Province snap at it as a set of hungry pike would at a tempting bait. There is no sort of decency in the thing—there is not even enough to conceal the miserable actuating motives. 'Chiselling' is at length the order of the day, and we have divers caucus meetings held accordingly. Common sense, even that of the House, points to fixing a permanent site for the seat of Government, but the members from the district of Quebec, join with those from the neighbourhood of Toronto, to keep up ambulating Parliaments, and thus combination makes a powerful 'log rolling' vote—perhaps a majority of the whole House.

. . . . The fixed site men are trying to checkmate things. . . . Any game of this sort seems to me to be justifiable as a *dernier ressort* to stop the present mad system,—better that the Government should be fixed at either Quebec or Toronto; and it is clear that if a few votes can be detached from either of these places, by the bait of getting the Government permanently at one of them, we shall get a fixed site and the disappointed gentlemen may be safely left to scream out until they are tired or their throats are sore. Now the question has become one of intrigue, the excitement is equal to that of horse racing, and the trickery practiced equals in morality that of jockeys.

110. (Toronto) *Leader*, November 13, 1854.

The seat of government question is one on which more selfishness is generally manifested, under the poor disguise of a pretended devotion of the public interest, than, perhaps on any other. Everyone wishes it to be understood that his conduct, in regard to the subject, is regulated by the highest principles of public justice, by an anxious regard for economy, and for the safety of the public archives; while in point of fact, nearly everybody directs his arguments to the great end of making his own city, town, or village the capital. . . . The advocates of Montreal, of Bytown, of Kingston, are shocked with the utter proligacy of the alternating system; but of course they are to the last degree unselfish in the matter: they would by satisfied with having their own particular locality the permanent seat of government.

111. *Ottawa Citizen*, November 18, 1854.

The debate upon the Seat of Government has brought out the most extraordinary amount of selfishness ever exhibited in any legislature. . . . One of the arguments made use of is that *faith* should be kept with Toronto in carrying out the resolution of alternating parliaments for as least four years more. If it were to return to Toronto for four years, that city would be satisfied. This would be doing whàt is called keeping faith with Upper Canada.—Upper Canada has always been treated by the family compact as if it belonged to Toronto—as if, in fact, its whole body and soul were concentrated within the walls of that town.

112. Address of H.J. Friel, Mayor of Bytown, at the close of the Town Corporation, January 3, 1855; The Town obtained a charter as a city (Ottawa), January, 1855 (PAC).

Permit me, gentlemen, to hope that the brightening prospect now opening on our young City is but a foreshadowing of its future greatness. The centre of the Ottawa Valley, its local importance cannot be questioned; the centre of a whole Province its general importance must be conceded. To this common centre all parties must turn ere long; the finger of destiny points hitherward, and I doubt not that metropolitan honours await the City just ushered into existence.

113. W. Patrick, member for Grenville, C.W., speaking in the Legislative Assembly, March 22, 1855.

. . . The city of Ottawa, which might be described as the Columbus of

Canada—scarcely in one Province or the other [an honorable member " 'tis nowhere"]—one of the finest situated cities in the world—the district one of the fairest and richest—the property ready purchased the ordnance property—ready prepared and well suited in every respect. And if honorable members would divest themselves of all prejudice— he thought that that was the place they would choose.

114. Legislative Assembly, March 23, 1855 (JLA).

Inexpedient to interfere with [the alternating] arrangement adopted in 1849 and re-affirmed in 1851 (see Figure 7).

115. *Montreal Gazette*, March 26, 1855.

Ambulatory Parliaments—We published the following intelligence in our Extra on Saturday:

> Gazette Office
> Saturday Noon, March 24, 1855
> By Special Telegraphic Despatch

Our Correspondent at Quebec sent us the following message, dated this morning:

'The House has decided to continue the Alternate System of Parliaments by a vote that took place at three o'clock this morning—the majority was seven for continuing the system.'

The public, we feel assured, will peruse this intelligence with no pleasure; but, on the contrary, with regret. We have seen something of the manner in which the Seat of Government question has been treated by the House of Assembly of late years, and must state it has been little creditable to that body. The general good has not been the object sought to be attained by members, but local interests have swayed them. From the first hour that the system was established, there has been what our neighbours across the frontier expressively call a "log-rolling" compact, between members in the interest of Quebec and Toronto, and the parties to this disgraceful compact have been unwilling to see anything beyond it. During the prolonged debates that took place on the Seat of Govt. last fall, dirty intrigues on behalf of different localities were the order of the day, and little, indeed nothing, was to be heard on the real merits of this important question. Members from this and that portion of the Province snapped at the Seat of Government, as a prize to be obtained for their respective localities, and did not, as we stated, look on it as a public question.

We cannot exempt the government from blame in the matter. No government consistently with self respect, or the very principles on

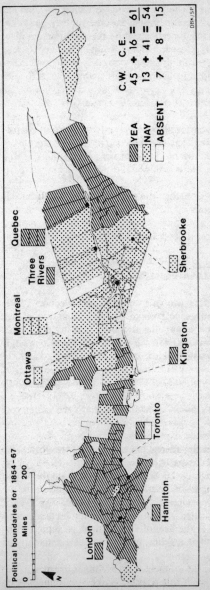

Figure 7. Inexpedient to interfere with the arrangement adopted in 1849 and re-affirmed in 1851; March 23, 1855. (See selection 114)

which the British system is founded, could leave such a question an open one, and it is no excuse for present ministers to say that they follow the bad and improper precedent set by their predecessors. A government that cannot, as a government, make up its mind on such a question, is not fit to remain in office.

We know the strong prejudices and jealousies against Montreal, and we know from what unworthy motives many of them spring; in view of them, although believing that Montreal has most claims to be the seat of government, rather than endanger the permanent fixing of it some where, we have all along steadily and sincerely advocated the claims of the City of Ottawa, and would have been glad to see it fixed there. We believe that the City of Ottawa has many of the necessary qualifications, and that the public interests would be consulted by taking the seat of government there. In this view of the case we have been personally disinterested, as we also believe that Montreal has been and can afford to be, to an extent that cannot be said of any other city in Canada. We look with no pleasure on the history of this system of nomadic Parliaments: it began in disgraceful cowardice, and has been continued in disreputable intrigue.

116. (Toronto) *Globe*, March 30, 1855.

[Toronto member, George Brown's amendment (selection 114)] bringing the seat of government to Toronto [has passed] in spite of the most strenuous opposition . . . our citizens may prepare for the inroad of the officials. Where they are to find room puzzles every one who knows the state of our crowded city.

117. (Toronto) *Leader*, March 30, 1855.

Montreal is for ever disposed of. . . . henceforth the claims of Montreal are nil.

118. Address from Legislative Council to Sir Edmund Head (Governor General), April 25, 1855 (JLC).

May it please Your Excellency.

We, her Majesty's dutiful and loyal Subjects, the Legislative Council of *Canada* in Provincial Parliament assembled, beg leave respectfully to represent to Your Excellency that in our opinion the time has arrived when the Royal Prerogative should be exercised in determining upon a permanent Seat of Government in this Province that the system of holding alternate Parliament at *Quebec* and *Toronto* is objectionable and detrimental to the Public Service, on account of its manifest and extreme inconvenience; that it involves a large expenditure of the Public Funds; and that by the frequent transportation from place to place of the several Departments connected with the Government, the security and safe-keeping of the Libraries, Records and Archives of the Country are seriously endangered.

We therefore pray that Your Excellency will be pleased, in the exercise of the Royal Prerogative, to fix permanently upon some convenient place for the annual assembling of Parliament, and we beg to assure Your Excellency of our cheerful concurrence in any proposition you may think fit to make for the appropriation of Public Money for the erection of suitable buildings for the accommodation of the three Branches of the Legislature at the place which may be so fixed upon by Your Excellency.

119. (Toronto) *Leader*, April 27, 1855.

The Legislative Council has determined to disturb the arrangement deliberately sanctioned by the popular branch of the Legislature. A question which has almost broken up existing party affinities during the present Session of Parliament is thus attempted to be re-opened. . . . The same antagonism between the two branches of the Legislature existed [in 1849] as exists now.

120. *Montreal Gazette*, April 27, 1855

. . . the final decision rests with the Governor General or the Colonial Office, that being a part of the absolute prerogative of the Crown. The exercise of that prerogative, however, may be checked by either House. The Lower may refuse to vote the necessary supplies; the Upper may refuse to sanction them. The question in its present shape is beset with difficulties for the Governor General.

121. Sir Edmund Head (Governor General) to Sir William Moles-worth (Colonial Office), (private), August 7, 1855 (PAC).

You are probably aware of the fact that in pursuance of an arrangement made some years ago it was understood that the Seat of Government after remaining four years at Quebec, was to be removed again to Toronto.

After some discussion in the course of last Session, this arrangement was virtually confirmed; although an Address in favor of a fixed Seat of Government was presented to me by the Legislative Council. Consequently it is now settled that in the course of this autumn, the residence of the Governor General and the various public departments necessarily connected with the Seat of Government will have to be transferred to Upper Canada.

This is not the place or time for discussing the question whether the moveable Seat of Government be a wise or economical arrangement. The disadvantages of such a system—among which I rate highly the inconvenience to the subordinate Officers and Clerks employed in the various departments, are obvious to every one; but it has without doubt produced certain benefits which are not less real because they do not catch the eye so readily as its evils. . . .

122. Speech at Cobourg, C.W., by Sir Edmund Head (Governor General), printed in *Farmers Journal*, Vol. 9, no. 7 (November, 1855).

Your Legislature has been settled in Lower Canada for four years. Your members from Upper Canada have been learning the nature of the country, and have been conciliating any prejudice that might exist, by living in good fellowship and brotherhood with their French brethren. And now that the French members from Lower Canada are coming up to live among you for a certain time, and are going to perform legislative duties in the midst of you, I have no doubt that you will heartily welcome them and receive them as brothers. It has struck me lately that it would be one of the most absurd things in the world if the French and English in Canada were to take to quarrelling just as the French and English in all the rest of the world are uniting to each other in amity. I think it would be one of the most foolish exhibitions that could be witnessed.—(Cheers.) And therefore it is that I have too much confidence in the good sense of the people both of Upper and Lower Canada, to expect ever to ever see any such thing.

123. George Brown, member for Toronto, C.W., speaking in the Legislative Assembly, March 17, 1856.

The great question was evidently not the abstract principle of a permanent Seat of Government, but whether Montreal should be selected. The justness of the abstract principle no one disputed; but the contingencies of the Union had to be taken into account. We were a different people—different in language and religion. And Upper Canada would never submit to the Seat of Government permanently in Lower Canada—so long as representation was not based on population.

124. *Montreal Gazette*, March 26, 1856.

Few things excite more intense interest in this House, and among out-siders, than this question of the Seat of Government. Every one seems determined to make it a personal matter. The galleries were filled last evening [March 17, 1856], in expectation of a close contest. The debate . . . was characterised by the same narrow-mindedness, the same local selfishness which has marked all previous debates of a similar kind. Montreal, poor Montreal, was the great bugbear that seemed to bestride men's minds; and weigh down their spirits like a nightmare: The Kingston people even, and all or nearly all from the vicinity of that city, turned traitors to the cause of a fixed Seat of Government because, forsooth, there was so great a prospect of Montreal being determined on as the site. . . .

Kingston men publically avow that they admit the evils of the present system, and are favorable to the establishment of the Government at some fixed site, yet vote against their convictions, because Montreal might benefit by it, and Kingston might fail to win the prize she covets. Not only did they vote thus, but called upon their friends to sacrifice their convictions in a similar manner, and violate the pledges given to their constituents.

The poor simpletons from the District of Quebec too, have deluded themselves with the idea that they will get the Seat of Government back there at the end of four years. Wait till the Government asks for a vote of money for the purpose of erecting buildings there, and they will see the result. Mr. George Brown will object until representation by population is granted, and will carry a sufficient number of Western men to vote with him upon this pretext and others to refuse the vote if Ministers should have the courage to propose it.

. . . Montreal has shown by her conduct throughout this matter, that she cared little about the Seat of Government. She, at least, can afford to condemn it. She has not intrigued for it.

125. *Montreal Gazette*, March 27, 1856.

The atmosphere of Quebec is not congenial to good Upper Canadian legislation we are told, nor is that of Toronto to Lower Canadians is retorted every day. In Ottawa or Montreal both might meet on neutral ground [where] a just, temperate and moderate middle course would be adopted, and the union cemented, not threatened with dissolution.

126. *Brockville Recorder*, April 3, 1856.

Despite the jealousies and trickery of interested parties, we sincerely trust a majority will set the question at rest. Kingston we think deserves the honour; but should the friends of Kingston fail, let them unite with voting for some other locality. Throw Quebec out of the list, and we are willing to submit to either Toronto, Ottawa or Montreal, as a permanent locality.

It is worse than foolish to stave off the question longer. Every removal cost the country nearly £100,000. No true man will vote to sustain this waste. Better apply the money in relieving the people from the burden of taxation in the articles to tea, suger, etc.

127. Legislative Assembly, April 14, 1856 (JLA).

In the opinion of this House the time has arrived when the present system of convening Parliament alternately at Toronto and Quebec should be discontinued (see Figure 8). [Sent as an address to the Governor General.]

128. (Toronto) *Globe*, April 16, 1856

We hope that Upper Canadians will quit themselves like men in the struggle. It will be a serious injury to our interests should Lower Canada win the day. The Seat of Government gives vast power to the views of those who possess it. Everybody knows what an influential priestcraft obtained over the government when it was stationed in the head quarters of Romanism, Quebec; and no one can fail to see the new power Upper Canadian opinions have gained since Parliament met in Toronto. Upper Canada should never allow such an advantage to be gained by the priest-party, so long as she is denied Representation by Population. The acquisition of her rights in that respect would enable her to cope in any place with her opponents, but before it is attained there should be no compliance even on the smallest point.

129. Sir Edmund Head (Governor General) to Legislative Assembly, April 16, 1856 (JLA).

The Governor General is ready to discontinue the present system of convening Parliament alternately at Toronto and Quebec, when the necessary information as to what is most convenient to the Legislature, and the requisite means for carrying out its wishes, are in possession of His Excellency.

130. E. Larwill, member for Kent, C.W., speaking in the Legislative Assembly, April 16, 1856.

If a fixed place must be found, do as they did in Michigan, where

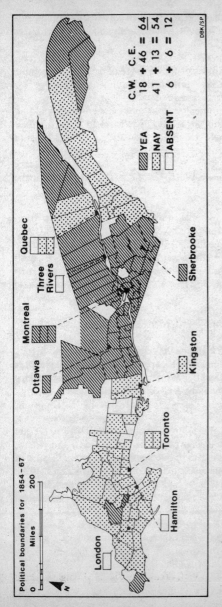

Political boundaries for 1854 - 67

0   Miles   200

Ottawa   Montreal   Three Rivers   Quebec

London   Hamilton   Toronto   Kingston   Sherbrooke

YEA   NAY   ABSENT

	C.W.	C.E.	
YEA	18 + 46	= 64
NAY	41 + 13	= 54
ABSENT	6 + 6	= 12

DBK/SP

Figure 8. Discontinue alternating system; April 14, 1856. (See selection 127)

they pitched on the middle of the State, which was also the middle of a bush, away from the influences which surrounded a Government wherever it was situated.

131. J.-E. Turcotte, member for Maskinonge, C.E., speaking in the Legislative Assembly, April 16, 1856.

I want the seat of government in a place where members could find an understanding ear; and an appreciative heart to listen to their speeches. Such a place could be Quebec, Montreal, or Ottawa, because all three have French-speaking populations.

132. A member from Canada West speaking in reply to Turcotte in the Legislative Assembly, April 16, 1856.

[Turcotte's reasoning] established a reason why the seat of government should not be fixed in the Lower Province. Why should Upper Canadian members be compelled to go down to Lower Canada, and to a people whose language they did not fully, and in many instances, at all understand? For it was a fact that the French members understood English much better than the Upper Canadian members understood French.

133. Legislative Assembly, April 16, 1856 (JLA).

Moved That in order to facilitate the selection of a proper place for a Permanent Seat of Government, it is expedient that no one place other than one of the Cities hereinafter named, be selected, or proposed for selection, as the place where the Seat of Government is to be permanently fixed, viz: Toronto, Quebec, Montreal, Ottawa, Kingston, Hamilton. . . .

Moved in amendment That all of the words after "That" to the end of the Question be left out, and the words "in the opinion of this House, the City of Ottawa is the most eligible place for the future Capital of Canada, and it is recommended that after 1859, the Parliament be permanently convened in that City, and that suitable buildings be forthwith commenced for the accommodation of the Legislature and Government" inserted instead thereof;

Moved in amendment That the word "Ottawa" be left out, and the word "Montreal" inserted instead thereof;

Moved in amendment That the word "Montreal" be left out, and the word "Kingston" inserted instead thereof;

Moved in amendment That the word "Kingston" be left out, and the word "Toronto" inserted instead thereof;

Moved in amendment That the word "Toronto" be left out, and the word "Hamilton" inserted instead thereof;

Moved in amendment That the word "Hamilton" be left out, and the word "Quebec" inserted instead thereof;

And the Question being put on the last proposed Amendment [that is, Quebec instead of Hamilton]: Yeas 70, Nays 46.

And the Question being put on the Amendment as amended, That the word "Toronto" be left out, and the word "Quebec" inserted instead thereof; the House divided: Yeas 71, Nays 50 (See Figure 9).

And the Question being put on the Amendment as amended, That the word "Kingston" be left out, and the word "Quebec" inserted instead thereof; the House divided: Yeas 67, Nays 54.

And the Question being put on the Amendment as amended, That the word "Montreal" be left out, and the word "Quebec" inserted instead thereof; the House divided: Yeas 65, Nays 55 (See Figure 10).

And the Question being put on the Amendment as amended, That the word "Ottawa" be left out, and the word "Quebec" inserted instead thereof; the House divided: Yeas 77, Nays 43 (See Figure 11).

And the Question being proposed on the Amendment to the original Question, as amended, That all the words after "That" to the end of the Question be left out, and the words "in the opinion of this House, the City of Quebec is the most eligible place for the future Capital of Canada, and it is recommended that after 1859 the Parliament be permanently convened in that City, and that suitable buildings be forthwith commenced for the accommodation of the Legislature and Government" inserted instead thereof;

Moved in amendment to the said Amendment, That the words "the Seat of Government be permanently fixed in Upper Canada" inserted instead thereof; and the Question being put on this Amendment to the said proposed Amendment to the original Question, as amended; the House divided: Yeas 53, Nays 67 (See Figure 12).

And the Question being put on the Amendment to the original Question as amended; the House divided: Yeas 61, Nays 59 (See Figure 13).

Then the main Question, so amended, being put, That in the opinion of this House, the City of Quebec is the most eligible place for the future Capital of Canada, and it is recommended that after 1859 the Parliament be permanently convened in that City, and that suitable buildings be forthwith commenced for the accommodation of the Legislature and Government; the House divided: Yeas 64, Nays 56 (See Figure 14).

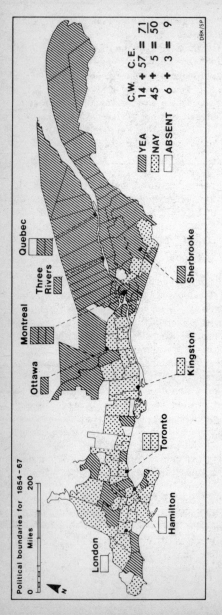

Political boundaries for 1854–67

0   Miles   200

N

YEA

NAY

ABSENT

```
        C.W.   C.E.
       14  +  57  =  71
       45  +   5  =  50
        6  +   3  =   9
```

London

Hamilton

Toronto

Kingston

Ottawa

Montreal

Three Rivers

Quebec

Sherbrooke

DBK/SP

Figure 9. Quebec instead of Toronto; April 16, 1856. (See selection 133)

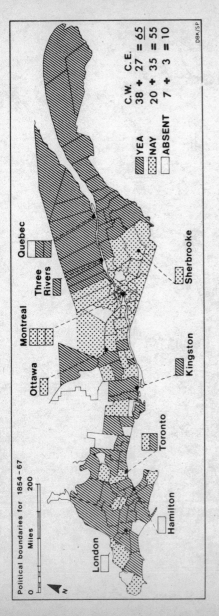

Political boundaries for 1854-67

Miles
0   200

N

London

Hamilton

Toronto

Ottawa

Montreal

Three Rivers

Quebec

Kingston

Sherbrooke

	C.W.	C.E.	
YEA	38 +	27	= 65
NAY	20 +	35	= 55
ABSENT	7 +	3	= 10

DBK/SP

Figure 10. Quebec instead of Montreal; April 16, 1856. (See selection 133)

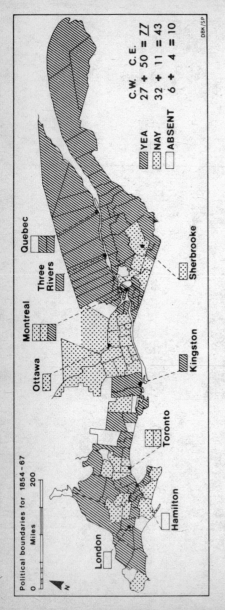

Figure 11. Quebec instead of Ottawa; April 16, 1856. (See selection 133)

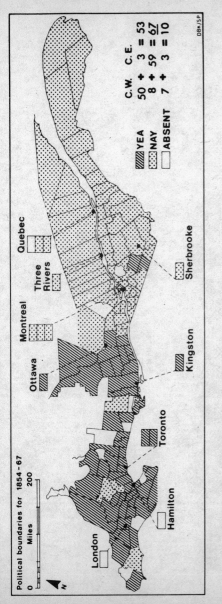

Figure 12. Permanently fixed in Upper Canada; April 16, 1856. (See selection 133)

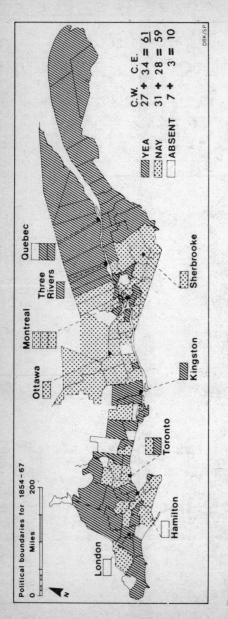

	C.W.		C.E.	
YEA	27	+	34	= 61
NAY	31	+	28	= 59
ABSENT	7	+	3	= 10

Figure 13. For Quebec after 1859; as amended from amendment supporting Ottawa; April 16, 1856. (See selection 133)

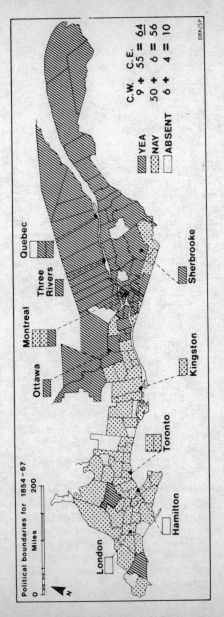

YEA

NAY

ABSENT

	C.W.		C.E.		
YEA	9	+	55	=	<u>64</u>
NAY	50	+	6	=	56
ABSENT	6	+	4	=	10

Quebec

Three Rivers

Montreal

Ottawa

Sherbrooke

Kingston

Toronto

Hamilton

London

Political boundaries for 1854-67

0   Miles   200

N

DBK/SP

Figure 14. Main question: Quebec; April 16, 1856. (See selection 133)

134. *Quebec Mercury*, April 17, 1856.

THE NEWS
QUEBEC TO BE THE PERMANENT
SEAT OF GOVERNMENT!!

The question finally settled by Parliament
at 2 o'clock this morning!!

The most important decision of the Session,—one saving a vast annual and needless expense to the Province, and at the same time terminating an agitation that seemed destined to be prolonged indefinitely to no benefit;—has at last been come to by the Assembly in Toronto this morning. The general votes in favor of Quebec may be thus computed:—majority for Quebec in preference to Toronto 40, Hamilton 22, Kingston 13, Montreal 10,—so that Montreal had the nearest chance after Quebec, and Toronto the most remote. We had expected the choice to result in favor of Montreal, as in the Estimates laid before the House on the 11th the outlay for the necessary buildings stood as follows, including the residence for the Governor General, would be as follows:-

At Quebec	£178,385
At Montreal	151,558
At Kingston	162,240
At Toronto	155,747

NEW GOVERNMENT
BUILDINGS AT QUEBEC

The decision as to the permanency of the seat of Government in this city, involves an outlay of some £300,000 in Buildings, that will have to be commenced at an early date. The Government have already recommended that the Parliament Buildings be erected on the Jesuit Barrack grounds, and that the Governor's residence be in or about the Castle Gardens. The city will gain, in addition, the location of a provincial Picture Gallery, and Museum, intended to be build in connection with the Halls of Legislature.

135. *Montreal Gazette*, April 24, 1856.

This debate on the seat of government question raises some reflections on party government in Canada which may be of use if properly acted on. Sectionalism in this matter more than any other has been rampant. The patriotism of each man, with rare exceptions, has been bounded by his county, or his immediate district. The few exceptions were those men from the district of Montreal and Upper Canadian constituences who voted for Quebec as the permanent seat of government rather than continue the absurd alternating system longer. There seemed no principle of cohesion between differing sections, no broad principle of any kind on which men from various portions of the Province could hang together. Alternate system men were found voting for a permanent seat of government where the country would not desire to see it, in order to defeat by a trick the previously declared intentions of the House. And some of the permanent system men were found voting against all but the particular place which suited them thereby endangering the chance of getting it fixed in any place at all.

136. (Toronto) *Leader*, June 9, 1856

Voting money towards the erection of public buildings in Quebec, with the idea of that city becoming the permanent seat of Government looks like a gigantic hoax. Every body feels that the thing is impossible; that any action which may now be taken in that direction is only a step to be replaced at some future time. You may force water up hill; but it will never be possible to force the whole population of the country down to Quebec to do the business of legislation. The tide of population flows westward, steadily and without recession. In a short time, the preponderance of Upper over Lower Canada will be immense. Rational men would aim to do the business of Legislation at the centre of population; and to this it might come at last, however the representatives of either section of the country may try to deceive themselves in the matter at present. The Government is made for the people, not the people for the Government; and the former must follow the latter instead of the latter following the former. Whoever seeks to reverse this inevitable law deceives himself; he cannot deceive posterity for whom a fixed seat of Government can only be required. In new countries, we live fast; and half a generation suffices to settle the knotiest questions. This seat of Government question, so difficult of solution at present, will one day settle itself. It is difficult of solution now because every thing is in a state of transition. Two United Provinces claim a population about equal to one another; but if this equality really exists, which we very much doubt, it is destined soon to be replaced by a positive and decided preponderance. Let people dispute as much as they may about the relative population of Upper and Lower Canada, at this moment every body sees the inevitable tendency of the population and can foretel with absolute certainty where its future centre will be. But while the population goes one way, is the government to set off the other? Is the government to run away from the people whose business it is required to transact? Is the great majority of the people to be dragged down hundreds of miles to the government, or is the government to take up its position among the bulk of the people?

137. Legislative Council, June 28, 1856 (JLC)

Resolved: That this House not having been consulted . . . and the other branch of the Legislative having resolved upon Quebec, . . . and having, moreover, passed a Bill of Supply, making provision for erecting Public Buildings at Quebec, this House feels itself imperatively called upon to declare that it cannot concur in the said Bill of Supply.

138. *Quebec Mercury*, July 1, 1856.

The rights of Quebec are sacrificed.

139. *Hamilton Spectator*, July 8, 1856.

. . . On the Seat of Government question there can be but one opinion among Upper Canadians, and that is, that the most central and accessible locality should be chosen. Where that locality should be, must be left to the good sense of the people to decide. For our part, we give the preference to Kingston, but should the decision be otherwise, we would willing acquiesce in it.—One thing is certain: the Seat of Government can never be located in either Quebec or Montreal. That, we firmly believe, is a fixed fact in so far as Upper Canada is concerned; but should it be otherwise we would not like to answer for the consequences.

140. Dunbar Ross, *The Seat of Government of Canada* (Quebec, 1856).

Railways and electric telegraphs have annihilated distance, and centrality has ceased to be a question,—thus adding materially to the preference already due to Quebec on a fair consideration of all the requisites for a proper site for the Government of this Province.

141. (Toronto) *Globe*, March 7, 1857.

[The Ministry wants] to get rid of a question which imperils its safety, without regard to considerations of policy or right.

142. (Toronto) *Leader*, March 10, 1857

Proof enough exists that there are sectional parties in the House who would not allow the Seat of Government question to remain undisturbed, whatever might be the desire of the Government in regard to it.

143. *Montreal Gazette*, March 11, 1857.

[Referral is right because] any decision whatever in our Parliament will hardly be regarded as a finality. We got a decision last session in favour of Quebec. The Government found it impossible to act upon it—to get supplies voted for the necessary buildings. Suppose Montreal, or Ottawa, or Kingston were decided on, is there any certainty that the appropriation would meet with any better fate? It may be decided 500 times, and there will be plenty of men found desirous of trying it over the 501st time.

144. *Brockville Recorder*, March 12, 1857.

The important subject, omitted in the Governor's speech, is not to be allowed to slumber. . . .

The selection of a permanent locality being a ticklish point for Ministers, they have shown to the country their want of moral courage in refusing to embody the subject in the Governor's Speech. They prefectly well know the country is disgusted with the expensive menageric up and away plan, and desire the permanent settlement of the Government.

Quebec cannot be chosen, neither, we are afraid, is Toronto likely to be the favoured spot. The race in our opinion will be between Montreal, Ottawa and Kingston. We would certainly prefer Kingston, but failing this city, then Ottawa. Montreal has had her day. . . .

We know no more eligible site on the banks of the St. Lawrence, except Brockville, but we suppose if Kingston loses, Ottawa is likely to come in for the next chance. Be this as it may, a permanent seat should be at once selected, to stop the squandering of public money. He is no friend to his country who will vote against the selection of a permanent Seat of Government.

145. *Carleton Place Herald*, March 19, 1857.

It is probable that the seat of Government question will be referred to the Queen, by way of compromise; and if so; the City of Ottawa, has as good a prospect of being selected, as any other place in Canada. It is too bad, however, that we cannot settle our own affairs; and this, of all others, is certainly a purely local matter.

146. George Cartier, member for Vercheres, C.E., speaking in the Legislative Assembly, March 17, 1857.

It was impossible to obtain a majority in the House for any one place, and if that were possible, it would still be impossible to obtain the concurrence of the Council. [Because of this,] the Ministry had now come to the conclusion that the question must be settled [by referral to the Queen] and to make a grant of money for the purpose, and this in conjunction with the other House.

147. John A. Macdonald, member for Kingston, C.W., speaking in the Legislative Assembly, March 19, 1857.

[Referral to London was] the only way in which the question could be settled. The fault was not with the Government, but with the sectionalism of the Legislature. By pursuing the proposed course the matter would be referred to a disinterested arbiter, one anxious only for the promotion of the interests of every section of the Country.

148. Legislative Assembly, March 20, 1857 (JLA).

That the present system of perambulation is highly injurious to the Public Service, and of the greatest possible inconvenience; that, therefore, this practice be abandoned, and a convenient and central place selected as the permanent Seat of Government, and that Ottawa be so selected (See Figure 15).

149. (Toronto) *Leader*, March 21, 1857.

The debate and the divisions of last night . . . only lead to confirm the opinion heretofore expressed in this journal, as to the impossibility of determining the question of a permanent Seat of Government in the present House of Assembly—or indeed in any Parliament subject, as ours must necessary be, to local influences.

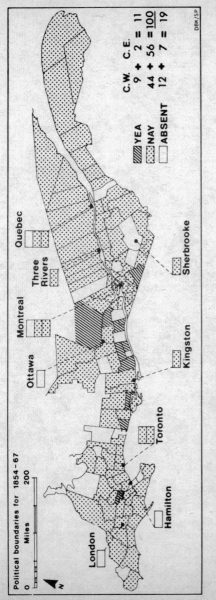

Figure 15. For Ottawa; March 20, 1857. (See selection 148)

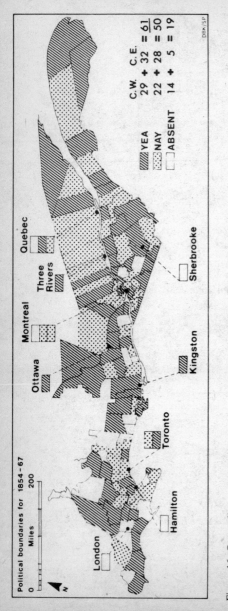

Figure 16. On sending an Address to the Queen for exercising Royal Prerogative; March 24, 1857. (See selection 151)

150. *Montreal Gazette*, March 24, 1857.

The seat of Government debate drags on its way and grows more personal and senseless the further it goes.

151. Resolutions accepted by the Legislative Assembly, March 24, 1857 (JLA).

1. *Resolved*, That the interests of *Canada* require that the Seat of the Provincial Government should be fixed at some certain place.

2. *Resolved*, That a sum, not exceeding the sum of Two hundred and twenty five thousand pounds, be appropriated for the purpose of providing for the necessary Buildings and accommodation for the Government and the Legislature at that certain place. [Yeas 64, Nays 48]

3. *Resolved*, That an humble Address be presented to Her Majesty, praying that She may be graciously pleased to exercise the Royal Prerogative by the selection of some one place as the permanent Seat of Government in *Canada*. [Yeas 61, Nays 50; see Figure 16]

152. Address from Legislative Assembly to Queen Victoria, March 24, 1857 (JLA).

To the Queen's Most Excellent Majesty.
May it please Your Majesty,
We, Your Majesty's dutiful and loyal Subjects, the Commons of *Canada*, in Parliament assembled, humbly approach Your Majesty for the purpose of representing:—

That the interests of *Canada* require that the Seat of the Provincial Government should be fixed at some certain place.

That we have resolved to appropriate the sums requisite for providing the necessary Buildings and accommodation for the Government and the Legislature at such place as Your Majesty may see fit to select.

And we therefore humbly pray Your Majesty to be graciously pleased to exercise the Royal Prerogative by the selection of some one place as the permanent Seat of Government in *Canada*.

153. Sir Edmund Head (Governor General) to Henry Labouchere (Colonial Secretary), March 28, 1857 (PAC).

I Forward, with the present despatch, two Addresses to Her Most Gracious Majesty, of an unusual character. They are respectively from the Legislative Council and the Legislative Assembly, and the prayer of both is the same.

2. That from the Legislative Council is as follows:

"To the Queen's Most Excellent Majesty.

"Most Gracious Sovereign,

"We, your Majesty's loyal and dutiful subjects, the Legislative Council of Canada in Provincial Parliament assembled, beg leave to approach your Majesty with renewed assurance of devotion and attachment to your Royal person and Government.

"We desire, may it please your Majesty, to express our opinion that the interests of Canada require that the seat of the Provincial Government should be fixed at some certain place.

"We therefore respectfully pray that your Majesty will be graciously pleased to exercise your Royal prerogative, and select some place for the permanent seat of Government in Canada".

3. The Address from the Legislative Assembly is founded on resolutions passed in Committee of the whole House, which resolutions contain the additional assurance that the House resolves to appropriate a sum not exceeding £225,000, for providing the necessary buildings and accommodation for the Government and Legislature, at such place as Her Majesty may see fit to select.

4. You are aware, Sir, of the difficulty which, in this Colony, has long surrounded the question of the seat of Government. After its removal from Kingston to Montreal, in 1843, certain circumstances caused the Legislature to adopt a migratory system, by which Parliament was to sit alternately five years at Toronto and five years at Quebec.

5. The inconvenience of this arrangement has been strongly felt. It is attended by great expense, and by a periodical suspension of public business in every office. At the same time it is impossible to deny that it has done good; prejudices have been softened and misconceptions removed by it.

6. In the last session, however, the Legislative Assembly asserted the necessity of a fixed seat of Government, by a resolution of their own, and a vote was carried in favour of Quebec. When the question of providing money for the erection of the public buildings at Quebec came up, a clause appropriating £50,000 for that purpose was struck out of the supplies by the Legislative Council, and the whole Supply Bill had to be introduced again in the Lower House. Practically, therefore, the main question at the commencement of this session remained yet undecided.

7. My own conviction was, and is, that the time has arrived when this matter ought to be definitively settled. To keep it open is to maintain in full flow a constant source of local bitterness and sectional animosity, which by a little management, can always be turned against the Government of the day; nor is this the worst consequence of its unsettled

condition. If the Province of Canada is to remain one, it is essential that its seat of Government should be fixed and recognised by all.

8. There can be no doubt that Her Majesty's prerogative enables her to summon the Parliament wherever she may please, but Her Majesty, with a desire to meet the wishes of the people of Canada, has, in practice, graciously left the matter to be determined by those most immediately interested therein.

9. It now appears to a majority of both branches of the Legislature that the question is one not likely to be arranged satisfactorily by themselves. They do not, I conceive, by their present Addresses, in any way renounce or disclaim their own capacity for self-government; nor do they, by referring this question to the Queen, intend to establish a principle in any way inconsistent with the free and unimpeded action of Parliamentary responsibility in the Colony.

10. The matter itself is one of exceptional character; nothing but this consideration, and a strong conviction that its speedy settlement is of the utmost importance, would induce me to recommend that so soon as the money necessary for erecting the public buildings at the spot which Her Majesty may select, shall have been placed at her disposal, the prayer of these Addresses should be complied with.

11. Under any circumstances, I apprehend that the Legislature and public offices will, in 1859, have to be removed again to Quebec, according to the present arrangement. What is asked of the Queen is to select the site at which, in the meantime, fit and suitable buildings may be erected, for the establishment of the permanent Legislative capital of Canada.

12. In order to lay fully before the Queen the claims of the several places which may be said to consider themselves entitled to selection as the seat of Government, I have caused a circular (of which a copy is annexed to this despatch) to be addressed by my Secretary to the Mayor of each of these cities. I have asked each Corporation to set forth the reasons in favour of their own city; and to forward the statement of such reasons to the Secretary of State for the Colonies, before the 1st of July.

13. In doing this I have, perhaps, presumed too much on the probability of Her Majesty complying with the request of the Legislative Council and Legislative Assembly: if so, I must entreat forgiveness; but I have thought it important that no time should be lost. The question must, of course, be decided after calm and deliberate consideration of the interests of the whole province, not of those of any particular city or place.

14. It would evidently be improper to convey to the Queen's advisers in England any opinion or advice in this matter, as on the part of the Executive Council here. The whole reference is, as I have observed, of an exceptional character, and if it were to be finally decided on the

advice of persons any of whom are responsible to the Parliament of Canada, the great object of removing it beyond the cross-action of local politics and sectional jealousies would be altogether frustrated.

16. This despatch has been shown to the members of my Council, and concurred in by them. With this observation I again submit my recommendation that Her Majesty may be advised to comply with the prayer of the Addresses now transmitted.

154. Henry Labouchere (Colonial Secretary) to Sir Edmund Head (Governor General), April 17, 1857 (PAC).

I have to acknowledge your despatch of the 28th ultimo, forwarding Addresses from the Legislative Council and Assembly of Canada, praying that Her Majesty will be graciously pleased to exercise the Royal prerogative by the selection of some place for the permanent seat of Government in Canada.

I understand the object of these Addresses to be the selection of some fitting place at which, under all ordinary circumstances, the Legislature of the Province should henceforward be called together, and where the necessary public buildings may be provided for that purpose, as well as for the general administration of the affairs of Canada.

I have to inform you that Her Majesty, on the advice of Her Ministers, and fully weighing the importance of the reference thus made to her by the Legislative Council and Assembly of Canada, has been graciously pleased to comply with the prayer of these Memorials.

I shall await the further information which your despatch promises and in particular the replies which may be received to the circular which you have addressed to the Mayors of the several cities, before taking any further steps to initiate the necessary examination into the relative advantages of the places indicated for the information of Her Majesty.

155. Extract from speech by Sir Edmund Head (Governor General) when proroguing Parliament, June 10, 1857 (JLA).

In submitting to the decision of Her Most Gracious Majesty the final choice of a Seat of Government for Canada, you have done that, which, without derogating from the rights of the Colonial Parliament, will remove from its walls a constant source of heart-burning and local jealousy.

156. *Times* of London, April 4, 1857

The Queen has been invited to discharge one of the most interesting and poetical duties of the empire, and one of very rare occurrence. She is asked to decide between the rival claims of as many as four or five cities to be the seat of the Canadian Government.

157. Letter from "Ego" (an Ottawa supporter residing in London) to the Editor, *Times* (of London), April 21, 1857.

. . . Let this decision, then, be in favor of Lower Canada, and you light a volcanoe in the heart of Upper Canada; let it be in favor of Upper Canada, and you sink a deep well of discontent in the heart of Lower Canada. But let it be in favor of Ottawa, which is on the boundary line between the two, with one-half its population French and the other English—let at this point, where the two provinces are connected by a magnificent suspension bridge, the Parliament Houses be erected in Upper Canada, and the Governor's Palace, or Government House in Lower Canada, and you hush the voice of discontent for ever, sink all that rivalry and jealousy between parties, and unite the two provinces and the two races in a bond that can never be broken.

CHAPTER VI

THE CITY MEMORIALS

Introduction

Governor General Sir Edmund Head was the leading figure in the 1857 decision-making process that followed referral to London by the Canadian Government. In 1856, Head had determined that Ottawa should be capital[1] and this belief was transmitted to the Colonial Office in writing and orally in 1857. Sir Edmund also asked that memorials from Toronto, Kingston, Ottawa, Montreal, and Quebec be sent to London laying out the case for each site.

Private letters with claims for different cities were sent to the Colonial Office by members of the Canadian Government even after John A. Macdonald had assured the Legislative Assembly that such would not happen. Also sent to London were memorials from Sarnia and Belleville, C.W., praying that Kingston should be made capital. Receipt of the Sarnia memorial prompted the Colonial Office to direct the officer administering Canada in Sir Edmund Head's absence not to forward any further such memorials directly to the Colonial Secretary. The despatch also indicated:

> I wish to point out to you that only places, the authorities of which were put directly in communication with Her Majesty's Government by Sir E. Head, are the several cities which have been named as those between which the selection of the future Capital of Canada must be made.[2]

From this despatch we can conclude that the capital of Canada was to be selected from only the five cities identified by Head. Clearly, this reservation also excluded Hamilton, even though the Colonial Office decided to accept the uninvited Hamilton memorial. Following the receipt of the latter, in May, 1857, the Colonial Office received six other city memorials—Quebec was represented by two groups.

Notes

[1]See A. Patchett Martin, *Life and Letters of the Right Honourable Robert*

Lowe, Viscount Sherbrooke (London: Longmans, Green, and Co., 1893), Vol.
II, p. 134.

   [2]PAC, PRO, CO 42/611, pp. 405-407, Henry Labouchere to Officer Administering Government of Canada, July 24, 1857. Interestingly, the despatch was
drafted in London by Sir Edmund Head.

Documents

158. R.T. Pennefather (Governor's Secretary) to His Worship the
      Mayor of Toronto, Montreal, Kingston, Ottawa, and Quebec,
      March 28, 1857 (PAC).

   You are probably aware that the Legislative Council and the Legislative Assembly of Canada have addressed Her Most Gracious Majesty to
exercise her prerogative in the selection of a permanent seat of Government for the whole province.

   In the event of Her Majesty complying with the prayer of these
Addresses, his Excellency is anxious that her advisers in England
should be enabled to place before her a full and fair statement of the
claim of each separate city which may be considered a candidate for the
honour of becoming the future capital of Canada.

   As a matter of course, the final selection must depend on a comprehensive survey of the interests, not of any one place, but of the
whole Province, as part of British North America.

   The claims, however, of each city are likely to be stated by the
persons most interested in supporting them better than they would be by
any other party.

   His Excellency, therefore, invites the Corporation of — to cause to
be prepared a paper setting forth the reasons which may, in their
opinion, favour the claims of that place to be selected by the Queen.

   With every wish to afford full time for preparing these statements,
his Excellency desires that it may be in the hands of the Colonial
Secretary by the first week of July in the present year.

   You will please, if you see fit to comply with his Excellency's desire,
to address the packet to the Right Hon. the Secretary of State for the
Colonies, London, and endorse it with the words: "City of —,
Canada."

159. Memorial of the Council of the Quebec Board of Trade, May 30,
      1857.

To the Queen's Most Excellent Majesty.

The Memorial of the Council of the Quebec Board of Trade humbly and respectfully Showeth

That Addresses, voted by the Legislative Council and Assembly of Canada, praying that your Majesty will be graciously pleased to exercise the Royal prerogative, by the selection of some place for the permanent seat of Government in Canada, have been forwarded to be laid before your Majesty, and are now awaiting the further information promised upon the question submitted, before any action is taken thereon.

That his Excellency the Governor-General, in transmitting these Addresses, was pleased to intimate that he had by circular letters, called upon the Mayors of the several places which may be said to consider themselves entitled to selection as the seat of Government, to set forth the reasons in favour of their own city, and to forward the statement of such reasons to the Secretary for the Colonies before the 1st of July.

That, the Mayor and Corporation of Quebec having prepared such statement, they are now forwarding the same accordingly.

That the Council of the Quebec Board of Trade, representing in their corporate capacity the mercantile interests of this the most extensive shipping port in British North America, whose splendid harbour is annually visited by a large amount of British tonnage, of great value, and carrying on extensive trade, and to which shipping and trade the seat of Government is of vast importance, beg leave, on behalf of these several interests, humbly and respectively to submit to your Majesty the following observations:—

That Quebec was for 230 years the capital of Canada; that during the period it was so, as a British Possession, the affairs of the Government, and the Legislative proceedings, were carried on in perfect tranquility and without interruption, in the midst of its peaceful inhabitants. The circumstances which led to the first removal of the Government and Legislature to Kingston, at the time of the union of the provinces, the next movement to Montreal, and the unfortunate cause of the abrupt change from that city to the system of alternate removals of the Government and sittings of the Parliament, every four years, to Toronto and Quebec, are already so fully before your Majesty, that it is only deemed necessary herein briefly to allude to these changes as public events that are past.

That the inconvenience of the alternate system having been strongly felt, the Legislative Assembly, in the session of 1856, asserted the necessity of a fixed seat of Government, when a vote was carried in favour of Quebec; the appropriation then made by the representatives of the people towards the erection of public buildings was, however, struck out by a small majority of the Legislative Council; the main question was thus left undecided, and the appeal to your Majesty to select a site has been the result, as above stated.

That Quebec having been selected as most suitable for a fixed seat of Government by a vote of the Representative Assembly, in preference to the other cities competing for the honour, this Council would venture to offer the following statement in support of that decision: The City of Quebec is now, in consequence of internal improvements in the country, in a position as central as is usually deemed requisite for the seat of Government, either for nations or provinces; throughout the year, railroads extending, expecially westward, nearly to the extent of the province are in constant use; splendid and fast steamers are running on the lakes and rivers during the open navigation; and, for immediate communication, electric telegraphs are established to all places of importance, thus making Quebec of as easy, and perhaps more ready, access from the extreme western sections of the province, than London is from the distant parts of the British Isles.

That during seven months of open navigation, Quebec connects with the mother-country by means of mail-steamers, even now, in the very short space of ten days, with the expectation of a yet greater diminution of time, and in the winter months the same connection is kept us (and soon, it is to be hoped, by railroad) through British territory to the open seaports of St. John's, St. Andrew's, and Halifax, in your Majesty's Provinces of New Brunswick and Nova Scotia.

That the situation of Quebec is most healthy; it is surrounded by natural scenery of great extent and grandeur; the necessaries and comforts of life are abundant, and reasonable as compared with other cities in the province, a fact worthy of consideration with reference to the many employed about a Government and Legislature; and it contains, within its walls, magnificent and commodious sites for Government and Legislative buildings, while abundant materials, in its neighbourhood, are available for their construction.

That an important advantage, perhaps the most important in favour of Quebec, and which is not possessed by other of the competing cities, is the great strength of its fortress, under the protection of which the proceedings of the Government and the deliberations of the Legislature would not be liable to interruption, nor the public archives, books, and documents to destruction, either from domestic commotion or foreign aggression; neither of these contingencies may appear probable, yet what has occurred before may occur again. Quebec, in addition to its own strength, is of convenient access to the fleet and army of England (the harbour is capable of containing any number of ships from the largest downwards): and if at any time hard pressed, would soon be relieved and supported, while, through it, other points in the province could be strengthened, if required; so long as the British fleet commands the sea, communication between the Imperial Government in London, and the Colonial Government in Quebec, could not be cut off; a foreign attack in winter is not much to be dreaded, the distance from the lines of the adjoining Republic, and the severity of the climate, form a strong bar in prevention.

That the selection of a fixed site for the seat of Government in Canada may also be considered with reference to another, and, perhaps, not distant, political change, namely, a Federal or Legislative Union of the British North American Colonies, a union often contemplated by statesmen, recommended by the late Earl of Durham, and looked forward to by many of the colonists themselves, as a means of consolidating their resources, strength, and power, of increasing their commercial prosperity, and extending the railway lines both to and in the neighbouring provinces. In the event of such a union taking place, it is believed to be conceded on all sides that Quebec would be most suitable and convenient as the seat of general Government for your Majesty's North American Possessions.

That, under all and several the advantages herein set forth, of future prospects, present suitableness and salubrity, ready means of obtaining naval and military aid, from the mother country, in case of need, and a strong fortified position, affording the requisite security for the Government, the Legislature, the public archives, books, and records of the province; it is humbly hoped that the claims of Quebec to be restored to its ancient privileges and public position, by being again selected and fixed as the site for the seat of the Canadian Government, may obtain from your Majesty favourable consideration.

160. Memorial of the City of Quebec, May 25, 1857.

To the Queen's Most Excellent Majesty

Your Majesty having graciously been pleased to accede to the request of your Majesty's loyal people of Canada, praying that your Majesty would select from among the cities of this Province the place for the future seat of Government and capital of this flourishing and important part of your Majesty's dominions, the mayor, councillors, and citizens of the city of Quebec beg leave to approach your Majesty with the fullest reliance upon your Majesty's wisdom and regard for the interest of this Province, and to lay before your Majesty a statement of the grounds on which they found the hope that the ancient city of Quebec may be honoured by your Majesty's selection as the future capital of Canada.

The choice of the capital of a county is a subject of the very highest importance, involving, in almost all cases, the destiny and greatness of a people. Accident has in some instances determined the selection, but, generally, a city has owed this distinction to the advantages of its situation for the purposes of commerce and navigation, and, above all, for the defence of the country, and the facility of communication and supervision over all parts of the subject territory.

The natural features of a country generally point out, of themselves, the place possessing these advantages of position. So true is this, that almost all the first towns founded by Europeans in both North and South America have ultimately become the capitals of their respective Provinces.

The first Europeans who ever visited Canada located themselves at Quebec. Although at a distance of 360 miles from the Gulf of St. Lawrence, and of more than 800 from the Atlantic, no other point between Quebec and the sea offered, to the first colonists of Canada, such a striking position as to induce them to form a permanent establishment. The wisdom of their choice has never since been questioned. A Governor of Canada, the Count de Frontenac, wrote to the Minister at the Court of France, in 1672:—

"Nothing struck me as so beautiful and grand as the location of the town of Quebec, which could not be better situated, even were it to become, in some future time, the capital of a great Empire."

It is a frequent practice, at the present, for some persons to speak of Quebec as though it was situated at one extremity of the Province, and on the margin of the sea; but this, as we have just seen, is an altogether erroneous impression. The situation of Quebec is far in the interior of the country, and, if renowned as a sea-port, it is that the town is situated on one of the greatest rivers in the world—a river whose waters bring to her door the largest vessels of the ocean.

It was this interior and commanding situation, and this vast and capacious port, which drew from the Count de Frontenac an expression of his opinion that Quebec was formed by nature to be the capital of a vast Empire.

Indeed, there is a striking resemblance, in point of situation, between the cities of Quebec and London, the respective geographical limits of Canada and Great Britain being considered. The situation of London, as a capital, has never been condemned; on the contrary, it is believed that the commercial and maritime greatness of England, arising out of her insular position, is due, in a great measure, to the situation of the capital on a sea-port, and where the Government and the Legislature had offered to their constant observation the importance of commerce and navigation as the source of wealth and power.

Peter the Great, when in England in 1698, impressed by these considerations, decided upon the abandonment of Moscow as the capital of his Empire, and the founding of St. Petersburgh on the shores of the Baltic, where the seat of Empire has ever since remained. Yet St. Petersburgh is 13° further north than Quebec.

While, in point of maritime situation, the city of Quebec is incontestably the first city of Canada, it is placed in the centre of a vast and fertile district whose mineral and agricultural wealth, and facilities for the establishment of manufactures yet in their infancy, promise, at no distant period, to place the city in the very first rank as to population and resources, an increase which would be much accelerated by the impulse which would be given by the possession of the seat of Government.

In determining this question, the policy of Government as respects the future development of British America must also be kept in view. The ever-increasing power of the United States necessarily points to the Federal union of the British Provinces under the protection of England as a measure which will ultimately become necessary. England herself is interested, even in view of her European policy, that a power should exist on this continent to counterbalance that of the great American Republic, in imitation of the European system. With this prospect in view, the choice of a capital for Canada could not possibly be uninfluenced by so important a consideration, and, in the event of such an union, Quebec would be not only the most accessible from the sea, but the most central city of British America.

The Duke of Wellington himself observed, that the whole of the British North American colonial system depended upon the possession of Quebec; and, indeed, Quebec is the stronghold of Canada, and history has proved, over and over again, under the French as under the English rule, that the possession of Quebec is always followed by that of the territory composing the British Provinces. Chosen, in 1535, by Cartier, in 1608, by Champlain, the promontory of Cape Diamond has ever been regarded as the key of the country, and on all occasions the fate of the Province has been decided under the walls of Quebec.

Of all the towns of Canada, also, Quebec is the least exposed to attack from the Americans, and the easiest of access to succour from England. It is remote from the frontier of the United States, and protected by the River St. Lawrence, on whose left bank it is built. It is well known that Canada is bounded, throughout its entire length, on the south by the United States, who have the superiority on Lakes Ontario, Erie, Huron and Superior, and that the most flourishing part of Upper Canada lies in an angle between those lakes, exposed to attack from all of them. The numerical superiority of the United States over Canada would permit any skilful Commander to cut off the communication with the interior at any point between Montreal in the east, and Lake Superior in the west. In the last war the Americans burnt Toronto, and marched as far east as the Cedars within thirty miles of Montreal.

Toronto and Kingston are immediately contiguous to the United States, exposed to the cannon of their ships; while they are also liable, from that contiguity, and close intercommunication with the Republic, to imbibe political opinions adverse to the integrity of the Empire.

But it is not merely as a fortified city that Quebec has exercised such an important influence on the fortunes of Canada. Its adaptation to the peaceful purposes of commerce also renders it a place of the first rank and importance. At Quebec the navigation of the largest class of vessels terminates, and at Quebec the inland navigation commences. The port is accessible to ships from sea long before any other place, as was strikingly exemplified this year by the arrival of the "City of Toronto" from Glasgow, at Quebec, on the 20th of April, when the St. Lawrence, above Quebec, was frozen over as far as Montreal, and inaccessible to navigation. Whatever may be the present course of trade, the time is fast approaching when the products of the Great West, illimitable in amount, will come to Quebec by river, canal, and railroad, as to a common centre of export to Europe.

Among the cities of Canada, Montreal might have some claim to enter the lists with Quebec, but since railroads have shortened the distance between these two cities to a few hours, the advantages which its more western situation might impart to Montreal are more than counterbalanced by its want of defences in case of war, and its exposure to an American army, which could penetrate, without obstruction, into its streets, and all the more easily when the Victoria bridge is finished.

The towns of Montreal and Kingston have successively been selected as the seat of Government, but have successively been abandoned after the experience of a few years; while, in the session of the Parliament of Canada, held at Toronto in 1856, the Governor-General, the Ministers of the Crown, and a majority of the Representatives of the people, by a solemn vote, decided in favour of the city of Quebec, and appropriated the moneys necessary for the erection of a House of Parliament, and it was only the defeat of this measure by the Legislative Council, by a questionable exercise of power, which rendered it necessary to adopt other means for the solution of this important question.

Your Majesty, in your choice, governed by a regard for the general interests of Canada and of the British Empire, will feel the importance of these influences, which tend permanently to connect Canada with England as an integral portion of the Empire; and, in this view, the city of Quebec may point to the tried fidelity of her citizens, who, when the English rule was menaced in America in 1775, in 1812, and 1837, rallied in defence of the Government, their peaceful and hospitable character, the harmony in which the two races destined to occupy the banks of the St. Lawrence, here live together, and have always lived together, and the familiar use of both languages prevalent in Canada.

Besides these considerations, Quebec may boast of the salubrity of its climate, the beauty and grandeur of its site, the extent and safety of its harbour, its fortifications, its impregnable citadel, its historical associations—all of them incidents which impart dignity to power.

For 230 years Quebec was the capital of Canada. During this long period fifty-three Governors here successively took up their residence. None of these ever expressed a wish to transfer the seat of Government from its original position.

161. Letter from the Mayor of Toronto to the Right Hon. H. Labouchere, June 15, 1857.

The Governor-General having called upon me to furnish Her Majesty's Secretary of State for the Colonies with a statement of the grounds upon which Toronto bases her claims to becoming the permanent seat of Government for the Province of Canada, I have now the honour of addressing you in compliance with his Excellency's request.

In order to estimate the value of the arguments on which I rely for establishing the justice of the selection I am advocating, it is necessary to state the considerations which will naturally influence Her Majesty's Government in determining upon the selection of a site for the permanent capital of Canada. In doing so, I have endeavoured to approach the question in a broad and extended view of those interests which concern the whole province, uninfluenced by the supposed claims of any particular locality to especial consideration; for this city repudiates the idea that it has any pretensions to the distinction of continuing to be the metropolis of this vast dependency of the British Crown other than those based upon an enlarged and prospective view of public policy, convenience, and justice to the people, considered as one great body of British subjects without regard to national distinction, which time is rapidly obliterating.

Among the considerations which may be presumed to influence the determination of this important question are:-

1st. The convenience of the people to be governed, keeping in view the direction in which the settlement of the unoccupied territories is advancing as indicated by past experience. The extent and availability of those territories for the purposes of colonization, and also the commercial energy of the people, as evinced by their commercial wealth and enterprize.

2ndly. Economy.

3rdly. The defence of the capital in the event of war with the adjoining States.

Although the exigencies which may arise during a state of war are not to be disregarded, it appears just to give the greatest importance to the considerations first named, and in relation to them I shall confine myself strictly to facts deduced from official documents which, without doubt, are within the archives of your office.

When the union of the two provinces was consummated, the districts bordering on the waters of Lake Ontario, at its western extremity, were looked upon as being coterminous with the western limits of Canada. In 1843 the population of the two provinces number 1,190,867, and of these there were in the home district (in which Toronto is situated), and westward of its eastern boundary, only 275,081, being 23.1 per cent of the whole population.

In 1851, by the census then taken, the population of United Canada was found to be 1,842,265 and of these there were to the westward of the same line 579,524, being 30.3 per cent of the whole; and exhibiting an increase in eight years of 110.6 per cent, west of the supposed line of demarcation, and of only 37 per cent, eastward of it. A similar rate of increase if maintained would, in 1859, make the population west of Toronto 1,220,477 and east of it 1,729,955, while in 1867 just ten years' hence, a similar ratio of increase will give a population west and east respectively, of 2,570,324 west, and 2,370,038 east.

If, in like manner, we estimate the density of population, embraced within circles described with equal radii, and having the various competing cities as centres, by the ratio of increase indicated by the census of 1851, as compared with that previously taken, we find that within a radius of—

	50 miles	100 miles	150 miles
Toronto will have	596,992	1,118,578	1,460,558
Montreal will have	551,667	841,185	1,182,868
Quebec will have	251,262	425,523	897,423
Ottawa will have	234,969	544,242	1,179,810
Kingston will have	180,646	521,383	833,567

Thus satisfactorily proving that within two years (as in all probability it now is) Toronto will be the centre, not only of the greatest wealth, but of the greatest number of inhabitants.

As the above calculations are based on data obtained from official documents, and represent a period of eight years, four of which were years of extraordinary depression, and inasmuch as the progress of settlement in the adjoining States exhibits parallel results, I can discover no reason for questioning the correctness of the deductions drawn therefrom. But doubts, however unfounded, may arise as to the extent of territory available for agricultural purposes west of this city being sufficient for so large a population as I have indicated: without checking the ratio of increase on which my figures are founded, by ceasing to afford the requisite inducements to settlers, as will presently be seen, no such check is likely to occur.

I shall hereafter refer to the Red River Settlement, and the Hudson's Bay territory, and their probably future connection with this province; but for the present I shall confine myself to the boundaries of Canada, as usually exhibited on maps. Thus limited, Canada extends from 64° to 91° of longitude west from Greenwich, and from the 42nd to the 51st parallel of north latitude. Toronto is in longitude 79° 25' west, and nearer as regards the east and west limits of the province to the geographical centre of the country to be governed, than any of the cities mentioned in connection with this question, and if we exclude from our argument the sterile coasts and territory bounding the Gulf of St. Lawrence, it will be found that the city lies, in fact, somewhat to the eastward of the centre; especially will this obtain if we exclude all territory which lies to the north of the mean temperature of Quebec (i.e. 41° of Farenheit), as we might justly do for all practical purposes of colonization. In this way the number of square miles of territory east of the meridian of Toronto would be reduced to 85,690, and west of that meridian there would be 108,484 square miles.

That the isothermal line of 41° of mean temperature which passes through Quebec is deflected by the influence of the great inland seas far to the north of the assumed Canadian Territory is an important fact, inasmuch as the moderate temperature which prevails over the vast tracts of finely timbered lands lying to the north of lakes Huron and Superior is a guarantee that an early period will see them settled by an agricultural population who will not only be able to supply the wants of those engaged in mining operations on the shores of those lakes, but will have a large surplus of cereals for exportation to Europe.

Recent explorations through the territories alluded to have proved it to be well adapted to colonization, and capable of immediately affording vast and almost unlimited supplies of timber of the finest quality.

In fact, therefore, the territory westward of the meridian of Toronto is greater in extent than that to the eastward of it; and if we take into account the vast prairies (and the magnificent uplands drained by the Sastrachewan and other rivers) within the British possessions, and if we add to the importance of these the value of the vast coal-fields and other mineral resources between this province and the Rocky Mountains, and bear in mind that the line of mean temperature before mentioned still trends towards the north, as we advance westward we shall be forced to the inevitable conclusion that the present generation will see interests in existence about the shores of Lake Superior equal in every respect to those which now render the trade of Lakes Huron, Erie, and Ontario so important an item in the commerce of America.

Apart from all these, however, the fertile districts of the Western

Peninsula, already surveyed and in a course of settlement, afford abundant space for a population far greater than I have indicated, without any portion of it becoming more thickly settled than the counties lately constituting the county of York now are; it is abundantly evident, therefore, that, both as regards population and territorial extent, this city occupies a more central position than any other city named as likely to be selected for the seat of Government.

It has been justly held that where railways are in existence, the activity of the traffic over them may be fairly taken as the exponent of the energy and enterprize of the inhabitants, as well as of the commercial, agricultural, and other capabilities of the country and people.

If we apply this test we shall find it an overwhelming evidence of that fact that, in all these particulars, the west is far in advance of the east; for not only in the gross amount earned per week, but in the average earnings per mile, the railways west of the city exhibit returns, both in the former and latter respect, nearly three times as great as those exhibited by the railways east of it.

It is difficult to separate from the gross amounts returned those portions either of exports contributed, or of the imports consumed, by any section of the whole country; but it is certain that much of both which appear in the official returns, as entered at the Custom-houses of Quebec and Montreal, is for account of that part of the province west of and bordering upon Lake Ontario. In tracing the exports, however, no insuperable difficulty exists, inasmuch as the quantities passing the St. Lawrence canals are a fair test of all the important quantities leaving this part of the province.

Referring to the Trade and Navigation Returns recently laid before Parliament, we find that the total quantities of wheat and flour exported in 1856 were equivalent to 9,491,531 bushels of wheat (1,186,441 quarters); of this there were apparently due to Quebec and Montreal 2,002,122 bushels (250,265 quarters); but by reference to the quantity of wheat and flour passing downwards through the canals, we find that, after deducting from that quantity the wheat from United States' ports, this part of the province not only contributed all the wheat exported, but no less than 2,064,606 bushels (314,117 quarters) for the consumption of the inhabitants east of the Ottawa. If we extend our investigation on this point to other articles of export, we shall find cognate results in every article exported except timber, and even in these the inquiry reverses the opinion commonly held in Britain, that the products of the forest are chiefly due to the country laying east of the Ottawa; and it is susceptible of demonstration that of the £3,146,446 currency reported as the value of the exports from Montreal, Quebec, and the lesser sea-ports of the province, fully one-half has been contributed by the western portion of the province, while of the remaining half no insignificant proportion has been drawn from the American States bordering on Lake Michigan.

In like manner it can be shown that a very large proportion of the imports via the St. Lawrence, which appear in the returns from Montreal and Quebec, are consumed west of Kingston, inasmuch as the returns of freight upward on the canals below this city indicate that more than half the tonnage reported inwards at the lower ports is re-shipped for the western districts of Canada. It follows, therefore, that of the total imports, amounting in value in 1856 to £10,896,096, fully £7,000,000 currency have been for the service of the inhabitants west and north of Lake Ontario. This conclusion is sustained by the ability of the people to purchase the imported luxuries of life; and the statistics of the annual creation of wealth in the various sections of the province, considered with reference to the same dividing lines as were assumed in relation to population, indicate results even more conclusive as to the westward tendency of wealth than were shown when considering the direction of the increase of population.

With reference to the economic bearing of the question, our arguments should have a wider application than to the mere construction of public buildings: they should apply to the effect which the determination of the question will have on the economy and convenience of that portion of the whole people governed who have occasion to resort to the seat of Government for the transaction of business; and this again has an intimate connection with the facilities afforded by the travelled routes over which the metropolis may be reached.

A glance at the map attached to this communication [not here reprinted] will show that while all the cities claiming the honour of being selected (except Ottawa) may be approached by navigable waters and by railway, Toronto is the only point upon which several railways converge, it being already the centre of no less than four important lines; and at a period not far distant, other important railways, already projected, and having Toronto for their terminus, will be brought into existence; nor should it be lost sight of that one of those railways—a work especially promoted by this city, and the first opened for traffic— connects, by the shortest possible link, the waters of Lakes Huron and Superior with those of Ontario, and thus affords the most direct access to those regions in the great north-west previously alluded to, and which are now exciting so much attention, not only here, but in the Imperial Parliament.

I have already drawn your attention to the comparative activity of railway traffic east and west of this city, to the greater and more rapidly increasing amount of business transactions, and to the relative number of the whole population interested in obtaining cheap and convenient access to the metropolis. By reference to that part of my communication, it will be made evident that if the selection falls on either Kingston, Montreal, Ottawa, or Quebec, the greatest proportion of the people will be placed at the greatest distance; while if it falls on Toronto, the counties most densely peopled, and where the greatest business activity exists, will be brought within a minimum distance.

This fact becomes all-important when we reflect that great numbers of the people have occasion to resort to the seat of Government on business connected with the Crown Land Department, and that of the whole business transacted in that office, 90½ per cent of the lands sold, and 96 8/10 percent of the value was, during the last three years, due to that portion of the province west and north of Toronto: that such is practically the fact could not be doubted for one moment by any attentive observor of the people who have resorted here from a distance since the Government has been established in this city.

If the same porportions obtain in reference to other classes, and all circumstances justify such a conclusion, it follows that with the seat of Government at Toronto the economy of the majority of those governed will be best consulted.

So again in relation to the minor consideration of public buildings: none are in existence elsewhere, having either been destroyed by the populace, as in Montreal, or by fires originating in unaccountable causes as in Quebec; but in Toronto, not only does the Government hold abundance of land for the purpose, but buildings amply sufficient for its wants are already erected and occupied, representing an immediate saving of at least half-a-million of money, an item of no small consequence to a colony whose debt in proportion to its revenue already exceeds that of the mother country.

It is not necessary for me to occupy time in discussing the capability of Toronto and the surrounding country, for offering resistance to an enemy in time of war, inasmuch as Her Majesty's Government is undoubtedly in possession of the best military opinions on that part of the question; but to such circumstances in this connection, as are most obvious to a civilian, I may be permitted briefly to direct your attention.

That Quebec may be considered impregnable is now a generally received opinion, and such being the case, that city would have no competitor were the question to be determined solely with reference to military defence; but the chances of war are, it is believed and hoped, so remote, that it would be unreasonable to allow such a contingency to override the convenience of the whole country, especially now, when, if a war should unfortunately occur, the railways afford every facility for the rapid transportation of the archives of the province to the chief military stronghold, if such a course should be deemed necessary.

In comparison with any of the other cities which his Excellency has called upon to state their claims to becoming the permanent seat of Government, it is confidently asserted that Toronto is best capable of defence. Montreal is within an easy day's march of the frontier, and no defensible position intervenes until the River St. Lawrence is reached; and in winter this may be crossed on the ice by the heaviest artillery, or in open boats in summer. Kingston is immediately on the frontier, and, as at Montreal, the St. Lawrence may be crossed in open boats in summer, or on the ice in winter. Ottawa is within forty miles of the frontier, and no defensible position intervenes. This city, on the contrary, is 100 miles by land from the National Boundary, where either the steep banks of the river, or the rapid current, renders a passage at all times extremely difficult; but even if passed, the strong position at Stoney Creek, the scene of the ignominious defeat of the United States' forces in the last war, has to be passed, and subsequently the position at Burlington Heights, which may be counted as impregnable if defended by a similar force to that which occupied it during the war of 1812.

With the command of the lakes, an enemy might assail Toronto by water, but the same applies to all other places along our extended frontier; this, however, is of small moment, when we take into account the fact that our provincial canals give access to all the lakes for a numerous fleet of gunboats which could be dispatched from Britain on the first appearance of hostilities, and which could effectually prevent the creation of a hostile fleet in those waters, and at once assume that position of superiority on those great inland seas which Her Majesty's fleets have never failed to sustain on the ocean, and inasmuch as Toronto possesses a harbour open at all seasons, this arm of defence would be at all times available.

Apart, however, from these considerations, Toronto might, if occasion required it, be rendered as safe as Quebec itself; the late war has demonstrated that stone walls are not essential for defensive works, and with the gallantry and loyalty which now animates Her Majesty's subjects in this part of her dominions, defences would rise as rapidly as the earth works did at Sebastopol, wherever a necessity for them might exist, and would be defended with equal pertinacity.

But I believe the time has passed when the defence of the capital should be held to be of prime importance: such reasoning is only applicable to despotic countries, where serfs are to be awed into submission; here, where every arm would freely rise in defence of the Crown and its rights, such arguments may be safely dismissed.

A desire to confine this communication within reasonable limits, as induced me to omit reference to many points which will, doubtless, have weight with Her Majesty's advisers, and will exert a favourable influence towards this city, but they will be referred to by the gentlemen who have undertaken to urge our arguments with you in person, namely, the Honourable John Hillyard Cameron, M.P.P., the Honourable Henry John Boulton, and George William Allan, Esq.

There are sent by mail this day a series of photographic views of various portions of the city.

162. Memorandum relative to the policy and justice of continuing the seat of Government for the Province of Canada at Toronto, July 9, 1857, from John Naylor, Actuary (in London).

In 1825 Lower Canada — 423,630 souls	Upper Canada 157,425
In 1831 Lower Canada — 511,917 souls	—
In 1835 No census for Lower Canada	Upper Canada census 344,500
In 1840 No census for Lower Canada	Upper Canada census 427,078
In 1848 No census for Lower Canada	Upper Canada census 723,332
In 1851 Lower Canada census 890,261	Upper Canada census 952,004

Upon the above data, what has been the annual progress of each, and how many fold has each advanced between the extreme periods; and at the same progression, what will be the population of each in 1860 and in 1870?

From the annexed data it appears that the population of Lower Canada has increased, during the twenty-six years from 1825 to 1851, at the uniform rate of 2 $8/10$ per annum, that it has been somewhat more than doubled during that period, and that if it continues to increase at the same uniform rate its amount—

> In 1860 will be 1,142,000 and
> In 1870 will be 1,506,000

It also appears that the population of Upper Canada has increased from—

> 1825 to 1835 at the rate of $8^1/_{10}$ per cent. per annum
> 1835 to 1840 at the rate of $4^4/_{10}$ per cent. per annum
> 1840 to 1848 at the rate of $6^8/_{10}$ per cent. per annum
> 1848 to 1851 at the rate of $9^6/_{10}$ per cent. per annum

The average rate of increase slightly exceeding 7 per cent. per annum. It further appears that the population has during the twenty-six years (1820-1851) increased by more than six times its amount, and that if it continues to increase at the uniform rate of 7 per cent. per annum, its amount—

In 1860 will be 1,750,000 and
In 1870 will be 3,443,000

163. Memorial of the City of Montreal, May 27, 1857.

The confidence which the citizens of Montreal have ever entertained
in the wisdom and justice of Her Most Gracious Majesty, and their
knowledge of her gracious consideration and regard for all her loyal
Canadian subjects would have withheld the City Government of
Montreal from submitting the reasons which they confidently believe
will induce Her Most Gracious Majesty, on a comprehensive survey of
the interests, not of any particular locality, but of the whole Province,
to select the City of Montreal as the future permanent seat of Government for United Canada; but respect for the wishes of Her Majesty's
Representative, expressed in the foregoing circular, now demands that
some, at least, of these reasons should be stated.

The present is not the first occasion on which the important question
has been mooted of the locality in which the seat of Government should
be permanently established in Canada. It was discussed and decided
upon by the Provincial Legislature, in the year 1843, when the Government was temporarily located in Kingston.

The reasons which induced the Legislature, at that time, to decide
upon fixing the seat of Government permanently in Montreal, are
embodied in the Report of a Committee of the Executive Council to his
Excellency the Right Hon. Sir Charles Bagot, then Governor-General
of British North America. This report was drawn up by the Chairman of
the Committee, the late Honourable Mr. Sullivan, an Upper Canadian
member of the Legislature, who was born, and resided all his lifetime,
in Toronto, and who was for many years the popular Representative of
that city in the Legislative Assembly of the Province. All the other
members of the Committee by whom the Report was adopted with the
exception of two, Messrs. Lafontaine and Morin, were Upper Canadian members resident in and representing constituencies in that section
of the Province. Such men could not have been charged, on such a
question, with indifference to the claims of any section of Upper
Canada, or with partiality or bias for the city of Montreal. The reasons
given in the report apply with even greater force and weight at present
than they did then: they so obviously proceed from a comprehensive
survey of the interests of the whole Province, and not from partial or
corrupt feelings for any particular locality; they are so cogent and
conclusive, and they are, moreover, so clearly and impartially stated,
that no excuse will be offered for their reproduction here:—

[See selection 25 for the Report of the Executive Council, 1843].

If any reasons require to be added to those so ably stated in the preceding report, why Montreal should be selected as the seat of Government, from a regard both to the present and future welfare of the Province, and the advancement of its interests, socially, politically, and nationally, the following may, with confidence and propriety, be urged:—

The central position of the City.

It is as nearly equidistant as possible from the eastern and western extremities of the Province. Gaspé, the extreme east, lies in the vicinity of the 63rd degree of longitude; Montreal, the centre, in about the 73rd; Sandwich, the extreme west, in close proximity to the 83rd. On the north, the settled country extends, as yet, but a short distance from Montreal: on the south, the United States boundary line lies at a distance of about fifty miles from it.

The Facilities of Access to the City by Sea and Inland Navigation.

Montreal lies at the head of ship navigation. By the deepening of Lake St. Peter, which, though a provincial undertaking, Montreal is now effecting and has nearly completed at her own cost, ships of war of almost any magnitude are able to anchor in her ports; whilst by means of the vast lakes, the noble St. Lawrence and the magnificent canals above the city, vessels capable of loading 3,000 barrels of flour can descend to Montreal from the far west, without breaking bulk.

The Railroad Inter-communication of the City.

The Grant Trunk Railway Company have thei principal depots at Point St. Charles in this city. The Grand Trunk Railroad is already completed to St. Thomas, below Quebec, and to Toronto, in Upper Canada; it also extends to the seaboard at Portland. The Victoria Bridge, which, when finished, will span the St. Lawrence at Montreal, at a breadth of about two miles, and may be justly classed among the wonders of the age, will complete the link in the Grand Trunk Railway, connecting the eastern and western extremities of the Province, and it is fervently hoped by all Canadians, but by none more earnestly and enthusiastically than by the citizens of Montreal, that this great achievement of engineering science and skill will, when perfected, be opened by Her Most Gracious Majesty in person.

As the main artery of railroad inter-communication in Canada, the Grand Trunk will ultimately extend from Montreal, as its centre, not merely to the extremities of the Province east and west, but unite with the railroads in progress in the Lower Provinces, and otherwise branch off from Montreal in numerous eradiations. It already links Montreal to Quebec at Point Levi, on the south shore of the St. Lawrence, and will in all probability, at no very distant day, connect Quebec with Montreal by the north shore, and extend along the banks of that noble tributary, the Ottawa, even as far as the Georgian Bay in the west.

Montreal is the Commercial Emporium of Canada, and the centre of extensive manufacturing interests.

Our Upper Canadian friends, and those intelligent American citizens who honoured us with their presence at the memorable celebration of the opening, in Montreal, in November last, of the Grand Trunk Railway, conceded those facts, and complimented us on their advantages. It is hither the masses of the Upper Canadian merchants come to purchase their supplies of merchandize, imported from Great Britain and foreign parts. It is here that, from the magnitude of our commerce and the extent of our commercial relations, the Legislature during the session could best obtain the greatest diversity of public opinion affecting the commercial interests of the whole Province. This remark would equally apply to the manufacturing interests. Montreal is the seat and centre of extensive manufactories, from which all parts of the Province to some extent draw their supplies, and commands within herself an immense hydraulic power, lying, as she does, on the banks of the St. Lawrence, whose rapids above the city furnish her with an inexhaustible supply of water for mill-seats and manufacturing purposes. Of this power she has already largely availed herself by establishing extensive and costly manufactories on the banks of the Lachine Canal at Montreal.

Her Population, its numbers and mixed character.

The population of Montreal, now more than 75,000, and probably amounting to 80,000 in number, greatly exceeds that of any other city in Canada. Besides being the most populous city, Montreal receives throughout the year the largest number of transient visits from persons residing in various parts of the province; and thus in fact possesses at all times within herself, the greatest amount of public opinion, affecting every interest of a nature to be legislated upon, available on the spot at all times to the members of the Executive Government, and to Parliament when in session. This is in itself of much importance; but the mixed character of her population is of infinitely greater. Composed as the population of United Canada is well known to be of the descendants of different nationalities, speaking different languages, and to some extent yet retaining their respective national peculiarities— the French predominating in Lower, the English in Upper Canada— the population of Montreal is happily, for the interest of both races, almost equally divided in number between Franco- and Anglo-Canadians, or the descendants of the two races, the number of the latter rather preponderating over those of the former. The city of Montgeal consequently affords to each race the greatest possible facility for acquiring a knowledge of the language, habits, and feelings of the other; and that these facilities are readily and extensively availed of by both races, is manifest from the fact that both languages are constantly and familiarly spoken by nearly all the inhabitants of the city.

If due regard, therefore, be paid to the dearest, the most sacred rights and interests of all Her Majesty's Canadian subjects, no other place so fitting as Montreal can be selected for the permanent seat of Government in Canada. The harmonious working together of both nationalities, for their common good, will be more readily secured by assembling the members of the Legislature together in Montreal, where both languages are equally and generally used, than by calling them together in any other city of Canada where only one of these languages is spoken or understood.

The opportunities afforded to the members of the Legislature in Montreal, for social intercourse with its intelligent and cultivated citizens of both origins, will tend more than any other means to extinguish those national antipathies and prejudices from which Canada has already suffered so much, and such harmonious intercourse will no doubt produce those feelings of mutual forbearance, goodwill, and esteem for each other, so necessary to the welfare and advancement of both races.

The progress of Montreal in Literature, Science, and the Fine Arts.

In these certain evidences of civilization, Montreal lays claim to no very marked superiority over other cities; but a large and liberal spirit pervades her citizens, and if she cannot boast of extensive literary or scientific reputation, she has certainly not been niggard in the promotion of science and the fine arts, in cultivating a taste for literature, and in founding and endowing institutions of learning. The High School, the University of McGill College, the Natural History Society, the Canadian Institute, the Mercantile Library Association, the Mechanics' Institute, and the Geological Museum, may all be referred to with confidence as honourable and gratifying results of her literary and scientific progress; and the fact that the American Association for the Advancement of Science has honoured Montreal by selecting her as the favoured city in which they will hold their anniversary meeting this year, testifies to the estimation in which her claims to consideration on the score of science and literature, are held by that eminently scientific and erudite body.

Her position for Military Defence.

In a recent communication to one of our city papers a competent military authority has shown that Montreal possesses the greatest possible natural advantage for military defence, and that by means of the lofty mountain which overshadows the city and river at its base, and which has most judiciously been named the Royal Mount, and by means also of the Island of St. Helen's and the Nun's Island, commanding the channel of the river above, below, and opposite the city, Montreal can easily, and at a comparatively trifling cost, be made impregnable to hostile attack. If defended on the modern European system, as illustrated at Coblentz on the Rhine, and Lentz on the Danube, and still more recently in the immense external fortifications of Paris, but at the same time in a more inexpensive and simple way—by a series of detached works, scientifically designed to strengthen a naturally strong position, and by that class of impromptu intrenchments which late events have shown to be "the cheap defences of nations," Montreal may be defended, not only till succour comes, but may be made so formidable as greatly to deter an enemy from coming at all.

Montreal of 1857 is not the Montreal of 1775, when Montgomery marched into it at the head of a few thousand continentals. The city then numbered less than 5,000 inhabitants; it now counts upwards of 75,000. It embraces within itself immense resources, the largest, best-disciplined, and most efficient volunteer force of all arms, Horse, Foot, and Artillery, in Canada; and features in its material progress have imperceptibly added to its military strength since the period of the American Revolution.

The writer adverted to, most correctly observes that Montreal possesses two fortresses of great natural strength in its well known "Mount Royal" and in the Island of St. Helen's. The Mount Royal, or Mountain of Montreal, immediately in the rear of the city, forms the apex of a defensible triangle, of which the River St. Lawrence forms the base. One foot of the triangle is planted on the Island of St. Helen's, the other on the Island of St. Paul, commonly known as the Nuns' Island. This outline embraces the system of an inexpensive but secure defence. The Mountain of Montreal consists in reality of a nest of hills, each, in a defensive point of view, bearing upon, but independent of the other. They abound in wood and water, and offer convenient and safe accommodation for troops. As a whole, with the employment of skill and labour in the improvement of natural advantages, the mountain may be made impregnable. So long as the mountain is held in force, no enemy can safely assail the flanks of the triangle, the eastern and western defences of the town; and it is, therefore, impossible, under these circumstances, that the town can ever be taken.

Many other and most cogent reasons might be added to the foregoing, why Montreal should be selected as the seat of Government; but the length to which this document has extended would cause their enumeration to be tedious, and the force and weight of the arguments submitted render any further reasons supererogatory.

In the name, therefore, of the city authorities of Montreal, I will conclude this document by repeating in the candid and unanswerable language of the late Honourable Mr. Sullivan's Report—as incontrovertible reason why the seat of Government should be established here—that Montreal is essentially a city of both the late provinces of Canada, the Upper and the Lower, one in which each claims an interest, and it is, moreover, a city familiar to Upper Canadians, as it is to the inhabitants of the section of which it forms a part; it is the place of all others in which to study the statistics and politics of the whole of Canada, in which there is the least chance of partial legislation, or of the interests of any part of the people of the province being overlooked or disregarded. There can be no stronger proof of the correctness of these opinions, than the claim set up by the inhabitants of the western country, long before the Union, to the city of Montreal, as a place built up with the result of their industry and sustained by their commerce; but of the resources arising from the wealth of which they were deprived in consequence of the city forming part of a different province. That the Lower Canadians resented and resisted a proposition for the dismemberment of their country, and the loss of their chief city, is undoubted, and surely this contest for a place in which both claimed a deep and obvious interest, shared by no other locality, ought to be conclusive evidence in favour of the disputed position when the inquiry is made, where shall be the united capital of these contending provinces? That the capital of the united provinces ought to be placed in the position which would enable Upper Canadians most effectually to look after the concerns of their own seaborne and outward trade, and in the place in which Lower Canadians can most effectually investigate and control the internal management of communications of which they share the expense, and in the advantages of which they expect to share, is as indisputable a proposition now as it was when first enunciated by the Committee of the Council, and afterwards confirmed by the Legislature of the province in 1843. That Montreal possesses these advantages is not to be disputed, and that there are facilities afforded to a Government resident in Montreal, of closely and constantly ascertaining what is for the public advantage of the whole community and what is the true bent of public opinion, superior to any offered by rival cities claiming the choice of the Government, is equally apparent. All the advantages of common and universal interest in one locality are found in Montreal in a superior degree to those existing in most capital cities; and, therefore, every disinterested and upright Canadian, every true patriot and lover of his country, feels a confident expectation that Her Most Gracious

Majesty, without giving much weight to local claims, or to desires naturally entertained of political preponderance in either section of the province, will make choice of Montreal as Her Majesty's Canadian capital.

164. Memorial of the City of Kingston, June 15, 1857.

In obedience to a circular addressed by his Excellency the Governor-General of British North America to the Mayor of the city of Kingston, we, the Corporation of that city, beg to lay before Her Majesty's Secretary of State for the Colonies the following reasons and considerations why the City of Kingston should be chosen, and permanently adopted, as the future seat of Government of the Province of Canada.

So many and so valid are the claims which can be urged on behalf of Kingston, that it is found difficult to select them in any order of precedence in importance; but we venture first to mention the centrality of its position, not only geographically considered, but also with regard to population.

Kingston is situated at the head of the River St. Lawrence, and at the foot of that gigantic chain of lakes whose outlet is that noble stream. It is almost equi-distant from the eastern and western points of the settled portions of the province.

It is immediately connected by railway or by water communication with all the principal cities and towns of Canada, and is within a reasonable distance of, and readily accessible from, any of them; whilst its relative position with respect to the American seaports on the Atlantic, renders them available, when occasion requires, and brings the most important of them within a few hours' travel by railway: New York being distant about 366 miles, and reached in about twelve hours; and Boston and Portland being respectively distant about 417 and 465 miles, and reached in about eighteen hours.

With regard to population, the census returns and other official documents show this city to be almost in the very centre of the population of Eastern and Western Canada. Of the sixty-three counties into which Canada is divided, about half (not counting a few remote and thinly-settled counties) lie east, and half west, of the County of Frontenac, in which the City of Kingston stands.

That apart from being thus central and accessible from all parts of the province, the United States, and Great Britain, Kingston possesses all the security that great natural strength, and extensive fortifications, naval and military, can afford; and on several occasions, when danger threatened the province, have the archives of the Government been sent here for safe keeping. Immense sums have been laid out on these defences, and no post in British America, save Quebec and Halifax, is so strongly fortified; it is acknowledged and well known to be the stronghold of Western Canada. It is, moreover, the outlet of that stupendous military work, the Rideau Canal, which unites it with the waters of the Ottawa, and adds to its resources in time of war or threatened danger.

Its harbour is not excelled by that of any lake-port in Canada; not only can it furnish safe anchorage to an almost countless fleet, but its natural features and extensive fortifications render it a refuge and safe roadstead in time of war. The naval command of the American lakes would always be secured to Great Britain while this post was held; in short, it is the only fortified harbour in Western Canada, and its importance in this respect would ensure the city being always garrisoned and defended, and make it a safe and secure place for the Government archives and Legislative buildings; this circumstance, we feel well assured, is well known to Her Majesty's Government, the naval depot of the province having been located here for many years, and some of the largest vessels of war having been constructed here.

That as a naval and military post this city can fairly be considered what it proved to be when first the flag of Great Britain floated over the rude walls of Fort Frontenac, the key to the whole of Western Canada.

That for salubrity of climate, and healthiness of locality, Kingston is not excelled, perhaps not equalled, in the province; the epidemics which have visited the land have touched it with a lenient hand. The army and navy returns, the comparative mortality bills, and all reliable statistics, show it to be as healthy a spot as any in Canada.

Another consideration worthy of attention is, that the Government possesses, in Kingston, a very valuable and extensive tract of land, admirably calculated for the site of public, legislative, and official buildings.

That on former occasions, whenever the selection of a locality for the seat of the Government of this province has occupied the attention of the British Crown, Kingston has always been the place considered most eligible, and has even received the sanction of the choice of his Grace the late Duke of Wellingston, whose prescient mind had well considered the circumstances of the country, both with a view to the construction of the Rideau Canal, and, subsequently, with regard to the site of its capital.

Lord Sydenham, whose best energies and judgment had been devoted to this subject, writes thus upon the question. In a letter dated April 9, 1840, he says: "I shall certainly make the seat of Government in the Upper Province, Toronto is too far, and out of the way; but Kingston or Bytown would do. The people, the soil, the climate, of the Lower Province are all below par. Marryatt has not said a word too much of Upper Canada; it is the garden of the whole North American continent, and is, in fact, the source of all the wealth and trade of the Canadas. The Lower Province, except the eastern townships, is nothing but a fringe, some seven or eight miles deep, along the St. Lawrence, with two cities, Montreal and Quebec, which being the shipping ports for the whole of Upper Canada, have become wealthy and populous: but the source of their prosperity, even, is all in the Upper Province; the wheat, the timber, the cattle, all come from there. Lower Canada will not even now support itself with bread. . . . All our efforts ought, therefore, to be directed to Upper Canada, and I shall turn mine all that way as soon as the Union is through. There is some pleasure in working with and for an intelligent and enterprising set of men."

On July 11, 1841, he writes: "I have every reason to be satisfied with having selected this place (Kingston) as the new capital. There is no situation in the province so well adapted for the seat of Government, from its central position, and certainly we are as near England as we should be any where else in the whole of Canada. My last letter reached me in fifteen days from London! so much for steam and railways."

In a letter to Lord John Russell, dated September 16, 1840: "I have no longer the slightest doubt about Kingston as the seat of Government; nothing would make me meet in Lower Canada, or hold the central Government there. I really had no notion of what Upper Canada is till I made this tour. I always thought the country a fine one, but the whole of that tract of land which lies between the three lakes, and is nearly as large as England, is, I believe, unsurpassed in any part of the world, and any one district of it already contains more real wealth and intelligence than all Lower Canada (excluding the townships)."

Under date June 12, 1841, he writes to Lord John Russell thus: "I think we shall do very well here. I have really a very fair house for the Assembly and Council to meet in, and the accommodation would be thought splendid by our members of the English House of Commons.

"The house I lodge in is really a very nice one; and the public offices are far better than either at Montreal or Toronto."

Mr. Scrope acknowledges the salubrity of Kingston, when in writing his brother's life he says, "His health rather improved under the influence of the purer air of Kingston."

Lord Durham, in a despatch to Lord Glenelg, dated July 12, 1838, writes: "Kingston is a highly important station, both in a commercial and a military point of view. It will be the depot of all the trade from the west by the St. Lawrence, and the Rideau Canal and the Ottawa, to Montreal and Quebec; and its harbour is excellent for ships of any size."

Sir Charles Metcalfe, in a message to the House of Assembly, on October 6, 1843, says: "Her Majesty's Ministers will be prepared to submit favourably to Her Majesty such Addresses as may be presented by either, or both, of the Legislative Houses, in recommendations of either Kingston or Montreal, . . . it being understood that the selection is now necessarily limited to one of those places; the former capitals, Quebec and Toronto, being alike too remote from the centre of the province, and the plan of alternate sessions at one or other of these last-mentioned, or any other, places, being deemed impracticable, on account of its manifest and extreme inconvenience.''

Her Majesty's Secretary of State for the Colonies, in a despatch to Sir Richard Jackson, the Administrator of the government of this Province, dated November 1841, writes thus:—

"I have received Her Majesty's commands to instruct you to acquaint the House of Assembly that Her Majesty is always desirous, so far as may be possible, of consulting the wishes of her loyal subjects in Canada, deliberately entertained and constitutionally expressed through their Representatives in the House of Assembly; but that the establishment of Kingston as the seat of the united Legislature was not adopted without full consideration, and that a change involving, among other consequences, largely-increased expenditure, ought not to be sanctioned, except upon the clearest necessity, and the general sense of the Province unequivocally expressed in its favour.

"Many and serious objections attach to the proposal of holding sessions for alternate periods of four years each, at distant and distinct places, which, upon reconsideration, Her Majesty can hardly doubt will induce the House of Assembly to take a different view from that which is expressed in the Address now submitted to Her Majesty.''

When, after much discussion, the Provinces of Upper and Lower Canada were united, it was made a pledge to the members of the Upper Canadian Legislature that the seat of Government should be in Upper, or purely British, Canada, and their assent to that measure was undoubtedly given upon such understanding. It was in accordance with the pledge that the seat of the Provincial Government was, "after the most mature consideration" (as stated in the despatch of the Colonial Secretary, dated in February 1842), established at Kingston. Expensive public buildings were erected, and much private expenditure incurred, on the strength of its permanency, but, after the death of Lord Sydenham, and about three years after its establishment, it was removed to Montreal.

When circumstances, against the recurrence of which there is no security, rendered it inexpedient, if not impossible, to continue the Government at Montreal, the system of alternate Parliaments at Quebec and Toronto was adopted, a system now unanimously condemned by both Houses of the Legislature, and by well-understood public opinion, on account of the reason given by Lord Metcalfe—"its manifest and extreme inconvenience,'' its expense and risk to public documents and the suspension of business caused in all the governmental departments.

On the abandonment of a plan so obviously open to serious objection, and keeping in view the pledge given, that the site of the metropolis should be in Canada West, it seems to us that the claims of Kingston cannot, with justice, be overlooked; no other city in the Province, which possesses the requisites for a capital, being so ready of access to the members of the Legislature from Eastern Canada, at the same time that it is within reasonable distance from the cities and towns of the West.

When the comparative claims of other Canadian cities are considered, the obvious superiority of Kingston appears too great to be passed over. Whilst Montreal would need an enormous expenditure to place it in a state of anything approaching to security, the forts, batteries, and towers of Kingston, already present a formidable barrier against the approach of a foe. Whilst the peculiar position of Montreal, its mixed population, its conflicting creeds and races, its opposing factions, religious and political, have on former occasions, and might again on future ones, render it the arena of bloodshed and the scene of conflagration; whilst party-feeling has, there, even contaminated the legal tribunal, and rendered powerless the arm of justice; Kingston has ever presented, and still presents, a spectacle of order, peace, and good local government, and can justly boast a population, order-loving and law-abiding in their conduct, loyal in their principles of attachment to British rule, and intelligent and capable of self-management in all their local and municipal institutions. Whilst Montreal, from its location and other causes, forms the rock on which the waves of contending parties break in their violence, Kingston, whilst near enough to Lower Canada to keep alive all the better feelings that an interchange of reciprocal good offices will create, is yet far enough from the line between the two divisions of the Province to escape the effects of the smouldering, but not extinct, conflicting elements of adverse races, creeds, and feeling.

Whilst the isolated and extreme easterly position of Quebec would place it almost beyond consideration in relation to this question, Kingston, second only to it in military strength, is in the very heart of Canada.

Whilst Toronto's western situation and unguarded and indefensible position place it, almost equally with Quebec (save as to its site in Upper Canada), beyond the question, Kingston, equally British in feeling, loyal and orderly in population, is already strongly defended, and possesses the claims we have urged of centrality.

Whilst the remote city of Ottawa (the recent town of Bytown) would possibly admit of fortification, though at an immense outlay, Kingston's defences are already built, and as the outlet of the Rideau Canal, the key to that military work, and the only protected harbour where a fleet could lie, it must ever be the stronghold on the possession of which the fate of Ottawa must depend.

Whilst for Ottawa it may perhaps be contended that its inferiority in size, in population, and in comparative importance, constitute claims as the location of a capital, on the principle acknowledged in America, that the Legislature should be removed from the influence of a large and wealthy community; even these claims, shared, as they may be considered to be, by every village in the country, fall valueless before the fact that the situation of Ottawa or the line between the two Provinces exposes it in a marked degree to the same unfavourable influences that exist in Montreal, whilst its actual location, partly in each division of the Province, and subject to two different codes of laws, makes it satisfactory municipal management almost impossible, and tends to unfit it for ever for a capital city. On the other hand, Kingston, without possessing so large or influential a population as to create a danger of pressure on the Legislature, is of sufficient size and consequence to render all the necessary accommodation that increased population and the wants of a capital would demand. Of Bytown a Committee of the Executive Council of Canada reports thus:—

"Its position makes it inconvenient both for Upper and Lower Canadians; it is, in fact, out of the way of both; and thus possessing disadvantages which would be equally felt by both divisions of the Province, it would, probably, unite both in one feeling, and that not in its favour."

Doubtless the gentlemen who composed this Committee felt that the highway of Canadian prosperity, progress, and refinement, must ever be, or must surely be for a period beyond which human legislation need scarcely look, on the St. Lawrence frontier.

One other consideration we beg to urge: that fertile peninsula, surrounded by the great Canadian lakes, which has hitherto drawn the emigrant westward, may now be considered as well settled; and land, at prices suited to emigrants of ordinary means, can scarcely be procured there. The policy of the Provincial Government, which has recently opened up roads through the country lying between Ottawa River, Lake Ontario, and the River Madawaska, will turn the tide of emigration northward of Kingston, and the valuable tract of territory thus brought into occupation, with the aid of projected railways, will find its natural outlet, the *entrepôt* for its commerce, and its channel of communication with surrounding countries and Great Britain, all at Kingston.

Apart from all these grave considerations, we believe that the selection of Kingston would be more satisfactory to the Province generally than that of any other spot that can be chosen, and also that one very great and important object of the union of the Provinces would be thereby attained, namely, gradually to remove sectional interests, to amalgamate the population, and make the United Provinces one people, "British in fact as well as in name."

165. Memorial of the City of Ottawa, May 18, 1857.

To the Queen's Most Excellent Majesty.
Most Gracious Sovereign,

We, your Majesty's dutiful and loyal subjects of the city of Ottawa, in the Province of Canada, beg leave to approach the foot of the Throne with assurances of our loyalty and fidelity to the Crown of Great Britain, and of our devoted attachment to the person of your Majesty.

We have approached the Throne, on the present occasion, at the suggestion of your Majesty's Representative in Canada, to lay before our Sovereign the claims of the city of Ottawa for selection as the future capital of this growing province.

Since the union of Upper and Lower Canada, in the year 1840, the subject of the adoption of a permanent site for the seat of Government has continuously agitated the public mind, and has annually given rise to excited and protracted debates in the Legislature of the country, gradually developing bitter feelings of jealousy in the two sections of the province, and at times, almost threatening a dissolution of the union.

To avoid, for the future, an agitation so injurious to our best interests, the present Provincial Parliament have, with the concurrence of the Government, wisely resolved to refer to the judgment of our Sovereign the decision of a question that they themselves have in vain endeavoured to settle; and we beg to assure your Majesty that this judicious course is approved of by a very large majority of the people of the two Canadas, convinced, as they are, that, in the discharge of so onerous a task, your Majesty will recognise the important bearing it will have upon the future greatness of this country, in cementing more firmly the union of Upper and Lower Canada, in extinguishing those national jealousies that have for years past mutually existed, and in developing the illimitable resources of both sections of the province.

That, without desiring to prejudice the claims of other cities in the mind of your Majesty, we may, nevertheless, be permitted succinctly to set forth reasons demonstrative of the superiority of Ottawa to every other place for selection as a capital.

Consisting, as Canada does, of an extended line of territory, lying opposite the frontier of a powerful and rapidly-increasing Republic, it is of the highest importance to its protection that the seat of Government should be at some point far removed from the possibility of hostile attack in time of war, and of foreign influences on the minds of its people in time of peace, and so situated that its connection with the rest of the country could never be cut off or intercepted by an invading enemy, an argument forming an insuperable objection to Toronto and Kingston, lying, as they do, in an exposed position, immediately opposite American territory, and, in the event of foreign invasion, liable, as they are to be at any time dissevered from the other parts of the province. A similar objection may also be urged against Montreal, and with nearly equal force, for it must be conceded that Montreal itself fell an easy prey to an American army during the revolutionary war, and, from the present navigability of the St. Lawrence, the descent by water from foreign territory to that city is a task of little difficulty, and one that would require but a few hours in its accomplishment. Quebec, lying also on the St. Lawrence, is undoubtedly a point of great strength, but, from its extreme eastern situation and exclusive population, it is rather adapted to protect the approaches to the province by sea, than suited for the capital of United Canada, and the connection of both Quebec and Montreal with the rest of the country might at any time be readily severed by an invading army. Similar objections cannot be urged against this city, which lies in the very heart of Canada, far removed from the American frontier, surrounded by a loyal population, composed equally of French and British origin, who have ever remained free from the stain of disaffection to the Crown of England, and which is situated on the banks of the Ottawa, one of the largest and most beautiful rivers in your Majesty's widely-extended dominions, running entirely through British territory, and forming, in its course, the boundary line of the Upper and Lower Provinces.

As a central military position it stands unrivalled, its natural capabilities for defence not being even second to Quebec, and with but a moderate expenditure its fortifications could easily be made equal to that city, a knowledge of which, we believe, your Majesty already possesses from the plans and reports furnished at various times by the late Colonel By, its founder, and by other scientific military authorities, and in the once projected construction of which, that distinguished soldier, the late Duke of Wellington, is said to have taken a warm interest.

The city is connected with Montreal, on the east by the Ottawa river, with Kingston on the south-west by that great military work the Rideau Canal, and when the improvements on the upper portions of the Ottawa river shall have been completed, and the connection with Lake Huron on the extreme west made navigable, a project that in a few years will doubtless be executed, the city of Ottawa will be the radiating centre from which will diverge to the distant sections of Canada, the great arteries of the country, bearing on their waters trade and commerce, during peace, and affording a constant communication with the natural capital of the province during war. Moreover it is now united by rail with every other city in the two Canadas; a railway from Ottawa, intersecting the Grand Trunk and the River St. Lawrence at the town of Prescott, thus bringing this city within seven hours of Montreal, and twelve of Toronto; as a centre it is equally distant from Kingston and Montreal, from Quebec and Toronto, and when, in the future that already seems to shadow forth the destinies of this country, the Red River Valley shall be united on the one side, and the Lower British Provinces on the other, it will still form the centre of that extensive Empire.

Were the seat of Government permanently located in Toronto, Kingston, Montreal, or Quebec, its effect would not be felt beyond the immediate limits of the metropolis, while it must be obvious that the location of it at this central point would tend to develop equally the growth of the two Canadas in the very region where a stimulus is imperatively required, by attracting emigration and capital to the Ottawa valley, now the only part of Canada where any large and valuable tracts of land suitable for cultivation are still held by the Crown, and thus, by settling the interior, giving to the province that depth and solidity so essential to its strength, and creating for Kingston and Montreal that back country so indispensable to their prosperity. The Ottawa valley, already containing over 100,000 souls, is capable of sustaining a population of 8,000,000, while it is rich in mineral wealth and possesses unlimited water-power on the various tributaries of the Ottawa river.

So far back as the year 1843 the Committee of the Executive Council when recommending the removal of the seat of Government from Kingston to Montreal, thus alluded to the claims of this city: "Of Bytown, it may be said that it is comparatively safe from attack in the interior; that when the country of the Ottawa comes to be settled, it promises to rise into importance, and that it is situated on the provincial boundary, but then its position makes it inconvenient for both Upper and Lower Canadians." The argument of inconvenience cannot now be urged since the introduction of our railways, which render it easy of access from all parts of the province. And, though a matter of minor importance, it may still not be unworthy of consideration that the city of Ottawa stands unrivalled on the continent of America for the beautiful and romantic scenery of its rivers, cascades, and mountains, yielding not only pleasure to the eye, but keeping the atmosphere in so healthy a state that Ottawa has hitherto been comparatively free from those epidemics, cholera and fever, that have so fearfully devastated other cities of Canada.

The city contains also ample grounds, in its very centre, belonging to the Crown, admirably suited for the requirements of the Government, with abundance of the best building material at hand, and a productive country around it to furnish the wants of the place.

It may not be out of place, your memorialists conceive, to explain the apparent minority of votes which this city received during the debate in the present Parliament, on the reference of the selection of a capital to your Majesty. The amendment to the original motion for the reference of the question, naming Ottawa as the permanent site, was introduced solely with a view of embarrassing the Government, and did not receive the support of those members of the House favourable to the selection of Ottawa, since they had previously expressed their approbation of the Government measure, and they felt that the amendment was capriciously brought forward.

In fine, we conceive that, situated as Ottawa is, within the territory of Upper Canada, but connected with the lower province by the "Union" suspension bridge, with a population ox French and British origin equally balanced, the political and social effect of its selection would be to forever set at rest any feelings of jealousy on the part of either section, and would tend more firmly to cement a union which has already been productive of the happiest results; a conclusion your memorialists are warranted in asserting from the frequently expressed opinions of the Lower Canadians that, next to the place they felt immediately interested in, they preferred Ottawa, and to which, moreover, they have never urged any objection in Parliament; and Upper Canada would have no cause of complaint, since the pledge that the seat of Government should be permanently placed within the territory of Upper Canada, said to have been tacitly given by the late Lord Sydenham when carrying out the union, would be fulfilled.

We beg to accompany this, our memorial, with the tracing of a comprehensive map of British North America, compiled from authentic sources. And again renewing our assurances of loyalty and attachment to your Majesty, and expressing our confidence in the exercise of your wise judgement, we remain your Majesty's devoted subjects.

166. Memorial from the Citizens of Hamilton (not dated).

To the Queen's Most Excellent Majesty.
Most Gracious Sovereign,

We, your Majesty's faithful subjects, Citizens of Hamilton, in the Province of Canada, in public meeting assembled, beg leave to approach the Throne for the purpose of stating our views in reference to the application made by the Canadian Parliament to your Majesty for the selectiom of the seat of Government for this province.

Your Memorialists beg to represent that the city of Hamilton, from its many natural advantages and commercial prosperity, is the most suitable place in the Canadas fog the seat of Government; that situated at the head of Lake Ontario, at the point from which the through trade and traffic from and to the far west diverge by railways in every direction, and also have direct communication with the Atlantic Ocean by the best navigable inland waters in the world; Hamilton is destined to become at no distant period the commercial emporium of your Majesty's North American possessions;

That the ratio of increase in its annual exports and imports is greater than that of Toronto, Montreal, or Quebec; that its facilities of defence to repel invasion, and to preserve the archives of the countgy, are unequalled by any city in the province;

That it is rapidly becoming the centre of population and wealth, and is accessible to the most remote rural constituencies by railroads, so that no inconvenience would be experienced by those whose duty would necessitate their attendance at the seat of Government; and that the tide of emigration moves westward, and if the numerical increase of the population of Upper over that of Lower Canada during the next ten years be proportionate to that of the last ten years, Hamilton will be too far eastward for the centre of population.

Your Memorialists beg further to represent that your Gracious Majesty, having conferred on the people of this colony the power of controlling their own local affairs, it is derogatory to their character to refer a measure so purely provincial as the selection of the seat of Government to your Majesty's decision. This is a question which, from its local character, your Memorialists contend ought to be left to the decision ox the people of Canada, whose interests it would be to make the most judicious selection.

Your Memorialists have much pleasure in referring to a dispatch of Lord Stanley, dated the 2nd day of November, 1841, in reply to an Address from the Provincial Legislature, in which your Majesty declined to select the seat of Government for Canada on the ground of its being a local question which should be determined by the people interested in and affected by it. The same strong adherence on the part of your Majesty to the principles of self-government which have been so graciously ceded to your Majesty's Canadian subjects has been ably set forth by the Right Honourable H. Labouchere in a recent dispatch to the people of Newfoundland relative to the fisheries question, which your Memorialists regard as indicative of your Majesty's indisposition to depart from those wise maxims of Colonial policy, the scrupulous observance of which has contributed so much to the prosperity of this

Colony, and the inculcation of feelings of loyalty in all classes of your Majesty's Canadian subjects.

Your Memorialists would further represent that the question of a permanent seat of Government should not be decided until the union of Upper and Lower Canada, which was effected by Imperial authority in 1841, shall have been settled on a satisfactory basis, your Memorialists cannot conceal from your Majesty the grave doubts they entertain of the continuance of the Union unless a fair proportion of representation in the Legislature be conceded to your Majesty's Upper Canadian subjects.

The rapidly increasing wealth and population of Upper Canada over those of Lower Canada, and also the unwillingness of your Majesty's French Canadian subjects to submit to the same systems of taxation and of Municipal Government that obtain in Upper Canada, loudly call for a change in the representation of the people in both branches of the Legislature. Your Memorialists are, therefore, of opinion that, until the problem of the Union shall have been solved, it is impolitic to determine the question which has been referred by the Canadian Parliament to your Majesty's decision.

Your Memorialists further represent that the Parliament of this your Majesty's loyal Colony, as at present constituted, does not represent the majority of the people, as your Majesty's Representative and Council have been petitioned by a majority of the principal constituencies for a dissolution without effect.

That the object aimed at by the Government in referring this important question to your Majesty's decision is manifestly to avoid responsibility on their part, while it cannot fail very seriously to embarrass your Majesty, as no Imperial decision of the question is likely to give universal satisfaction to your Majesty's Canadian subjects.

In view of the foregoing facts, your Memorialists, in public meeting assembled, do most earnestly and respectfully pray your Majesty not to accede to the Address of the Canadian Parliament in reference to the seat of Government, but to refer the settlement of this question back to the people of this Colony.

167. Centrality data from table on map compiled to accompany Ottawa's 1857 memorial to the Queen.

DIRECT DISTANCE FROM THE CITY OF OTTAWA

Place		Miles	Place		Miles
To Montreal	C.E.	100	To St. Johns	N.B.	480
To Kingston	C.W.	95	To Sault St. Marie	C.W.	475
To Three Rivers	C.E.	175	To Pictou Coal Mines	N.S.	665
To Port Hope	C.W.	172	To L.S. Copper Mines	C.W.	660
			To Halifax	N.S.	612
To Quebec	C.E.	240			
To Toronto	C.W.	233	To St. John	N.F.	1150
			To Ft. Garry Red		
To Fredericton	N.B.	455	River Settlement		1140
To Windsor	C.W.	440			
			To New York		336
To Pt. Chicoutimi			To Moose Fact James		
Sagenay		322	Bay		492
To London	C.W.	334			

CHAPTER VII
THE DECISION FOR OTTAWA

Introduction

The city memorials and several other documents were published in a limited edition for use within the Colonial Office, the British Cabinet, and by the Queen.[1] Since Sir Edmund Head was in London during the period of decision making there, and took part in some Colonial Office decisions on related matters, it is highly likely the he also helped Arthur Blackwood and Herman Merivale in deciding on the sequence of the items in the published collection of documents. The order of the documents was a deliberate one, for the items were not arranged in the order received. Indeed, it is easy to conclude that the sequence was selected to deliberately guide a reader to conclude that Ottawa was the best site.

Following some general items (some official correspondence, the Addresses from the Legislative Council and Assembly, and copies of the Assembly's proceedings), the order of documents was (as in the previous chapter) the two memorials from Quebec (with their many strong claims), Toronto (with its very parochial claims), the Toronto supplement, Montreal (with the reliance of 1843 reasons, and an overextended declaration of possible defenses), Kingston (with a rather sad groping into the past to find reasons of support for its claims), and Ottawa (with a positive, eloquently written set of claims, and with no degrading comments about the other sites). There followed Hamilton's quickly dismissed document.

After the city memorials there followed three other documents which, with one other memorial, are presented in this chapter. Again, the order they appear in this book is the order in which they were originally published. The single most important document of the collection was that written by Sir Edmund Head.[2] It was an undated confidential memorandum that was known only by Colonial Office personnel, the British Cabinet, and the Queen, Prince Albert the Prince Consort, and the latter's private secretary, Sir George Grey. The memorandum, which reached the Colonial Office before the end of July, 1857, may have been written while Head was still in Canada and sent to London from there, or perhaps it was written while he was aboard ship and returning to Britain, where he hand delivered it to the

Colonial Secretary, Henry Labouchere (Head arrived at Liverpool on July 3rd, and was in London seeing Labouchere the following day). On the other hand, Head may have written it once he was back in England after having spoken to Labouchere. Whatever the case was, the document was conclusively in favour of Ottawa.

By the time any impartial reader had read through the several city memorials, Sir Edmund Head's memorial, and the two military views that followed, it would be clear that the only plausible choice to be made was in favour of Ottawa. There was a dissenting view, however, but it was published separately, having arrived late at the Colonial Office.[3] The author of the dissenting view was Sir Francis Bond Head (no relation to Sir Edmund). Sir Francis had been Lieutenant Governor of Upper Canada from 1836 until 1838. He was convinced that Toronto was the best place for the capital. However, in an aside about Ottawa, he unknowingly provided support for one of Sir Edmund's observations. Sir Francis wrote: "It is probable that, for a moment, the majority would be less annoyed by the success of Ottawa than by that of any of their great competitors."

The decision made within the Colonial Office was to accept Sir Edmund Head's recommendation in favour of Ottawa. This information, along with printed copies of the supporting documents, was relayed by Henry Labouchere to the British Cabinet for approval and it was given. The Queen's advisors thus recommended to Her Majesty that Ottawa should be selected as Canada's capital. Clearly, the "Queen's choice" was not arrived at in a vacuum, for in private meetings she received the decision in favour of Ottawa as well as receiving the private views of Labouchere (who had been in Canada many years before). The Queen may have recalled the 1841 reference from Canada that was refused, while Labouchere would have reviewed for her the complicated history of the divisive issue. The Queen also received guidance from within the Royal household, for her husband, Albert, took a great interest in the Canadian seat of government question. And General Grey also acted as a discussant, at least with Prince Albert and presumably with the Queen. Grey supported Head's decision. The Queen saw at least two maps. One was submitted by Sir Francis Bond Head and it excluded most of Canada East, including Three Rivers and Quebec! The other map we know the Queen saw showed all of British North America—with Ottawa in the centre. This map was probably compiled in the Colonial Office and one of its principal sources seems to have been a map submitted by Ottawa along with its city memorial.[4] Finally, it is worth noting that Sir Edmund Head and possibly his wife spoke with Queen Victoria and Prince Albert on more than one occasion while they were in England and it is reasonable to assume that the Canadian seat of government question was discussed.

The final decision to select Ottawa was made while Sir Edmund and Lady Head were still in Britain and Sir Edmund likely knew of the choice before they left on November 3rd to return to Canada. If he did not travel with knowledge of the decision then he learned of it soon after his arrival back in Canada, for he was requested by Henry Labouchere secretly to secure whatever land might be required in the vicinity of Ottawa for public purposes.

A draft of the despatch officially informing Head that Ottawa was the choice was sent from the Colonial Office to Queen Victoria on December 7, 1857, for her consent, and the formal despatch from Labouchere to Head was sent from London on December 31, 1857.[5]

Notes

[1] *Papers Relative to the Seat of Government in Canada* (London: Colonial Office, October, 1857).

[2] This has previously been republished in James A. Gibson, "Sir Edmund Head's Memorandum on the Choice of Ottawa as the Seat of Government of Canada," *Canadian Historical Review*, Vol. XVI, no. 4 (December, 1935), pp. 411-417.

[3] *Further Papers Relating to the Seat of Government in Canada* (London: Colonial Office, October 24, 1857). Sir Francis Bond Head's memorandum was later published in Toronto along with the City of Toronto's memorial to the Queen: *Toronto: The Grounds Upon Which Are Based Her Claims To Be The Seat Of Government Of Canada* (Toronto: Thompson and Co., 1858).

[4] The maps are too large to be reduced for republication in this volume, however, copies of them appear in Knight, *A Capital for Canada*, *op.cit.*, pp. 214, 224-225.

[5] PAC, PRO, CO 42/609, pp. 465-466, rough draft of despatch informing Sir Edmund Head that Ottawa was the choice. Notation in the margin indicates that a copy was sent to Queen Victoria on December 7, 1857. The official despatch is in PAC, PRO, CO 43/151, Labouchere to Head, December 31, 1857.

Documents

168. Confidential Memorandum by Sir Edmund Head, containing reasons for fixing the seat of Government for Canada at Ottawa (not dated).

1. The periodical transfer of the seat of Government from one place to another was declared inexpedient by a resolution of the Legislative Assembly in 1856. The adoption therefore of a fixed seat of Govern-

ment in 1857 became a matter of necessity, not of choice. The expediency, moreover, of putting an end to the migratory system, was obvious at all events. To keep the question open was to afford to any Opposition the opportunity of thrusting, in some form or other, on any Government a question on which four places of importance could always be made to direct their influence against any proposal of that Government. This question too, above all others, supplied a constant stimulant to the hatred of race and the conflict of religious feeling.

Irrespective then of the periodical expense, the suspension of public business, and the personal inconvenience caused by the change from one place to another, the interests of Canada as a whole, and the security of the Union, demanded a solution of the difficulty.

2. Ottawa is the only place which will be accepted by the majority of Upper and Lower Canada as a fair compromise. With the exception of Ottawa, every one of the cities proposed is an object of jealousy to each of the others. Ottawa is, in fact, neither in Upper nor Lower Canada. Literally it is in the former; but a bridge alone divides it from the latter. Consequently its selection would fulfil the letter of anyhpledge given or supposed to be given, to Upper Canada at tht time of the Union. The population at present is partly French, and partly English and Irish. The settlement of the valley of the Ottawa is rapidly increasing, and will be at once stimulated by making it the capital.

3. This circumstance is an incidental advantage of great value. Canada is long and narrow; in fact, all frontier. The rapid extension of settlement up the Ottawa, and on each side of it, would give breadth and substance to the country.

4. Ultimately, indeed in a short time, the question will arise, "which is to predominate, Upper or Lower Canada?" Upper Canada is conscious of its increasing strength, and of the fact that it pays the larger share of the taxes. The cry for increased representation to the most populous and the richest portion will soon be heard, or rather it is already raised. The only solution of the difficulty will be the chance that the district of Montreal, and the English population about it and in the townships, may be got to side wpth Upper Canada, and thus turn the scale in favour of that section, which, for reasons beyond our control, must in the end prevail. All real conflict would then be useless, and Quebec must succumb. It is most important, therefore, that the middle district should be made to feel its importance, and should connect its interests with Upper Canada. This object will be greatly promoted by the choice of Ottawa, linked to Montreal by its trade, and literally in Upper Canada, but close on the border of the other section of the province.

5. Montreal, as the most populous and the most central city, may be

said to have the strongest *prima facie* claim to be the seat of Government of the whole. The objections to it are the following:—

Its selection, though more agreeable to Upper Canada than that of Quebec, would not fulfil the supposed promise alluded to above, and would long leave open a pretext for reviving the question hereafter, when the increased wealth and population of the Upper Province shall have materially augumented its weight in the Legislature.

The choice of Montreal, therefore, would scarcely perhaps be accepted as a final compromise.

Montreal has been a turbulent town: it may not be so again; but it is supposed to be particularly subject to American influences of various kinds. In Canada, the direct influences brought to bear on a Ministry and a Parliament by the people of the place where the Government is carried on, are not to be overlooked or despised. The importance and character of their influence for the promotion of jobs of various kinds in Upper or Lower Canada has been visible according as the seat of Government has been Toronto or Quebec. The pressure which would be brought to bear on a weak Government at Montreal would always be considerable.

Montreal is, no doubt, the most important place in Canada in a military point of view. The attack of any regular army would probably, in the first instance, he directed against this city from the side of Lake Champlain.

Its defences are inadequate, and could not be completed except at a very great outlay. This outlay the jealousy of Upper Canada would not allow to be made at the expense of the colony.

6. Quebec is well secured against any military hattack, and is most readily accessible from England; but its selection would exasperate Upper Canada, and would rouse the jealousy of Montreal. The influence of Quebec is decreasing. The tendency of growth in wealth and trade is westward; and Quebec is practically at one extremity of the colony: all below it is of secondary importance.

7. Kingston is well situated and central, but it is what may be called 'a dead place,' when compared to Montreal and Toronto. Within a few years Ottawa will probably rival Kingston in population and in wealth. Kingston is accessible to an enemy, and though partially fortified, can scarcely be said to be secure from attack at any moment.

The choice of Kingston would cause discontent in all Lower Canada, and would rouse the jealousy of Toronto and Hamilton, both of which are, and will continue, to be far more flourishing.

8. Toronto, though increasing every day in commercial importance, is so situated as virtually to stand at one extremity of the united provinces. Its selection for the seat of Government would not be willingly acquiesced in by Lower Canada, and would tend to unite

Montreal with Quebec in renewed jealousy of the western section. Were this feeling to be created, the future conflict of which I have spoken as impending between Upper and Lower Canada would have to be fought out with much more equal power, and would be much more bitter in its character and more doubtful in its results. In short, Toronto would, in no sense, be accepted as a compromise: its choice would be considered as a complete triumph to the western section of Upper Canada.

Besides this, Toronto is indefensible against even a *coup-de-main*. Its position is such as to preclude efficient protection, except by the constant presence of a superior naval force on Lake Ontario.

9. The main objection to Ottawa is its wild position, and relative inferiority to the other cities named. But this wild position is a fault which every day continues to diminish. The present population may be called 8,000 or 10,000, not of the best description. It will be six years before the Government can be actually transferred thither, and the settlement of the fertile country on the Ottawa would be accelerated by the very fact of the certainty of such transfer, even before it took place.

According to my view, neither legislation, nor the action of the Executive Government, gain much by the casual presence of strangers, each of whom usually takes the opportunity afforded by the transaction of his own business, to press on the Ministry the 'jobs' which affect himself or the district to which he belongs. It is questionable whether in America legislation is best carried on in a great commercial city. The same might perhaps have been said of London in the days of Wilkes or Lord George Gordon. The Legislature of the State of New York would hardly have ventured to pass the law which destroyed the iniquitous jobbing of the Corporation, if it had held its sittings in New York itself. Ottawa is accessible by water from Montreal and from Lake Ontario. In the former communication there are still some difficulties, but they are not important. It is accessible too by a branch railroad from Prescott, where the line joins the Grand Trunk. The distance from Montreal may be called 100 or 120 miles, but its connection with Montreal is such as to cause its selection to be readily acquiesced in by that great city. I have heard persons of influence at Montreal say that they would as soon have the seat of Government at Ottawa as at Montreal itself. The latter city considers itself as the natural outlet to the Ottawa country, and believes that the opening of the valley of that river would establish its own communications with the western lakes, independently of Lake Ontario. In this they may be wrong, but the impression undoubtedly exists, and is important for our present purpose.

In a military point of view (I speak of course with submission to higher authorities), Ottawa is advantageously situated. Its distance from the frontier is such as to protect it from any marauding party, or even from a regular attack, unless Montreal and Kingston, which flank the approach to it, were previously occupied by the enemy. Stores and troops could be sent to Ottawa either from Quebec or Kingston, without exposure on the St. Lawrence to the American frontier.

A secondary consideration, but one of some importance as affecting the popularity of the choice, is the fact that the Rideau Canal, now handed over to the Provincial Government, would probably increase its traffic, and become more productive by the transfer of the seat of Government to Ottawa. At present this great work is a dead loss so far as money is concerned.

It may be added, that as Kingston stands at the outlet of the canal on Lake Ontario, the probable increase of traffic by this route would in some degree compensate Kingston for the preference of a rival city.

10. On the whole, therefore, I believe that the least objectionable place is the city of Ottawa. Every city is jealous of every other city except Ottawa. The second vote of every place (save, perhaps, Toronto) would be given for Ottawa. The question, it must be remembered, is essentially one of compromise. Unless some insuperable bar exist to its selection, it is expedient to take that place which would be most readily acquiesced in by the majority.

If Quebec were taken, all Upper Canada would be angry at the choice. If any place in Upper Canada (with the exception of Ottawa) were taken, all Lower Canada would raise an outcry.

If Ottawa is chosen, Montreal will acquiesce in the choice, and the majority of Upper Canada will not in any way resist, for to them it is a partial triumph. The whole matter is a choice of evils, and the least evil will, I think, be found in placing the seat of Government at Ottawa. Whichever section predominates, and however far westward the commerce of Canada may extend, Ottawa will be a convenient position.

If the Red River Settlement and the Saskatchewan country are finally to be annexed to Canada, the Ottawa route to Lake Huron and Lake Suerpior will be available, and may possibly turn out the shortest and the most advantageous of all.

I have written this Memorandum with no wish to thrust on Her Majesty's Government advice in a matter specially referred to the discretion of the Queen; but I have thought that I may be expected not to avoid the responsibility of expressing an opinion of my own.

I would also suggest that the military authorities in Canada should be forthwith consulted on this question. 'How far each of the places named is, or is not, exposed to attack by an enemy, and how far each such place may easily protected in time of war?'

169. Opinion of the Inspector-General Fortifications (J.F. Burgoyne) as to the place which, in a Military point of view, it would be

most desirable to select for the Seat of Government in Canada, September 26, 1857.

Whatever may be the expediency of political considerations, and the wish to reconcile rival local interests, and the irritation of races, there can, I think, hardly be a question but that the principal military establishments should be centered in Quebec.

Quebec must be the base of action for the military, and the receptacle for the military resources.

It is the only port in the Province; the only point having free communication with England; the only stronghold in the country; the first to start from, and the last to retire to; the only situation not immediately exposed to hostile aggression, in a country which presents one entire long line of frontier: Ottawa being no exception, as its security will be entirely dependent upon that of Montreal. And as regards the co-operation of all the British North American States with Canada, it is in a reasonably central position; but the value of a strictly central position is much reduced by the facilities of intercourse afforded by inland navigations, railways, and electric telegraphs.

A thorough personal knowledge of the country and of its military attributes, might afford means of giving a better opinion; and it is to be regretted that the present General in command there, had not had the opportunity of expressing his sentiments; but there is one of the best military authorities now in Dublin, General Lord Seaton, who was for several years in command in Canada in very troubled times, and during some period, it is believed, directed the Civil Administration also, whose judgment on the question would be of much consideration.

Unfortunately Lord Elgin is out of reach, but there is another former Governor-General, and a military man, Sir Francis B. Head, Baronet, residing at Oxendon, Northampton, who might perhaps also be consulted to advantage.

170. Confidential letter from General Lord Seaton to the Secretary of State for War, October 3, 1857.

With reference to your Lordship's letter of the 20th of September, relative to the question under the consideration of Her Majesty's Ministers, 'As to the most eligible place for establishing the seat of Government in Canada,' I have the honour to state, that if Quebec should be selected for the seat of Government, no doubt can be entertained that public business, and the proceedings of the Legislature, would be less liable to be disturbed than by establishing it either at Montreal, Ottawa, Kintston, or Toronto.

We may conclude that Quebec would not even be menaced by an

invading force. Its strong citadel, and improveable fortifications; the difficult and dangerous lines on which an army from the United States must act in moving in that direction; and a certain communication with the mother-country and the Lower Provinces, would afford, when the St. Lawrence is open, sufficient confidence, under any circumstances, to enable the affairs of Canada to be carried on without interruption at a seat of Government thus protected.

Montreal might probably be defended by constructing detached fortifications at an immense outlay; but military operations against this place would be much facilitated if the United States should obtain the command of the Chambley river from St. John's to its own confluence with the St. Lawrence. The northern part of the Island of Montreal would probably be constantly exposed to attack from Sorel; and it must be expected, in case of war, that one of the most important commercial towns in North America would be seldom free from alarm.

Ottawa, although only two marches from Ogdensburgh by Prescot, would be sufficiently remote from the St. Lawrence to prevent any sudden attack from the United States; and the position in which part of Bytown stands, between the Rideau and the Ottawa, might be easily fortified and protected.

Kingston cannot, I am persuaded, be considered a suitable place for the seat of Government, from its vicinity to the frontier of the United States, and the apprehension of attack, in winter particularly, on the part of the Canadians, which could not fail to be promoted by demonstrations from the towns and ports on the opposite side of the St. Lawrence.

Toronto could not be satisfactorily fortified, and would therefore invite invasion and attack; and it would appear, on military grounds, inexpedient to select this increasing city for the seat of Government.

171. Memorial of Sir Francis Bond Head, October 18, 1857.

[Section omitted on general facts about Canada written to support the claim that 'the heart or centre of the whole is, as nearly as possible, the City of Toronto.' Also omitted is a section on the defence of Canada.]
On the Locality in Canada which, for the general interests of the
    Province and of the Empire, should be selected as its Capital.

In theory, it might naturally be supposed that the capital of every country ought to exist, as nearly as possible, in its centre.

In practice, however, the opposite rule has been followed. Dublin, Edinburgh, London, Paris, Lisbon, Stockholm, Copenhagen, Amsterdam, Berlin, St. Petersburgh, Constantinople, and Washington in the United States, being all, either on the outside, or at an extremity of their respective countries. Indeed, as a negative proof, it may be remarked that Madrid, the only centrical capital, is the least flourishing country in Europe. In India, the Great Mogul reigned internally in Delhi, as the Emperor of China still reigns in Pekin; but in the one country, Calcutta, and in the other, Canton—both on the outside—are the real capitals.

As it would be absurd to suppose that, in a living animal, the heart could exist at any other point than at the terminus of its arteries, so must the heart or capital of a country necessarily exist in the centre of its business and of its commerce, or, in other words, at the termini of its main arterial railways and lines of water communication, which, in the map of every country, are the real indices or exponents of both.

Now, it is impossible for any unprejudiced man to study the map of Canada, without perceiving that almost the whole of the main arterial lines, of railway (especially those of the Grand Trunk and Great Western), and of lake navigation, converge upon, or diverge from, Toronto, which . . . is not only in the centre of the best land, the commerce, and the business of the province, but is also the heart of that fighting portion of it which, in case of invasion by the United States, would form its only defence.

This is no idle theory. In the rebellion and invasion of Canada by the American people, armed with the muskets and artillery of their Government, in 1837-8-9, Toronto, by two Lieutenant-Governors, was maintained as the point of Civil government and of military rendezvous; and if, from every direction, in the depth of winter, the fighting postion of the population hurried through the wilderness to it on foot, at a moment when the whole of Her Majesty's troops were concentrated in the Lower Province, how much easier could they be assembled by the railways, which, from Toronto now radiate in almost every direction.

In the city of Toronto, which for nearly half a century has been the seat of Government and metropolis of the Upper Province, and latterly of both, there exist, ready made, a suitable residence for the Governor-General, a Parliament-House, public offices, barracks, banks, and the other various requirements of a capital.

As regards its military position, it is a hundred miles from the United States by land, and once and a-half the distance from Dover to Calais by water.

In case of war, Toronto, like all the other lake-cities of Canada and the United States, would be liable to be attacked by the vessels of the most powerful of the two naval forces, whichever that might be. But, before such an event could occur, it would no doubt be deemed prudent to collect artillery, throw up earth-works, and transmit by railway to an inland position of perfect security all public archives of importance.

As regards the position of the other candidate cities, a very few remarks will, it is believed, suffice.

Of all of them Kingston would be the most unsafe, in consequence of its being divided from the United States only by the St. Lawrence, which in summer could be crossed by boats, and in winter in less than an hour, at any time by day or night, on ice.

Montreal, the populous, wealthy, and important metropolis of the Lower Province, lies not only within a day's march of the United States, but at the eastern extremity of 173 miles of the St. Lawrence, which, studded with islands, and averaging only two miles in breadth, could throughout the greater portion of that distance be crossed with the greatest facility by the enemy, who, by cutting the electric telegraph, breaking up the rails, and destroying the lockage of the navigation of the St. Lawrence, could completely isolate Montreal from that fighting portion of the population which, throughout the Province, constitutes its main defence.

Of the impregnable fortress and city of Quebec (which, like Montreal, is connected by railway with Portland, Boston, and New York), it may briefly be said that, on account of its position, as a metropolis, and even as a citadel, it is (especially during winter) *hors de combat*.

Of all the candidate cities, Ottawa—formerly called Bytown— would be the most inefficient for the capital of Canada.

In a northern and secluded locality—cut off from every arterial line of railway in the Province, and removed also from the navigation of the St. Lawrence, except by a branch railway greater in length than between London and Brighton—in time of peace it would be utterly impracticable to govern and transact from such a point the commercial business of the Province, especially that connected with the sale of public lands, as also with the valuable 'through' and home-traffic which exists between the cities on the five great lakes, and the vast corn-growing region of 'the Great West.' Ottawa, it is true, communicates with Montreal by the lockage of the Ottawa river; with Kingston, by the lockage of the Rideau canal; and with Brockville, on the St. Lawrence, by the long branch railway already described. But in time of war, of these three communications the termini of two, in the course of an hour, and of the third in the course of a day, might be in the possession of the enemy, who, of course, would also cut the wires of the electric telegraph; and as the St. Lawrence for 85 miles east, and for the same distance west of Brockville, would be crossed by them at any point, assistance by troops from Toronto might be either seriously impeded, or totally cut off; and the Provincial Parliament would then feel that it would be infinitely better for them 'to dwell in the midst of alarms than reign' in a desolate region, cut off from the wealth, commerce, business, and fighting population of the Province.

Actuated by the intense feelings with which the great cities situated on the main arterial or trunk-line are seeking, on the one hand, to be selected; and, on the other, to combine together against any one rival; it is probable that, for a moment, the majority would be less annoyed by the success of Ottawa than by that of any of their great competitors. But, though by order of Government, trade may occasionally be diverted unfairly from one sea-port to another, yet, in the selection of a capital for a great country, it is confidently submitted that the laws of nature must be implicitly obeyed, and that, in the language of Holy Scripture, 'where your treasure is, there will your heart be also.'

Now, by figures and facts which it will not be easy to gainsay, it has been shown that, as regards the wealth, business, commerce, and military defence of Canada, Toronto is the heart of the Province.

As regards its locality, as a convenient point of rendezvous for the 130 members of the House of Assembly, and the 48 Legislative Councillors who form the Provincial Legislature, the following figures will show, in that respect, a very remarkable resemblance between Toronto and the position of the Houses of the Imperial Parliament of Great Britain:—

DISTANCES

		Miles
1.	From London to Inverness 572 miles	
	to Aberdeen 508 miles averaging	540
	Toronto to the northern city of Quebec	501
2.	From London to the metropolis of Edinburgh	400
	Toronto to the metropolis of Montreal	333
3.	From London to York city	189
	Toronto to Kingston	160
4.	From London to Birmingham	112
	Toronto to Huron	95
5.	From London to the west port of Bristol	112
	Toronto to the west port of Sarnia	172
6.	From London to Liverpool (or great Western Ocean)	202
	Toronto to Detroit (and regions of 'Great West')	221

In the selection by Her Majesty of the city which is to form the capital of the Province of Canada, the inhabitants of the six great Republican States which form its frontier are vitally interested. If the heart of this magnificent British territory be deliberately inserted, unscientifically, in the wrong place, it will be physically, morally, and politically impossible for its wealth and commerce to maintain a healthy circulation. For the disease that must ensue, the people of the United States will offer to the people of Upper Canada, as the only remedy, annexation.

172. Henry Labouchere (Colonial Secretary) to Queen Victoria, October 16, 1857 (RA).

Mr. Labouchere sends Your Majesty, with his humble duty, Papers relating to the future Seat of Government in Canada, the decision of which has been submitted to Your Majesty. Sir Edmund Head is of opinion that the decision had better arrive in Canada about Christmas.

173. Henry Labouchere (Colonial Secretary) to Queen Victoria, October 30, 1857 (RA).

With Mr. Labouchere's humble duty to Your Majesty, Mr Labouchere sends 1. A memorandum from Sir Francis Head (who was formerly Governor of Upper Canada) upon the Seat of Government question. . . .

174. Pencil memorandum written in Lieutenant-General Hon. Charles Grey's hand, October, 1857 (RA).

An attentive perusal of the Papers relative to the Seat of Government in Canada leads to the conviction that the choice of Ottawa will be the right and politic one. Quebec may be the strongest and most acceptable situation for communication with the Mother Country, but great Military strength lies in contenting the people of both Provinces and rendering them therefore more determined to exert themselves to the utmost in the defence of their Capital.—Ottawa is reported by no means deficient in natural strength. It ought to have a Citadel planned on the best Military design, commanding the Town, but detached from it so as not to impede the natural growth of a Metropolis, destined to assume the largest dimensions.—Great care ought to be taken to leave sufficient space round the fortress, so that the town shd. not act as a covered way for its attack; Plans of the locality ought at once to be submitted to the Home Government and the necessary ground reserved, before its value has been increased by the Government decision.—

In order to secure future beauty and healthfulness, space ought at once to be acquired for laying out a large Park, which American towns do not in general possess, and would form the best site for the future Public Offices.—

The Military strength of the Position wd. be much increased by two fortified Ports in advance on the St. Lawrence,—say at Prescott or Brockville and Cornwall, which an American force crossing the St. Lawrence to attack the new Capital cd. not with safety leave in their rear.—

175. Sir Edmund Head (Governor General) to Arthur Blackwood (Colonial Office), (private), November 21, 1857 (PAC).

The despatch about the seat of Government had better be delayed till January first or the first mail after that day, which is the 2nd (Saturday).

The reason for this delay is the fact than an general election will not be well over till the beginning of January.

176. Henry Labouchere (Colonial Secretary) to Prince Albert, December 15, 1857 (RA).

The interest that your Royal Highness has taken in the question of the future Seat of Government for Canada induces me to bother you with the accompanying Papers [not reprinted].

They have been sent to me by Sir Edmund Head in reply to a confidential letter which I wrote to him on the importance of endeavoring to secure whatever land might be required in the vicinity of Ottawa for Public structures.

Sir Edmund Head informs me that it will be better that the decision of Her Majesty should not reach Canada until the Provincial Elections are over & the new Administration completely formed—& I shall therefore keep back my despatch for a few posts.

177. Prince Albert to Henry Lebouchere (Colonial Secretary), December 18, 1857 (PAC).

I return the enclosed papers with very best thanks.

Ottawa must indeed be a beautiful situation and all the detached descriptions must tend to confirm the impressions that the choice is the right one. We must now trust that the Province will look upon it in the same light, when it becomes known.

178. Henry Lebouchere (Colonial Secretary) to Sir Edmund Head (Governor General) December 31, 1857 (JLA).

By my despatch of the 17th April last, I informed you that Her Majesty had been graciously pleased to comply with the prayer of the Addresses presented to Her by the Legislative Council and Assembly of Canada, namely—that she would exercise the Royal Prerogative by the selection of some place for the permanent Seat of Government in Canada.

This question has now been considered by Her Majesty and by Her Government, with that attention which its great importance demanded.

The statements and arguments contained in the various memorials laid before them, in consequence of your invitation to the Mayors of the several Cities chiefly interested, have been fully weighed.

I am commanded by the Queen to inform you that in, the judgment of Her Majesty, the City of Ottawa combines greater advantages than any other place in Canada for the permanent Seat of the future Government of the Province, and is selected by Her Majesty accordingly.

CHAPTER VIII
REJECTION AND ACCEPTANCE

Introduction

The announcement in Canada that Ottawa had been selected as the capital of the country was met with a mixture of joy, surprise, anger, and shock. Delight was expressed in Ottawa, but city centred and also sectional jealousies led to resentment being expressed elsewhere when the news was released. A public debate began over whether the Queen's decision was a recommendation or an award.

Ottawans hoped that the Government would make a bold statement decreeing that since the choice had been made the Parliament now must accept it. Instead, at the opening of Parliament on February 25, 1858, there was but a glancing reference to the topic at the end of the Government-written Speech from the Throne: "Correspondence . . . will be laid before you, as well as an answer to your address presented to Her Most Gracious Majesty on the subject of the Seat of Government."[1] Thus hopes for a strong statement on Ottawa's behalf were shattered and Ottawans feared the result. Observers of the scene asked, what was the Macdonald-Cartier Ministry's policy? Was the issue to be regarded as an open one or a party one for members of the Assembly? What would the effect of the Government's nervousness be on some supporters, especially those from Quebec, but also those from Toronto, Kingston, Montreal, and even Ottawa? In fact, the Cabinet could not agree on what to do and the dissension prevented a policy from being developed. Ottawans pressured John A. Macdonald to make the question a Cabinet one, but he could do so only at the expense of splitting his ministry.

Finally, on June 22, 1858, a member of the opposition (who was from Montreal) moved that

> this House has had no opportunity of expressing its opinion as to the selection of Ottawa, and that before any expenditure of moneys be made for Public Buildings at the said City, the Government ought to submit the selection made to the consideration of the Legislature.[2]

In making the motion, the member said that "neither Mr. Labouchere nor the Government here had as yet given the reasons for [the] selection. He purposed of giving them an opportunity of doing so now."[3]

The Speaker ruled that this amendment was out of order but a debate on the seat of government question did take place.

On July 16 the topic was again raised (see selection 190). To the charge that they were disloyal to the Queen, opposition members retorted that they were not challenging any choice made by the Queen but that made by Labouchere and the Imperial Government. Opposition members variously proposed Quebec and Montreal for the capital. The vote on the Dorion motion (no. 190) was regarded as a want-of-confidence motion for the Government. The opposition were sure that the ministry had been caught in a trap, thus they were crushed when the House voted Yeas 45, Nays 63 in support of the ministry. However, the ministry was still in a difficult position, for it was known that the matter would again be dealt with on July 28. That evening's debate was very bitter and when the vote came on the motion against Ottawa (selection 193) it was accepted by a vote of Yeas 64 to Nays 50 (see Figure 17). The opposition, led by George Brown of Toronto, were ecstatic. Brown was quickly on his feet and he declared that the vote against Ottawa really represented "an express declaration on the part of the House of its dissatisfaction with the whole policy of the Government, and he would therefore move a direct want-of-confidence in the Administration."[4] Brown said that if the ministers were willing to accept the test right then, he would move that the House do now adjourn, "with the understanding that all who voted for the adjournment were to be considered as recording their opinions against the Government, and those in favour of non-adjournment as expressing their confidence in the Administration."[5] John A. Macdonald accepted the challenge for the Government. After a noisy discussion and amid high tension, the votes were then cast, with the result being Yeas 50, Nays 61 (see Figure 18). The Government was thus sustained, with men who had voted against Ottawa returning to vote for non-adjournment.

There followed one of the great dramas in Canada's constitutional history, for the Macdonald-Cartier ministry used the "insult to the Queen" as an excuse to resign, thus forcing the Governor General to ask the opposition to form a ministry. Brown, as the recognized leader of the opposition, was asked to form a government and this he elatedly set out to do. He had firm support from his Upper Canadian followers, but he had to work hard to achieve Lower Canadian support. His chief Canada East supporter was A.A. Dorion. Four of their new ministry were identified with Montreal. Indeed, it seems that Brown and Dorion agreed that the seat of government issue should become a cabinet measure to be dealt with after sectional problems within the union had been remedied, and that Montreal would be the place.[6] However, the Brown-Dorion ministry did not have an opportunity to inform the

House of their policies. When Brown presented the names of his cabinet to Sir Edmund on the morning of August 2nd, and they were sworn into office at noon, the ten men were obliged to resign their seats in order to seek re-election. Thus it was that when the House assembled that afternoon, the members of the ministry were absent. On their behalf, a supporter informed members that the new ministry did not yet have a fully defined policy and he asked for the House to be prorogued. He also moved an election writ, whereupon another member moved a non-confidence motion against the new administration. The result was inevitable: Yeas 71, Nays 31. A similar vote of want of confidence was carried in the Legislative Council. The Brown-Dorion cabinet asked Sir Edmund Head to dissolve the Parliament and to call a general election, however, to their surprise and shocked dismay, Head refused to accept this suggestion, so the Brown-Dorion ''two-day ministry'' was forced to resign on August 4th.

On August 6th, a new Cartier-Macdonald ministry was sworn in, just one week after the Macdonald-Cartier ministry had resigned. There were but two changes in membership of the cabinet, although new positions were held. In order to avoid vacating their seats for re-election in the manner followed by Brown and companions, the new ministry all switched portfolios just one day later, thus taking advantage of the law which declared that a minister need not resign if his portfolio was changed within thirty days of appointment! The switching of seats came to be called the ''double shuffle'' and heralded the rise of a major constitutional debate that cannot be developed here.[7]

The Governor General felt personally slighted by the Assembly's rejection of Ottawa. And the Parliament again stood in conflict with itself, since the House had declared that Ottawa ought not to be the permanent seat of government while the Legislative Council had resolved to accept the Queen's choice. Clearly, the new Cartier-Macdonald ministry had to find some means for reconcilling the Legislative Assembly's rejection of Ottawa with the existing law as agreed to in 1857, and also for reconcilling the differences between the two houses.

When Cartier met the Assembly on August 7th, and spoke about the policy of his new government—''the same as was announced in the Speech from the Throne''—he added that

> The Government felt itself bound to carry out the law of the land respecting the Seat of Government, but in the face of the recent vote on that subject, the Administration do not consider themselves warranted in incurring an expenditure for public buildings until Parliament has an opportunity of considering the whole question in all its bearings.[8]

Some people took this statement to mean that the Government had decided to leave the issue an open question, but the truth was that the ministry still simply could not agree on a course of action. Cartier did, however, tie the seat of government question to the possibility of a federation, but the session closed with no further reference to the question.

George Cartier and John A. Macdonald were subject to intense pressure from the Governor General and also representatives from Ottawa as efforts were made to have the ministry agree to make a firm decision in order to reconcile the dilemma. Finally, the members resolved that they would declare their support for the Queen's choice, even if their personal first choices were elsewhere. The reasoning behind the ministers' decision is interesting. The Queen had responded to the solicitation that she use her undoubted prerogative in making a decision, and the Canadian Parliament had passed an act which, by anticipation, adopted *as their own* the decision of the Queen, and appropriated money to carry it out. As Head noted,

> On these grounds, therefore, the Executive Council view the action taken by the Queen, as being, in reality, the action of the Legislative of Canada. They consider that the issue is not between the Government of the colony and that of the mother country, but between the Parliament of Canada and itself.[9]

Clearly, the Governor General was instrumental in guiding the cabinet to its decision. Indeed, Head happily wrote a friend in England to say that he had been able to get his ministers boldly and openly to face the question in the next Speech from the Throne.[10] However, one (Montreal area) member of the ministry refused to accede to the decision, and, when his conditions for remaining a minister were not met, Sicotte resigned.[11]

News of the resignation leaked out and it became clear to the public that the ministry meant to support Ottawa. Accordingly, pressures began to build as the time for the opening of Parliament approached. Great scheming took place as members from one area or another tried to forge plans for either supporting or upsetting the acceptance of the Queen's choice. Part of the plan for support as developed by the ministry was to promise to Quebec members that relocation to Quebec would occur in 1859 and that their city would remain as capital until the necessary buildings in Ottawa were completed.

Once Parliament met, the Legislative Council quickly agreed with the choice of Ottawa, but there was a sharp reaction to the provision in favour of Quebec. In the Assembly, there was a debate which lasted several days and attempts were made to have the members accept

Montreal as capital. However, on February 10, 1859, the ministry managed to squeeze a majority to vote down a motion which was against the Crown's interference and against Ottawa (see Figure 19).
This was the crucial vote. Thus by a majority of only five votes Ottawa was accepted as Canada's capital. In Canada East, 16 members voted contrary to their normal alignments (all but one normally voted with the ministry). In Canada West, outside of the Ottawa district, where differing political alignments were set aside by three opposition members as they voted with the Government, most members voted along "normal" lines. The most interesting cluster of votes was in the Quebec region where eleven members voted with the opposition against Ottawa, while seven others voted with the Government. Significantly, three of the latter seven members represented the City of Quebec, and thus they voted in contradiction to a resolution of their City Council which had directed them to vote against Ottawa. In so voting, these three men recognized that if, as Quebec members, they had voted to reject the act of permanence and award to Ottawa, then the Government would in no way be bound to adhere to the agreement to go to Quebec on a temporary basis.

Beyond the walls of the Parliament there was widespread, but reluctant, acceptance of the fact that Ottawa would be the capital of Canada. The Toronto *Globe* acknowledged simply that "the agony of the Government is over."[11] The *Globe* was correct as far as the House was concerned, for it shortly thereafter agreed in full to the selection of Ottawa and to locate temporarily in Quebec (see Figure 20). However, the members of the Legislative Council remained angered over the Quebec removal and so they voted against passing the supply bill. The bill had to be resubmitted before it was accepted.

A final effort at getting a majority vote against Ottawa was made in the Legislative Assembly in May, 1860, but the effort failed.

Ottawa thus became capital because of two basic ministerial decisions, namely to refer the issue to London and second, following the 1858 rejection, to make the issue a ministerial matter. Since there was little support in the Legislative Assembly for Ottawa on its own terms, and since many men voted for it only because the Government's life was at stake, one can only conclude that Ottawa became capital because of compromise.

Notes

[1]Legislative Assembly, *Journals*, Vol. XVI, February 26, 1858.
[2]*Ibid.*, June 22, 1858, p. 733.
[3](Toronto) *Leader*, June 23, 1858.

4(Toronto) *Leader*, July 29, 1858.

5*Ibid*.

6(Toronto) *Globe*, August 9, 1858.

7See, for example, PAC, MG 27, I, D8. Alexander Galt Papers, Vol. 5, pp. 2118-2125, manuscript by Galt entitled "Double Shuffle, 1858"; Careless, *Brown of the Globe, op.cit.*, pp. 269-280; Creighton, *John A. Macdonald, op. cit.*, p. 265 forward; Kerr, *Sir Edmund Head, op. cit.*, pp. 183-201.

8(Toronto) *Colonist*, August 9, 1858, and (Toronto) *Leader*, August 9, 1858.

9PAC, PRO, CO 42/617, pp. 7-8, Head to Lytton, January 8, 1859.

10Lewis Papers, Head to Lewis, February 12, 1859, cited in Kerr, *op. cit.*, p. 201.

11Sicotte wanted the choice, when fixed, to be confined to some locality (preferably Montreal) within the bounds of Canada East. He agreed with other policies of the ministry, but he felt honourbound to resign over the seat of government question.

Documents

179. (Toronto) *Leader*, January 27, 1858.

Her Majesty the Queen, in compliance with the expressed wishes of the Canadian Legislature, has selected the future capital of United Canada. The City of Ottawa is the favored place. This announcement will probably surprise few persons, since a very general notion—we cannot call it conviction—prevailed that Ottawa would be selected. This supposition arose chiefly from the position which that city occupies in Upper Canada.

To suppose that the choice made by Her Majesty of the future capital of United Canada would not be generally acquiesed in, is to suppose the Legislature and people of Canada the most fickle and unstable legislature and people on the face of the globe. The Queen has done what we asked her to do; neither more nor less. She has settled a question which we were too divided, too selfish, too local in our views and aims to settle for ourselves. We appointed Her Majesty arbiter of our dispute; begged her acceptance of the office, and she has complied with our request. . . .

180. *Ottawa Tribune*, January 30, 1858.

OTTAWA THE SEAT OF GOVERNMENT

. . . Ottawa is now destined to advance with rapid stride on the road to prosperity. Her natural advantages will be brought prominently before the country, and the time is not far distant when she will rank as one of the first rate cities of Canada. This city alone will not reap all the advantages to be derived from this wise selection of Her Majesty's Government, the entire Ottawa country will be a gainer. Real estate will be doubled in value, and all the unoccupied lands will speedily be settled by a sturdy and industrious people.—Hamlets will spring, as if by magic, into villages, villages into towns, and towns into cities. . . . The Ottawa country has long been kept in the background,—always looked upon by both Eastern and Western men as the fag end of Canada, belonging to neither sections, and therefore unworthy of notice. This can be the case no longer. The goddess of fortune has at last deigned to smile upon us benignly. . . . It will be some years, however, before the voices of United Canada will assemble in our midst. The necessary buildings for Legislative accommodation, and that of the Public Offices, must first be built, and this will take little short of four years.—This must cause the expenditure of a 'small pile,' which will be of vast importance. Ottawa has been fortunate in drawing such a noble prize.

181. (Montreal) *Pilot*, January 28, 1858.

That fearfully vexed question of the Seat of Government has at length been fixed, and the Opposition scribes are loud in their denunciations of the decision which has been come to. We confess ourselves to somewhat of regret that Montreal has not been the choice of the Imperial Govt. We cannot help thinking that our good city is the place which should have been chosen; and that it has, in any respect which could be mentioned, advantages superior to any other city or locality in the Province. But the matter having been deliberately referred to the decision of Her Majesty, and that noble lady having accepted the reference and made the award, as loyal, true and honourable citizens, it becomes us to accept the decision and submit to it. Next to Montreal, the City of Ottawa is certainly the best that could have been chosen. . . .

. . . objections would have been found to the Garden of Eden, had it been possible to fix upon that elysium as the metropolis of Canada. And we might have gone on fighting about localities until doomsday had not the happy expedient been hit upon of referring the question to the Queen, as the person most likely to give it a calm, impartial and unbiassed decision. The fiat has now gone forth; the choice has been made with much wisdom; and we congratulate the good folks of Ottawa on its good fortune in being chosen.

182. *Montreal Transcript*, January 28, 1858.

The great battle of the Session will be that of the Seat of Government. . . . There will be, as in former years, a keen struggle for the prize on the part of the respective friends of the various localities . . . and in the conflict of these clashing local interests, there will be manouverings and stratagems, plottings and counterplottings. . . . These considerations of local feeling, of party spirit, and of the respect due to our Gracious Queen, being all gathered around this question, it is impossible to predict what the action of Parliament will be.

183. *Montreal Transcript*, January 28, 1858.

Ottawa is certainly nearer being the seat of Government than ever it was before; but there are two old Proverbs, which do not seem to be altogether inapplicable to the case. One is, that 'near dead never fills the churchyard,' and the other, that 'there's many a slip 'twixt the cup and the lip.'

184. (Ottawa) *Bytown Gazette*, February 4, 1858.

The announcement . . . has caused considerable ferment amongst some of the members of the Provincial press, the more rational and temperate of them, after the display of a little disappointment at the choice not falling on their own pet localities, bowing to destiny and declaring their willingness to have Her Majesty's decision carried out in good faith, whilst the others have declared against this course being pursued, and threaten to make the question still a bone of contention and the source of agitation in Parliament.

185. (Ottawa) *Bytown Gazette*, February 25, 1858.

To those who now raise a howl against Ottawa, it matters not what the real merits of the case are. The City of Ottawa may be the very best, all things considered, for the location of the future capital of the Province, but this with them makes no difference. Nothing is considered of any account but what will enable them to strike an effectual blow at the Ministry.

186. *Hamilton Times*, February 12, 1858.

Right glad are we that the question of the permanent Seat of Government for this country is at last settled, though we confess it has not been settled in accordance with our wishes on the subject. . . . We accept that decision fairly and frankly, and we hope no attempt will be made to disturb it. The country has suffered enough already from the action of sectional jealousies on the question, and now that both branches of the

Legislature have pronounced, no matter on what grounds, that the Royal choice of Ottawa is to be maintained, no true patriot will endeavour again to kindle discussion on the subject.

187. Letter from "An Onlooker" to Editor of (Toronto) *Globe*, February 20, 1858.

. . . Ottawa must not be like Toronto, or Hamilton, or Kingston, or Montreal, raised into importance by the industry and enterprise of their inhabitants; it must be fed with pap from the public kitchen, raised into independence by public money.

188. Resolution passed by the Municipal Council of the City of Ottawa, April 5, 1858 (JLA).

Resolved: This his Worship the Mayor, be and he is hereby authorised to communicate to His Excellency the Governor General, in Council, and to both Houses of Parliament, that in order to aid in carrying out the decision of Her Majesty in favor of Ottawa as the Seat of Government, with the least convenient delay, this Council will furnish the necessary Buildings to accommodate the Legislature and the officers of the Government, until the permanent Government Buildings be erected in this City.

189. Henry Labouchere (Colonial Secretary) to Prince Albert, July 16, 1858 (RA).

Your Royal Highness took so much interest in the question of the future Seat of Government for Canada, that you may like to see the private letter which I have received from Sir Edmund Head about it, and the extracts from Canadian newspapers which accompanied it.

I see no reason to change my opinion that Ottawa is the best choice which could be made. It appears to have been as well received in Canada as could be expected in a Country where local considerations exercise so great an influence, of which Ottawa perhaps a much less share than any of her rivals,—I am, Sir, with great respect Your Royal Highness's most obedient humble servant.

190. Motions by A.A. Dorion, Member for Montreal (West), C.E., in the Legislative Assembly, July 16, 1858.

This House is duly grateful to Her Majesty for complying with the Address . . . this House deeply regrets that the City of Ottawa . . . is not acceptable to a large majority of the Canadian people. (Defeated by 45 Yeas to 63 Nays).

This House humbly prays Her Majesty to reconsider the selection she has been advised to make, and name Montreal as the future Capital of Canada [withdrawn].

191. Richard Scott, member for Ottawa, C.W., speaking in the Legislative Assembly, July 16, 1858.

[The first motion] was a very injurious one, as it was framed to secure the support not only of what might be termed the legitimate Opposition, but of members from various sections who desired the Seat of Government to be fixed in their respective localities, and therefore wished to have the question re-opened.

192. George Cartier, member for Vercheres, C.E., speaking in the Legislative Assembly, July 16, 1858.

Had the Queen been advised to select a commercial centre, Montreal should have been the choice; if a stronghold, Quebec; but if a compromise was wanted between the two Provinces, Ottawa was the place. [Ottawa] was far more a Lower Canada than an Upper Canada city because it was part French. . . . But what was the design of this [Dorion's] motion? Neither more nor less than a censure of her Majesty.

193. Legislative Assembly, July 28, 1858 (JLA).

In the opinion of this House, the City of Ottawa ought not to be the permanent seat of Government of this Province. (Accepted by a vote of Yeas 64, Nays 50; see Figure 17.)

194. Legislative Assembly, July 28, 1858 (JLA).

Motion to adjourn; regarded as a want of confidence motion (see Figure 18).

195. (Toronto) *Globe*, July 29, 1858.

IGNOMINIOUS DEFEAT OF THE GOVERNMENT
MR. LABOUCHERE'S DECISION REVERSED!
OTTAWA NOT TO BE THE CAPITAL

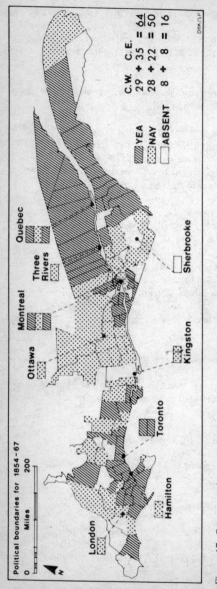

Figure 17. Ottawa ought not to be the permanent seat of government; July 28, 1858. (See selection 193)

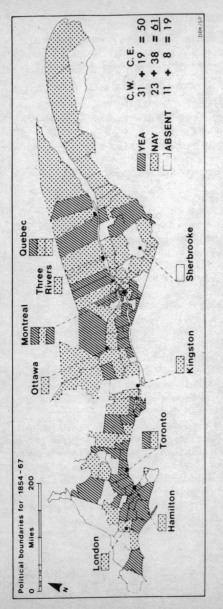

Figure 18. Motion to adjourn; regarded as want-of-confidence motion; July 28, 1858. (See selection 194)

196. *Montreal Transcript*, July 30, 1858.

This vote leaves all the exciting questions connected with that [seat of government] question open, and will revive another cause of dissention which we thought was disposed of for ever.

197. Sir Edmund Head (Governor General) to Sir E. Bulwer Lytton (Colonial Secretary), July 31, 1858 (PAC).

On Friday, the 16th of July, the following proceedings took place in the Legislative Assembly of Canada—

"The order of the day for the House to go again into Committee of Supply being read,

"And the question being put that the Speaker do now leave the Chair;

"Mr. Dorion moved, in amendment, that Mr. Speaker do not leave the Chair, but that it be Resolved:

"That this House is duly grateful to Her Majesty for complying with the Address of Her Canadian Parliament, praying Her Majesty to select a permanent Seat of Government, but that this House deeply regrets that the City which Her Majesty has been advised to select is not acceptable to a large majority of the Canadian people.—Yeas 45, Nays 63."

The proposal of Mr. Dorion was therefore negatived by a majority of 18.

2. I now proceed to give an extract from the votes of the House on Wednesday, July 28:

"Mr. Dunkin moved that it be Resolved,—

"That an Address be presented to Her Majesty to represent that this House humbly prays Her Majesty to re-consider the selection she has been advised to make of a future Capital of Canada, and to name Montreal as such future Capital.

"Mr. Brown moved, in amendment, that an Address be presented to His Excellency the Governor General, praying that no action may be taken towards the erection of Buildings in the City of Ottawa, for the permanent accommodation of the Executive Government and Legislature, or for the removal of the Public Departments of that City.

"Mr. Piché moved, in amendment to the said amendment, that in the opinion of this House the City of Ottawa ought not to be the permanent Seat of Government of this Province.—Yeas 64, Nays 50.

"The question being then put on Mr. Brown's amendment as amended,

"Mr. W.F. Powell moved, in amendment thereto, that in the opinion of this House the City of Quebec ought not to be the permanent Seat of Government of this Province.

"Mr. Brown moved that the House do now adjourn.-Yeas 50, Nays 61.

"The question being then put on Mr. Powell's amendment, and a debate arising.

"Mr. Cimon moved that the debate be adjourned.—Yeas 35, Nays 68.

"Mr. Turcotte moved that the House do now adjourn.—Yeas 95, Nays 5."

3. Thus, notwithstanding the rejection of Mr. Dorion's motion on the 16th, the Legislative Assembly on the 28th asserted that they did not approve of Ottawa as the "permanent" Seat of Government. No proposal has yet been made to embody that assertion in an address or to bring it under my notice in an official shape.

4. On the morning following this division, the two leading Members of the Administration waited on me, and tendered the resignation of themselves and their colleagues. I had no alternative but to accept such resignation, and to send for the most prominent member of the opposition Mr. George Brown, Member for the City of Toronto.

....

6. Mr. Brown has undertaken to form a Government, and he is to wait on me on Monday for the purpose of submitting the names of those whom he would propose to associate with himself.

7. Until some address or some legislative action is taken in consequence of the proceedings of the 28th, it is impossible to say what is the precise meaning of the vote of the Assembly. It may signify that they think Her Most Gracious Majesty has been advised to select the wrong place for the Seat of Government, or it may signify that the Assembly, contrary to the express votes of the two last sessions, would prefer to continue the system of transferring the Seat of Government from one place to another.

8. If the former of the two meanings is the right one, then I presume some other place will be suggested as preferable to Ottawa,—that is to say:—The Parliament, having referred the decision to the Queen, will itself say what that decision ought to be. At any rate until a clew is obtained to the precise wishes of the Assembly by definite action on their part, and until their ultimate acceptance of the New Government shall have been expressed, any advice or recommendation from me would be premature and useless.

9. I cannot however forbear offering the following observations:

I. The address of last session to the Queen was the act of both Houses of the Legislature, not of one.

II. The Act 20 Vic. c. 17, s.2, expressly provides that a sum of £225,000 shall be expended at such place as the Queen may select for the Seat of Government.

That choice, having been made, the section in question has, I apprehend, operated, and as it contains no provision for a change of place, the section itself must be repealed before it could cease to be binding, or before the money could be laid out elsewhere.

III. As regards myself, I desire to express my unfeigned regret for having, in my despatch of March 28, 1857, recommended that Her Majesty should be advised to accept the reference in question. In palliation of so grave an error in judgment, I can only urge that it might have seemed ungracious to refuse a spontaneous reference of this kind, and that it appeared to me impossible to conceive any form in which a Legislature could bind its successors more solemnly, or commit itself in its corporate capacity more conclusively than was done by the Parliament of Canada with reference to the Seat of Government, more especially because their address was coupled with the Legislative provision in the 20 Vic c. 17, referred to above.

10. It would now seem however that my view of the binding character of the action of a Legislature differs essentially from that taken by the majority of the Legislative Assembly of Canada.

My present duty will be to carry out the Government of the Province in such a manner as may best lead to the ultimate settlement of the difficulty without deranging the administration of affairs.

11. So soon as I am able to afford further information on the deliberate opinion of Parliament, and the course they wish to pursue I will communicate again. In the meantime I am ready to act in all ordinary business cordially and frankly with the new Ministry as I have done with their predecessors.

198. John A. Macdonald in a speech made in St. Catherines, C.W., n.d. (PAC).

If there is one thing, gentlemen, that has been trumpeted from one end of the country to the other, it is the course the Government pursued when they resumed office after the disastrous and humiliating defeat of the Two-Days administration. [Hear, hear.] I allude to what has been called the "double shuffle." [Laughter.] . . . Sir, when we resigned over positions in 1858, we had a large majority in Parliament. We were not then driven out because we had lost the confidence of the House; on the contrary, we had a very large working majority; but we, who 'cling to office for the sake of public plunder,' resigned our places at once, rather than see our Queen insulted on the Seat of Government question. We might have retained our position without difficulty, for that very day, half an hour after the vote was taken, I appealed to the House on the question of confidence, which Mr. Brown, with his usual want of judgement, brought up, and when I accepted the vote on the adjournment as one of confidence, a majority of 14 sustained us.

199. *Ottawa Union*, reprinted in (Toronto) *Globe*, August 7, 1858.

To the miserable trucking of the fallen administration* may be attributed to the temporary misfortune which has befallen the country. Time and again have they been called upon to grapple manfully, and as became ministers of the Crown, with this national issue. They had a splendid basis for their operations—an act of Parliament granting them the necessary funds, a vote of the Legislature referring the question to solemn arbitration—the arbitration given, and the legalized decree of the Sovereign in their hands. Why dally with the question? Why keep it dangling between earth and heaven as a tempting bait for interested localities and greedy demagogues? The answer is simple—because ministers were not sincere; they desired to make a shew of obedience to the Sovereign, and regard for the national welfare, while at the same time they endeavoured to provoke outside interference, advance local interests, preserve corrupt parliamentary support, and retain Government patronage, pelf and power. It was their duty to have pushed on the work; and if storms threatened, like men of principle, have stood or fallen with the robe of decency around them, as they pledged themselves to do, by the decision of their Royal Mistress. Their disloyalty and treachery is as marked and as indelible as that of the abused aspirants to their vacant portfolios.

200. (Toronto) *Globe*, August 2, 1858.

The organs of the fallen Government are inclined to harp upon the question which proved the final stumbling block for its feeble steps, and ring the changes upon the "Queen's decision," "an insult to Her Majesty," "an invasion of the prerogative," while they endeavour to take credit to ministers for their devoted loyalty in resigning when the choice of the Crown was reversed. The truth is, that although the Administration received the *coup de grace* on the Seat of Government question, their fate was not decided by it. Had the question not been brought before the House at all, they would still have been compelled to resign office. As Mr. Macdonald himself admitted, the defections from the ranks of their supporters, evidenced by the vote of want of confidence which he himself demanded, proved to the Government that they were lost. Had they continued in office a few days longer, more than one question would have been brought on the *tapis* which would have supplied as effectual a finishing blow as that of the Seat of Government. The reference of the question to the Queen in 1857 was carried in the House of Assembly by a narrow partizan majority, and was not sup-

*(Macdonald-Cartier)

ported by public opinion either in the House or the country. People were induced to support that method of settling the question only by the most positive assurances that the places in which they were interested respectively would be chosen. Quebec was the place, it was said, which the military authorities would choose, Montreal was the commercial centre, Ottawa the compromise between Upper and Lower Canada, and Kingston the British place. Each was to be the favoured spot, according to the assurances of members of the Administration, and but for these assurances, the reference never could have been carried. It was passed however, by a majority of two only, a fact which ought to have induced Mr. Labouchere to decline the responsibility placed upon him. Besides that fact, however, the Colonial Minister was warned by Canadian gentlemen whom he consulted on the subject that his decision would not be final, that it would assuredly be upset if it did not find general approval in Canada.—In spite of all this, Mr. Labouchere proceeded, and we can only account for his doing so, on the supposition that he did not care whether his decision was sustained or not, that he made the choice to please the Canadian Government which pressed the task upon him, and was perfectly willing to submit to any change which might take place.

Since that time a general election has taken place, and the whole policy which referred the matter to the Imperial authorities has been condemned by the people of Canada. It is not the choice made which has been set aside, for the elections were over before the secret was revealed, it was the policy of reference which received the mark of public disapproval. Under such circumstances, is the Legislature not at liberty to declare the result of an appeal to the people? Is it not free to say to the Sovereign, that whereas the last Parliament left to the decision of her Colonial Secretary the Seat of Government question, the present one disapproves of that step, and would prefer to do the work itself? Are the fiats of Colonial Secretaries—of whom we have had three within the last three or four months—like the laws of the Medes and Persians, unalterable? The absurdity of talking of her Majesty's views of the matter, it is not necessary to dwell upon. Neither the Queen, nor, for that matter, her ministers, care one straw about the seat of Canadian Government. Mr. Labouchere undertook a duty pressed upon him by our provincial ministry, whose sole motive was to get rid of a question which affected their fortunes, and if, after a general election, and after other difficulties connected with the matter have approached a solution, a new Ministry and Parliament declare themselves prepared to choose a Seat of Government themselves, we are quite convinced that neither Her Majesty nor her Colonial Secretary (even were Mr. Labouchere himself in office) will have any objection.

As to the language of the resolution which was carried on Wednesday night last, it was not intended for the eyes of Royalty. When the address on the subject is passed it will, we have no doubt, be perfectly satisfactory in its respectful devotion even to the flunkies who are now so indignant against any interference with what they are pleased to call "the Queen's decision."

201. (Toronto) *Leader*, August 9, 1858

After some ten days of ministerial crisis the machinery of Government is again in working order. With the exception of two names, the Macdonald-Cartier Administration have been reinstalled. The new Government naturally takes the policy of the old one, in other words, it adheres to the policy which, in its previous phase, it announced to Parliament at the beginning of the Session. The recent vote of the House, on the subject of the Seat of Government will render it necessary that Parliament should have an opportunity of reconsidering the whole question. The law directs the Government to expend £225,000 on public Buildings, in Ottawa, and there is a resolution of one branch of the Legislature declaring that the law ought not to be carried into effect. Parliament being thus at cross-purposes with itself, on the question, any immediate action by the Government on the subject becomes impossible. Parliament must become consistent with itself; it must find some means of reconcilling its late position, in taking a stand against Ottawa, with the existing law, which authorizes the expenditure of £225,000 on public buildings in Ottawa. We cannot see how the Legislature can give due consideration to the question this Session; if indeed the rules of the House would permit of its being brought up again.

202. Sir E. Bulwer Lytton (Colonial Secretary) to Sir Edmund Head (Governor General), September 10, 1858 (JLA).

In reviewing the history of the Session of the Canadian Parliament now terminated, it is impossible for Her Majesty's Government to avoid expressing their regret that after having deliberately invited the award of Her Majesty on the question of the future Seat of Canadian Government, the Assembly should have thought proper deliberately to reject that award. They are not in possession of the reasons which may have led to so unexpected a decision; but they are too strongly assured of the loyalty of the representatives of the Canadian people, to believe that any individual among the Members who joined in that vote intended a slight to his Sovereign.

203. *Montreal Transcript*, December 28, 1858.

The question of the future course to be adopted with reference to the carrying out of the Queen's choice of Ottawa, it has been whispered during the past week, has been the bone of contention in the Cabinet, and Mr. Sicotte has been represented as firm in the determination that Ottawa must be set aside, and a choice made by the Cabinet Ministry of some place in Lower Canada to enjoy the metropolitan honours. His colleagues, on the other hand, were said to be firm in opposition to anything that would imply a revocation by the Cabinet of her Majesty's decree. This radical difference, it was felt, would be found difficult of solution. Still, so many dissensions have sprung up amongst our statesmen of late years, and been either plastered up or reconciled in other ways, that little attention was given to the reports of a probable break-up of the entirety of the present Administration. It therefore took people by surprise when they learned yesterday that Mr. Sicotte had actually resigned his seat in the Cabinet, and on the very question which, according to public rumor, was the actual stumbling block. . . .

The reference to the Queen of the Seat of Government question has from the first been viewed with public disfavour; and if the Ministry thought to relieve themselves from difficulty by it they have been egregiously mistaken. It has been, and promises to be, a never-ending theme of discontent, breaking down or rendering unpopular every one who sustained it. . . .

204. *Montreal Transcript*, December 31, 1858.

The Seat of Government has again . . . given rise to a ministerial crisis [with the resignation from the Executive Council of Sicotte who favored Montreal], and it certainly is to be deplored, that such an element of disunion and discord should exist among public men, and the political parties of this country. So long as the Seat of Government remains an unsettled question, the country will be exposed to constantly recurring divisions and disruptions in cabinets and political parties.

205. Sir Edmund Head (Governor General) to Sir E. Bulwer Lytton (Colonial Secretary), January 8, 1859 (PAC)

I have the honor to inform you that the Hon.able Mr. Sicotte has tendered to me, through Mr. Cartier, the resignation of his seat in the Executive Council, and of his office as Chief Commissioner of Public Works, which I have accepted.

Mr. Sicotte resigns because he differs from his colleagues on the policy which it is their duty to pursue with reference to the question of the seat of Government.

It is therefore necessary that I should state what I now understand that policy to be. . . . the members of the Canadian Government, as at present constituted, believe that it would be an entire misapprehension of the real state of the question of the seat of Government to represent the issue as being one between the Legislature of Canada and the Government of the Queen.

According to this view, it has no analogy whatever to those differences which formerly, from time to time, arose between the Colonial Secretary and the Government of the Colony. They know that no interference of any kind was thrust upon the Canadian Government by the advisers of Her Most Gracious Majesty in England.

The Canadian Parliament, after more than one resolution to adopt a fixed seat of Government, apparently found themselves unable to select any one place for that purpose, and in the most solemn manner they solicited Her Majesty to exercise Her undoubted prerogative in making such solution—thereby acknowledging expressly Her Majesty's constitutional power to take such a step, whilst they asked for its discretionary exercise. They passed, moreover, an act which by anticipation adopted as their own the decision of the Queen, and appropriated money for carrying it out. This act remains unrepealed.

On these ground, therefore, the Executive Council view the action taken by the Queen, as being, in reality, the action of the Legislative of Canada. They consider that the issue is not between the Government of the colony and that of the mother country, but between the Parliament of Canada and itself. They think it essential that the Parliament of Canada should show respect for laws yet unrepealed which it has itself enacted, and should adhere in honour and good faith to a course of action deliberately adopted, and to pledges solemnly given.

Such, Sir, I understand to be the principles in the maintenance of which Mr. Sicotte does not entirely concur with his colleagues, and he has accordingly resigned office.

206. *Journal de Quebec*, reprinted in (Toronto) *Leader*, January 8, 1859.

Nothing . . . not even fifty general elections, held one after the other, would make Lower Canada, and especially the District of Quebec, renounce the hope of possessing the Seat of Government. . . .

207. (Toronto) *Globe*, January 20, 1859

The [Toronto] *Colonist* copies from the Montreal *Commercial Advertizer*——being ashamed, we presume, to give such an absurd story on its own authority——a statement that it was the Queen herself, and nobody but the Queen, who made choice of Ottawa for the Seat of Government. The thing would be a good joke, if it were not intended to deceive some innocent people. Every well-informed person knows that all such matters are decided by the advice of responsible ministers, but we dare say that there are some people ignorant enough to believe that Her Majesty put on the Crown of State and the Royal robes, and, looking over a map of Canada, laid her finger on Ottawa and declared that there the Canadian Parliament should meet, and nowhere else. One thing is certain, that neither the Queen nor ministers will contradict this story, announced by the veracious editor of the Montreal *Commercial Advertizer* and we have no doubt that ministers will use it freely.

208. (Toronto) *Leader*, January 28, 1859

[Did] the Queen [select] Ottawa simply as an arbitress or in the exercise of the Royal prerogative[?] Nominally, the selection of the place at which the Queen, through Her Representative in the Province, will convoke the Chambers is a matter of prerogative. In strict right, it belongs to Her Majesty by an exercise of the royal prerogative to decide what Canadian city shall be the Seat of Government. But this had long since been numbered with the dormant or disused prerogatives. Over and over again, the Provincial Parliaments had exercised the power of determining where the Seat of Government should be. In 1843, the Legislature decided to leave Kingston, and fix the Seat of Government at Montreal. In 1849, one branch of the Legislature advised the Executive to take the Seat of Government from Montreal and on many subsequent occasions, the Legislature has treated the question as one entirely at its disposal. In remitting the decision of the question to the Queen in 1857, the Legislature has treated the question as one entirely at its disposal. In remitting the decision of the question to the Queen in 1857, the Legislature only asked Her Majesty to step in as arbiter and settle what local disputes, prejudices, and interests rendered impossible to settle in this country, The Queen, it is clear, acted the part of an arbiter, and did not undertake the settlement of the question by an exercise of the Royal prerogative. . . . The Queen in selecting Ottawa did so simply as an arbiter acting on reference.

209. (Toronto) *Leader*, February 1, 1859.

Anyone who has watched, with ordinary attention, the late movements in regard to the Seat of Government question, must have observed that almost the entire opposition, to the Queen's decision is in the interest of Montreal. . . . As the question stands at this moment, it is Montreal against every other place, including Ottawa, in the country.

The object of the attempt to set aside the Queen's award is to make Montreal the capital. . . .

The question, which is at this moment paramount to all others, is viewed in very different lights by different people. There is a class of men who will not consent to argue whether or not they should keep their ward; whether it is allowable to cater to a solemn engagement and then repudiate it. This class of persons value their own honor higher than any other earthly possession. Another class of persons look at the question solely as one of local interest. The expenditure occassioned by the Government they believe beneficial to any place where it may happen to be; and that consideration with them is paramount. If they live in the district of Quebec, they will listen to nothing but that Quebec should be the permanent Seat of Government; if they live in Montreal, they advocate that city, on the same grounds. It is the same if they live in any other place. Another class are only anxious to use the question for political purposes. If they can so manipulate the question as to defeat the ministry, a great point would, in their estimation, be gained. But this is not the only advantage. An Upper Canada politician by agreeing to give his influence in favor of Montreal, may obtain allies from the city and district interested in the success of such a scheme.

210. Extract from Speech from the Throne at opening of Parliament by Sir Edmund Head (Governor General), January 29, 1859 (JLA).

It is my duty, on the present occasion, to call your attention to the question of the Seat of Government of Canada.

The Legislature of Canada, having resolved that a fixed Seat of Government should be selected, solicited our Gracious Queen, by an Address of either House, to exercise her prerogative in making such selection.

An Act, moreover, was passed, adopting beforehand the decision of Her Majesty, and appropriating the necessary funds.

This Act of the Canadian Parliament and the decision of the Queen are binding on the Executive Government of the Province, and it will be their duty to carry out the understanding which existed at the time when the reference was made, by which the Government will be transferred to Quebec for a fixed period, until the necessary arrangements shall have been completed.

The Correspondence with Her Majesty's Government will be laid before you, and I cannot doubt that you will recognize a selection made by Her Majesty at your own request, and that you will duly acknowledge Her gracious compliance with the Addresses which you yourselves caused to be presented to Her.

211. Legislative Council, February 2, 1859 (JLC).

Resolved: That this House cannot perceive that the transfer of the Seat of Government to Quebec, for a fixed period, until the completion of the necessary buildings at Ottawa, is involved in the duty which devolves upon the Executive of carrying out the Queen's decision—or that any such arrangements has ever been recognized by any resolution of the Legislature; and this House deprecates the expenditure attending a double removal of the Seat of Government after the Queen's selection of a fixed site has been promulgated (accepted by 24 Yeas, 14 Nays).

212. Sir Edmund Head (Governor General) to Sir E. Bulwer Lytton (Colonial Secretary), February 4, 1859 (PAC).

I have the honour to enclose a copy of the speech from the Throne with which I opened the Session of Parliament on the 29th ultimo.

2. I also enclose a copy of the address from the Legislative Council in answer to the Speech which has this day been presented to me.

3. You will see that the Legislative Council explicitly recognize, as they have already done, the Queen's selection of Ottawa—they dissent, however, from the avowed intention of my present ministers to transfer the Government to Quebec for a certain fixed period according to what it was thought was understood at the time of the reference. This latter question is one entirely of expediency, and is in no way involved in, or connected with the decision made by Her Most Gracious Majesty.

4. The address from the Lower House is still under discussion.

....

6. This amendment is of a general and abstract character, but as it will, (if carried) remove from the address the immediate recognition of Her Majesty's solution of the seat of Government, it would in fact place the Legislative Council and the Assembly at direct issue with each other on this very important subject.

213. (Toronto) *Leader*, February 3, 1859

. . . This is an unequivocal defeat of the Government, but it cannot be regarded as of serious, much less fatal, import. We have only to go back ten years to find a removal of the Government from Montreal, in opposition to the expressed opinions of the Legislative Council, and what has happened once may happen again. Since the Government cannot go to Quebec with the consent of the Second Chamber, it is within the range of possibility that it may go there without that consent.

214. (Montreal) *Pilot*, February 4, 1859.

The question one is asked at every street corner here, is, Will the Ministry have a majority on the Seat of Government question? The answer is generally in accordance with the wishes of the person asked. . . . The members of the District of Quebec have the decision in their hands, and if they do not sacrifice the interests of their constituents to their own ends, there can be no doubt of the course they will pursue. In the first place, they are given the Seat of Government for four years, with all that the 'chapter of accidents' may bring forth in those years; in the second place, if the Ministerial proposal in favor of Ottawa be voted down, Montreal must win the coveted prize, and Quebec may whistle for metropolitan honours for ever and a day, federation or no federation of the Provinces.

215. Richard Scott, member for Ottawa, speaking in the Legislative Assembly, February 1, 1859.

Every member must admit that, from the way the debate had been carried on, one would think that the question was not, if Ottawa should be selected as the Seat of Government, but whether the present Premier was to remain in office or not. . . .

The selection of a capital ought not to be made subservient to the upholding or upsetting of any Government, and he called upon the members to give a vote which they could in future years reconcile to their consciences, their God, and their country. It appeared to him that they had but one duty to discharge, and that was to carry out the Queen's decision.

216. Legislative Assembly, February 10, 1859 (JLA).

Question: That we shall give our earnest attention to the question of the Seat of Government of Canada.

Moved in amendment: that all the words after "That" to the end thereof, be left out, in order to insert the words, "the fundamental principle of the representative system, and one of the most important advantages resulting from it, is the right of the majority to have their views and opinions prevail in the Administration of the country; and it is the duty of this House to repel any attempt which might endanger a principle which for centuries has preserved, in a wise measure of progress, the franchises and liberties of England." That, in declaring, on the 28th July last, "that in the opinion of this House the City of Ottawa ought not to be the permanent Seat of Government of this Province," this House, without intending any want of respect to the

Sovereign, expressed its views and opinions on the subject of the Seat of Government in the ordinary and constitutional exercise of its privileges," instead thereof.

And the Question being put on the Amendment to the original Question, the House divided: Yeas 59, Nays 64 (See Figure 19).

Then, the Question being put on the second paragraph [that is, the motion above which was to form part of the House's reply to the Speech from the Throne]; the House divided; and it was resolved in the Affirmative.

217. (Montreal) *Pilot*, February 15, 1859 [regarding division on February 10, 1859; Figure 19].

Two minutes must elapse after the ringing of the peal before the vote can be taken—they seem to all an age. The seats begin to change their look—well-known forms rush in to occupy them. From the gallery, we see the crowd of heads more closely packed than we ever noticed them before. Ah, Scott, of Ottawa, well may you nervously twitch your fingers, and look in fifty places for that division-list you put there not a moment since. Calm and unruffled though you try to look, you cannot deceive a close observer! Powell, of Carleton, thin and pale as death, wrapped in his furs, walks in upright; but we see how great an effort it is for the sick man as he sinks down into his chair. . . . Silent as the ice-covered Bay outside, are all the members. With one impulse, yet without noise, the Opposition rise as Mr. Speaker invites the ayes to the amendment to declare themselves. . . . The numbers increase; fifty-seven, *fifty-eight*, FIFTY-NINE! . . . . How will the tide of battle turn? For whom will be the victory? The Honorable Attorneys General Cartier and Macdonald lead the van. There are a few "hear, hears" when Dubord votes, a few when Holmes is found all right. But the anxiety becomes too great to cheer as we count sixty, sixty-one, sixty-two. Now we are safe. . . . Yeas 59; Nays 64—says the clerk. The Ottawa men shout hurrah! Scott goes into extacies of joy for once. A burst of cheering follows. . . .

218. A.T. Galt (member of the Cartier-Macdonald Ministry), to B. Pomroy, February [11], 1859 (PAC).

We got a vote on the Seat of Government last night, and had a majority of 5—rather too close to be pleasant—but it affords no indication of the strength of the Ministry on other question.

219. Sir Edmund Head (Governor General) to Herman Merivale (Colonial Office), (private), February 12, 1859 (PAC).

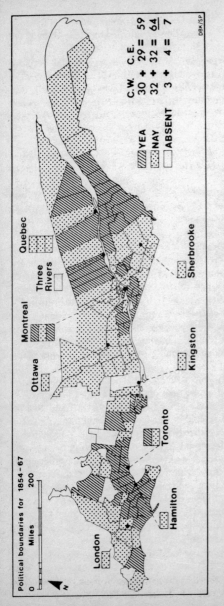

Political boundaries for 1854 - 67

0   Miles   200

London
Hamilton
Toronto
Kingston
Ottawa
Montreal
Three Rivers
Quebec
Sherbrooke

	C.W.	C.E.	
YEA	30 +	29 =	59
NAY	32 +	32 =	64
ABSENT	3 +	4 =	7

DBK/SP

Figure 19. Against Crown's interference and against Ottawa; February 10, 1859. (See selection 216)

I cannot send you the result of our debate on the address by this mail because it is not yet over—The Ministry defeated Sicotte's amendment by a majority of five and last night they put aside another proposed change—It is now *extremely probable* (though by no means certain) that the recognition of the Queen's decision and the virtual reversal of the vote of last session about Ottawa will succeed completely.

Cartier deserves great credit: he has parried great abuse and odium from his Civil Supporters most manfully.

The whole matter of Brown's Government has been debated over and over again and I am none the worse for what has passed. . . .

If the vote on the seat of Government goes right I am quite satisfied, and whether I stay the remainder of the session or not will be immaterial—I care only for this. . . .

If the Government were to be defeated tomorrow I could never form another Cabinet without Mr. Brown—but I think the chances are greatly in Cartier's favour.

220. Extract from Address to Sir Edmund Head (Governor General) from the Legislative Assembly in Reply to Speech from the Throne, February 14, 1859. [Third paragraph was accepted by Yeas 59, Nays 47; see Figure 20]

May it please Your Excellency,

We, Her Majesty's dutiful and loyal subjects, the Commons of Canada in Parliament assembled, humbly thank Your Excellency for your Gracious Speech at the opening of the present Session of the Provincial Parliament.

Your Excellency may rest assured that we shall give our earnest attention to the question of the Seat of Government of Canada.

The Legislature of Canada having resolved that a fixed Seat of Government should be selected, and having solicited our Gracious Queen, by an Address of either House, to exercise Her prerogative in making such selection,—and an Act, moreover, having been passed adopting beforehand the decision of Her Majesty, and appropriating the necessary funds,—We agree with Your Excellency that the Act of the Canadian Parliament and the decision of the Queen are binding on the Executive Government of the Province, and that it will be their duty to carry out the understanding which existed at the time when the reference was made, by which the Government will be transferred to Quebec for a fixed period, until the necessary arrangements shall have been completed.

Any Correspondence with Her Majesty's Government which Your Excellency may be pleased to lay before us will receive our most respectful consideration; We are prepared to recognize the selection

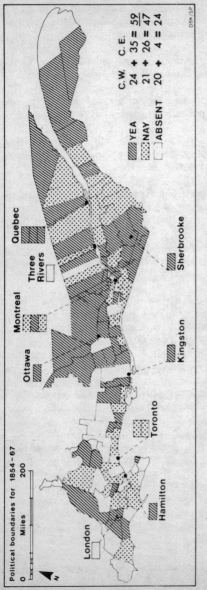

Figure 20. Agree with Queen's choice and to locate temporarily in Quebec; February 14, 1859. (See selection 220)

made by Her Majesty at our own request; and we shall not fail duly to acknowledge Her gracious compliance with the Address which we ourselves caused to be presented to Her.

221. Sir Edmund Head (Governor General) to Sir E. Bulwer Lytton
      (Colonial Secretary), February 15, 1859 (PAC).

I have the honour to enclose a copy of the Address in reply to the Speech from the Throne presented to me this day by the Legislative Assembly of Canada.

You will see that the . . . Address recognize[s] fully and completely the selection of the Seat of Government made by Her Most Gracious Majesty as communicated in Mr. Labouchere's Despatch of the 31st December, 1857.

The several votes on Montreal go far to show that it would be very difficult to ensure the settlement of the question by the selection of any one place by the voice of the majority of the Legislative Assembly of Canada.

222. Sir Edmund Head (Governor General) to Sir E. Bulwer Lytton
      (Colonial Secretary), March 19, 1859 (PAC).

. . . . The vote by which the address from the Legislature in answer to the speech from the throne was carried was, as you will see by reference to my despatch of February 15, a small one. The majority, such as it was, in support of the selection of Ottawa was obtained only by a combination of interests of a peculiar kind. All the Quebec members would, on local grounds, have been unwilling to reverse the adverse vote of last Session, had not the ministers at the same time professed to adhere to the understanding that the Government would be transferred to Quebec for the interval which must elapse before buildings can be erected, and arrangements made, at Ottawa.

223. Sir E. Bulwer Lytton (Colonial Secretary) to Sir Edmund Head
      (Governor General), March 17, 1859 (PAC).

I have to acknowledge your Despatch of the 15th ultimo, enclosing a copy of the Address of the Legislative Assembly in reply to the Speech from the Throne. That Address, as you observe, recognises the selection of the Seat of Government made by Her Majesty in compliance with the former reference of the question to Her decision by the Province.

I must refer you to my Despatch of the 10th September last on the subject, in which, while expressing the regret felt by Her Majesty's

Government at the rejection of that decision by the Assembly, I assured you that they were persuaded that no slight was intended to Her Majesty or Her Majesty's decision by any individual who joined that vote. As on that occasion, so on the present, they are convinced that the welfare of the Province has been, as it ought to be, the object aimed at through much difference of opinion in the course of these proceedings. But I must nevertheless express their satisfaction that the ultimate judgement of the Assembly has been in accordance with those views which first prompted the submission of the question to Her Majesty.

224. (Kingston) *British Whig*, February 17, 1859.

The question of the Seat of Government is now happily settled, so far as the present House of Assembly can settle any question. . . . an immense country, hithertoo neglected by emigrants . . . will now become properly settled. We allude particularly to the counties of Lanark and Renfrew, and the newly surveyed townships, . . . To say nothing of the immense valley of the Ottawa, and the hithertoo partly neglected townships lying between Kingston and Ottawa. These fertile though now waste lands will, in the course of a few years following upon Ottawa's being established as the Seat of Government, be densely filled with an industrious population, and Kingston, being their outlet to the United States and as well, as to the more western parts of Canada, must reap the benefit of their productiveness.

225. *Montreal Transcript*, February 19, 1859

In the Legislative Council last night, in reply to De Blaquiere's enquiry, whether the Government intended, in defiance of the vote of the [Legislative] Council, to carry the Seat of Government to Quebec, Mr. Vankoughnet replied, that no decision had yet been arrived at by the Executive. We are pleased to see that the Government are hesitating, and we sincerely hope that the country may be saved this unnecessary expenditure of half a million of dollars. The whole Province is raising a cry for retrenchment, and, if this half million is thrown away, there will be wide-spread discontent. No paltry savings, effected by the dismissal of a few clerks and the paring down of the salaries of those who remain, will appease the popular clamour, if Quebec is paid its enormous bribe out of the public chest.

226. Expenses Connected With The Several Removals of the Seat of Government, 1849-1858 (JLA).

	1849	1850	1851	1852	1853	1854	1855	1856	1857	1858	Total
	£. s. d.	£. s. d.	£. s. d.	£. s. d.	£. s. d.	£. s. d.	£. s. d.	£. s. d.	£. s. d.	£. s. d.	£. s. d.
Actual Expense of Removal, &c	6188. 2. 0	—	8965. 9.11	282.10. 0	—	—	18164.15.10	7674. 5. 1	807. 6. 5	67. 7. 6	42149.16. 9
Allowances to Clerks and others, in consequence of Removal	—	—	—	130. 4. 2	—	—	—	—	7289. 6. 2	193.11. 8	7613. 2. 0
Rents, Repairs, &c., &c.. To Public Buildings at the existing Seat of Government	3900.18. 2	19747.16. 0	1928.19. 5	38643.15. 8	10584. 6. 0	27548. 7. 9	37012.10.10	35193.12.11	15235.12. 2	7486. 2. 8	197282. 1. 7
Rents, Repairs, &c.. &c.. To Public Buildings elsewhere than at the existing Seat of Government	2258.19. 3	3417. 1. 8	20169.14. 7	1302.16.11	1118. 9. 7	6853.12.11	4461. 3. 2	5354. 1. 4	4301.15. 8	1824. 8. 1	51062. 3. 2
Total	£12347.19. 5	23164.17. 8	31064. 3.11	40359. 6. 9	11702.15. 7	34402. 0. 8	59638. 9.10	48221.19. 4	27634. 0. 5	9571. 9.11	298107. 3. 6

227. (Toronto) *Globe*, April 30, 1859.

THE MINISTRY DEFEATED IN THE UPPER HOUSE THE SUPPLIES THROWN OUT!

This morning at one o'clock the Government received the fitting penalty of their reckless extravagance, their perfidy, and their disregard of the feelings of the people of Upper Canada. The Supply Bill was thrown out by the Legislative Council, by a vote of 23 to 20, after the Government had used the most extraordinary exertions to overcome the adverse majority. . . .

Hon. Mr. Vankoughnet having moved the second reading of the Supply Bill, Mr. DeBlaquiere moved an amendment refusing to go into supply unless the Government pledged themselves to spend no money on the removal to Quebec, without the sanction of Parliament. . . . Mr. Allan, who seconded the resolution, stated his reason for so doing, in a clear, precise way, capable of no misconstruction, and with irrisistible force of argument. The removal of the Government to Quebec was a part of the system of bribes or equivalents which was demoralising our public affairs, as an act of extravagance in the present state of the finances, and was an insult to the Council.

228. (Toronto) *Globe*, May 3, 1859.

The machinery of government is at a standstill. The Legislative Council, having thrown out the Supplies, has checkmated the move of the ministry, and created a crisis which the boldest partizan cannot afford to despise. It is the Council backed by the people, *versus* the Assembly, driven by Mr. Cartier and his whip. The antagonism is not accidental, or on an immaterial issue. It has been forseen from the commencement of the session, and is the natural result of the attempt to subject both branches of the Legislature to the caprice of the present ministers. And the issue is vitally important. A government can outlive the defeat of an ordinary bill; but a stoppage of the Supplies cannot be disregarded; impeding as it does Executive action, and implying in the most marked manner a want of confidence in Executive integrity.

. . . . Aware that in a fair contest they would be again defeated— aware that a majority of the Council, being averse to the removal to Quebec, will not consent to any proceeding calculated to give to the Executive command over the Supplies—ministers intend to muster their forces secretly, and then, without notice, and in an unexpected moment, to bring up again the bill of Supply and push it through without further debate. The manoeuvre is almost too base to obtain credence.

229. (Toronto) *Globe*, May 4, 1859.

THE SUPPLIES ARE FORCED THROUGH
THE COUNCIL

It was as we stated yesterday morning, Ministers set all their agencies to work—bribery, persuasion, intimidation—and yesterday, four days after the refusal of the supplies, they were prepared to force the Council to stultify its action of Friday night. Three members of the Opposition who were present on Friday returned to their homes on Saturday, not thinking of a re-consideration, and were not able to return. . . . The Government brought up three Lower Canadians, and Colonel Prince rose from his bed to serve his masters in their time of trial. This gave the ministry a majority of four, the vote being 24 to 20.

The result might have been different, but for the attitude assumed by Mr. Vankoughnet, in moving the second reading of the bill. He said that it did not matter to the ministry what the Council did; they might do just what they pleased; the Government would go to Quebec this year, and Parliament would meet there next session. If the Council refused the supplies, the Government would at once stop all public business, Parliament would be prorogued, and the removal commenced. This threat was not, of course, resorted to without the consent of the Head of the Government.

230. Extract from Speech by Sir Edmund Head (Governor General) when proroguing Parliament, May 4, 1859 (JLA).

The answer of Her Majesty's Secretary of State to my despatch, announcing the final settlement of the question of our Seat of Government, has been placed in your hands. You will see that such answer expresses satisfaction on learning your ultimate judgment on this long-agitated matter—consistent as such judgment is with the honor and good faith of the Provincial Legislature. [Refer to selection 223]

231. (Toronto) *Leader*, May 24, 1859.

House rent, it is true, never reached the exorbitant figure in Quebec that it did in Toronto, on the return of the Government. But everywhere the same result substantially is produced. The increased demand for any particular thing naturally increases the price; but in these cases something like the impositions proverbially put upon travellers are practiced upon the helpless officials. Houses form precisely that description of commodity which does not respond readily to the demand. If ten thousand extra barrels of flour are required, they can be imported in a few days; but houses cannot come into existence upon short notice, and they constitute altogether another species of property. In the one case, there is a temporary investment; in the other a permanent one. And who will enter into a permanent investment for the accommodation of a passing population: a population that is here today and off again in four years? The results of these official migrations are inevitably to create considerable social perturbation. They put things out of joint; and as soon as they have been set right, another move upsets everything again. There is no help for it, but in that changed system which Parliament, with the consent of the Crown, has decreed. If ever the Government can get settled down permanently in some one place, the evil will be cured. But, at the very moment when we are told everything is to settle down into a position of permanency, we are threatened on the one hand with a dissolution of a Union, and on the other with a Federation of all the Provinces of British North America. . . .

232.   Sir Edmund Head (Governor General) to Duke of Newcastle (Colonial Secretary), August 29, 1859 (PAC).

I have the honor to inform you that as the various public Departments are about to be transferred to Quebec my address after the receipt of this Despatch will be in that City.

233.   (Toronto) *Leader*, September 14, 1859.

Today, His Excellency the Governor General, his family and staff leave Toronto for Quebec, the ancient as well as the present capital of Canada. Two or three ministers may remain a few days longer; and perhaps a stray member of the Government may not depart till the end of the month. But with the departure of the Governor General Toronto ceases to be the capital of the Province, and Quebec rises to the importance which that position is capable of conferring upon it.

234.   *Ottawa Citizen*, November 4, 1859 [from the Quebec Correspondent of the *Citizen*.]

The ancient as well as the present capital of the Canadas is dull— very dull indeed at the present moment. . . . Were it not for the number of Government employees I meet at every step I take in our narrow, dirty thoroughfares—I would fain make myself believe that the establishment of legal authority was not in Quebec at all. What good it will do daring its stay remains to be seen. . . .

Very many people are still under the impression that Ottawa will never become the Seat of Government. What folly to believe in any such thing. What a delusion! As sure as the Government left Toronto to come to this city—as sure will it depart from the ancient capital for Ottawa.

235. *Ottawa Citizen*, May 12, 1860.

THE SEAT OF GOVERNMENT QUESTION BEFORE THE HOUSE!
OTTAWA STILL THE FAVORED LOCALITY
Her Opponents in a Minority of Sixty-Four!

The telegraphic report of Wednesday night's [May 9, 1860] proceedings in the House of Assembly . . . shows the complete failure of the long threatened attempt to cheat Ottawa out of becoming the Seat of Government for United Canada. On this question it was reserved for its introducer, Mr. Piché, and his followers, to suffer a most inglorious defeat, they being in a minority of *sixty-four*! This miserable failure to upset the Queen's decision and the people's choice, must have the effect of convincing Mr. Piché, and those who supported him in his unsuccessful effort, that they cannot find a respectable minority in the present House to wink at even a disguised attempt to treat with disrespect the expressed wish of our Sovereign. After Mr. Piché's poor success we dare say few can be found to broach the subject again. So we may now consider the matter finally settled.

CHAPTER IX
THE LATER YEARS

Four government buildings were to be constructed in Ottawa at a cost of no more than £225,000 (about one million dollars): the Parliament Building, two departmental buildings, and a residence for the Governor General. Despite having less than three months to develop plans, eighteen different architects submitted thirty-three separate designs, sixteen of which were for the Parliament Building. The design selected for the latter building was Gothic, being submitted by a newly arrived Englishman who obviously was influenced by the style of the recently completed (1852) Houses of Parliament in London. Anthony Trollope visited Ottawa in 1861 and later commented: "The glory of Ottawa will be—and, indeed, already is—the set of public buildings which is now being erected on the rock which guards, as it were, the town from the river. . . . I know of no modern Gothic purer of its kind, or less sullied with fictitious ornamentation. . . . I know no site for such a set of buildings so happy as regards both beauty and grandeur."[1]

When Trollope visited Ottawa, he visited a site of discord. The relative happiness in Government over the laying of the corner stone for the new Parliament Building by the Prince of Wales on September 1, 1860, was shortlived, for it soon became evident that something was wrong. Mismanagement and over-expenditures became the order of the day.[2] For instance, the original plans omitted heating and ventilating arrangements, so these had to be added, at great expense because of the extra digging; no preliminary examinations of the Barrack's Hill site had been made, so that it was not realized the costly rock excavations were needed; and the design selected for the Parliament Building was too grand and costly for the $300,000 appropriation. Indeed, by the end of 1860, over $423,000 had been paid to the contractors, and the buildings were not then above ground. By September, 1861, all of the appropriations were exhausted and so the work was halted. In 1862 a royal commission was appointed to examine the situation. New contracts were signed in April 1863 and work was resumed. However, even by July 1, 1867, when Confederation came into being, the library, the main tower roof, and the surrounding roads and gardens were still incomplete. Once the buildings were complete, the Ottawa landscape was completely dominated by the grand new structures. The impact of the Government's decision was not only felt on the landscape, for approximately 1600 workmen were employed in the construction of the buildings and these men supported perhaps 5,000 people in Ottawa, the town itself having doubled its population by 1861 to 14,669. In total, by the time the buildings were completed, they cost nearly $2,600,000. It was largely because of this tremendous cost that the delegates to the conference at which the concept of Confederation was accepted reluctantly agreed to make Ottawa the federal capital.

In 1864, the delegates from the various provinces toured the future confederation. They were welcomed in Ottawa on October 31st by an immense torchlight procession. Next day the delegates were shown over the new buildings and they "warmly expressed their admiration at the exterior design and construction of the edifices, and what promised to be the splendor of the interior arrangements."[3]

Ottawa, as seat of government for the proposed federation, represented a compromise for Maritimers. The principal non-Canadian to agree to Ottawa was Dr. Charles Tupper of Nova Scotia. Some men were openly against such a compromise, however, including another Maritimer, anti-confederation politican Joseph Howe, who sought continued ties with England. He later said that there was no need to seek a capital

> in the backwoods of Canada and [that we] may be pardoned if we prefer London under the dominion of John Bull to Ottawa under the dominion of Jack Frost.[4]

But if there needed to be a capital for the new federation, then, Howe asked, "Is Halifax . . . so poor an outlook for an orator?"[5] The Maritime newspapers which gave print to their thoughts generally favored Quebec for the federal capital.

Resentment continued to be expressed in the Province of Canada over the expense of buildings in an obscure town, but other realities partially distracted the thrust of concern and continued jealousies. Notably, the rupture between the north and south in the United States, and the distinct possibility of a northern movement by United States troops and fear of annexation introduced dangerous tensions into Canadian life. And in later years, during the Fenian threats, specific plans were discovered for blowing up the new Parliament Buildings.[6] These plans were not acted upon, nor were they ever made public, but Canadians felt that Ottawa could be defended even by "a single Company of Artillery" because of its distance from the United States border.[7]

Newcomers to Ottawa seem mostly to have been very favorably

impressed by the buildings under construction. For instance, George Brown told his wife that "the buildings are really magnificent. . . . They grow upon you very much."[8] However, the Governor General Viscount Monck while agreeing that the buildings were "magnificent," declared to George Brown that "every day I spend here impresses me in the conviction that it would be impossible to select a worse place than this for the seat of government."[9] Many others agreed with Monck. For example, politicians who arrived for the first session of the Legislature in 1866 were not favorably impressed and there was "an almost unanimous desire . . . to get away from [Ottawa] as soon as practicable."[10] Soon after the legislature first met, George Brown himself observed that

> everyone is quite disatisfied with the new Buildings. You cannot hear what the speakers say and it is very unpleasant to speak. The whole thing is a superlative piece of folly—and hardly a man can be found here who is not already [of the opinion] to remove the Govt. to Montreal.[11]

Civil servants, about 350 of whom had been relocated to Ottawa in 1865-1866, were distressed by living conditions in Ottawa and clearly desired a return to favored Quebec.[12] After questioning the new arrivals to Ottawa a reporter wrote that

> The society of the Old Capital, or even Toronto, is, in their estimation, far superior to that they meet with in the "forest city." Houses are not to be found at moderate rents, living [costs are] higher, and even the public buildings for comfort and convenience are inferior, in their opinion, to those in Quebec.[13]

But, because of a Governor General's choice, the acceptance of it in London, and compromise forced by the support of a Ministry more concerned for its own continued existence than for a particular place, Ottawa had become the seat of government for the Province of Canada. And, because financial necessity forced further unhappy compromises, Ottawa remained as capital of the Dominion of Canada. The British North America Act (Canada's constitution) states that "until the Queen otherwise directs, the seat of Government shall be Ottawa."[14]

Notes

[1]Anthony Trollope *North America* (London: Chapman and Hall, 1862), Vol. I, pp. 104-106.

[2]The remainder of the paragraph is based on the following: Province of Canada, *Sessional Papers* (No. 57) 1860, (No. 4) 1861, (No. 3) 1862; Legislative Assembly, *Journals*, *op. cit.*, 1860-1866; PAC, MG 24, B40, George Brown Papers, Vol. 5, pp. 1021-1026, Brown to Anne (wife), August 28, 1864; Eggleston, *op. cit.*, pp. 127-130; Hodgetts, *op. cit.*, pp. 198-204.

[3]Edward Whelan, *The Union of the British Provinces*, edited and with an introduction by D.C. Harvey (Toronto: Garden City Press, [1865] 1927), pp. 137-138. See also (Ottawa) *Union*, November 5, 1865.

[4](Halifax) *Morning Chronicle*, June 9, 1866.

[5]*Ibid*.

[6]PAC, MG 27, I, B1, Monck Papers, F.W.A. Bruce (British Legation, Washington) to Governor General Monck, September 8, 1866. The informant told Bruce that ''They have all the ammunition they require for the destruction of Parliament Buildings. It has been sent to Ogdensburgh, New York, in care of Dr. McMonagh. They have 1,000 lbs powder, 50 10 inch shells, & 6 torpedoes each capable of containing 200 lbs powder which are to be placed in the air ventilators or conductors leading from the banks of the Ottawa river under ground and under the buildings for the purpose of airing the Halls of Assembly. The ammunition will be kept on this side [of] the [boundary] line until they [Fenian raiders] are about to make the move on Goderick, Sarnia, etc.'' (*Ibid.*, Bruce to Monck, September 18, 1866) Two members of the attack group lived in Ottawa (*Ibid.*, Bruce to Monck, September 9, 1866).

[7]Opinion of leading politician Thomas D'Arcy McGee (*Ibid.*, McGee to Lady Monck, June 4, 1866). Brault, *op. cit.*, p. 153, relates that one newspaper in the United States thought that Ottawa's defences were excellent since any ''invaders would inevitably be lost in the woods trying to find it.''

[8]PAC, MG 24, B40, George Brown Papers, Vol. 6, pp. 1377, Brown to Anne, December 14, 1865.

[9]PAC, MG 24, B40, George Brown Papers, Vol. 7, Monck to Brown, May 17, 1866.

[10]PAC, MG 24, I9, Hill Collection, Vol. 20, p. 5338, G.H. Perry to Daniel McLachlin, June 12, 1866.

[11]PAC, MG 24, B40, George Brown Papers, Vol. 7, p. 1440, Brown to Anne, June 14, 1866.

[12]C.C.J. Bond, ''The Canadian Government Comes to Ottawa, 1865-1866,'' *Ontario History*, Vol. LV, no. 1 (1963), pp. 23-34.

[13]*Brockville Recorder*, July 5, 1866.

[14]Clause 16 of ''The British North America Act, 1867.''

INDEX TO THE DOCUMENTS

Chapter III

Chapter V

Chapter VI

Chapter VII

Chapter VIII

SELECTED BIBLIOGRAPHY FROM CITED WORKS

Books

Brault, Lucien. *Ottawa Old and New*. Ottawa: Ottawa Historical Information Institute, 1946.

Careless, J.M.S. *Brown of the Globe*. 2 volumes. Toronto: Macmillan Company of Canada, 1959, 1963.

———. *The Union of the Canadas: The Growth of Canadian Institutions 1841-1857*. Toronto: McClelland and Stewart, 1967.

Cook, F. *The Struggle for the Capital of Canada*. Ottawa: By the author, 1938.

Cornell, Paul G. *The Alignment of Political Groups in Canada, 1841-1867*. Toronto: University of Toronto Press, Canadian Studies in History and Government No. 3, 1962.

Creighton, Donald. *The Empire of the St. Lawrence*. Toronto: Macmillan Company of Canada [1937] 1970.

———. *John A. Macdonald*. 2 volumes. Toronto: Macmillan Company of Canada, 1952, 1955.

de Blij, Harm. *Systematic Political Geography*. New York: John Wiley and Sons, 1973.

Dent, J.C. *The Last Forty Years: The Union of 1841 to Confederation*. Toronto: McClelland and Stewart, Carleton Library No. 62, [1881], 1972.

Doughty, Arthur, editor. *The Elgin-Grey Papers 1846-1852*. 4 volumes. Ottawa: King's Printer, 1937.

Eggleston, Wilfred. *The Queen's Choice*. Ottawa: The Queen's Printer, 1961.

Goheen, Peter G. *Victorian Toronto, 1850 to 1900: Pattern and Process of Growth*. Chicago: University of Chicago, Department of Geography, Research Paper No. 127, 1970.

Harris, R. Cole and Warkentin, John. *Canada Before Confederation: A Study in Historical Geography*. Toronto: Oxford University Press, 1974.

Hodgetts, J.E. *Pioneer Public Service: An Administrative History of*

United Canada, 1841-1867. Toronto: University of Toronto Press, 1955.

Kerr, D.G.C. *Sir Edmund Head: A Scholarly Governor*. Toronto: University of Toronto Press, 1954.

Kesterton, W.H. *A History of Journalism in Canada*. Toronto: McClelland and Stewart, Carleton Library No. 36, 1967.

Knapland, P., editor. *Letters from Lord Sydenham to Lord John Russell*. London: George Allen and Unwin Ltd., 1931.

Knight, David B. *A Capital for Canada: Conflict and Compromise in the Nineteenth Century*. Chicago: University of Chicago, Department of Geography, Research Series, 1977.

Monet, J. *The Last Cannon Shot: A Study of French-Canadian Nationalism, 1837-1850*. Toronto: University of Toronto Press, 1969.

Morton, W.L. *The Critical Years: The Union of British North America 1857-1873*. Toronto: McClelland and Stewart, 1964.

Nish, Elizabeth, editor. *Legislative Assembly Debates of the Legislative Assembly of United Canada, 1841-1866*. Montreal Presses de l'Ecole des hautes etudes commerciales, 1970- .

Scott, R.W. *The Choice of the Capital: Reminiscences Revived on the Fiftieth Anniversary of the Selection of Ottawa as the Capital of Canada by Her Late Majesty*. Ottawa: The Mortimer Company, 1907.

Spelt, J. *Urban Development in South-Central Ontario*. Toronto: McClelland and Stewart, Carleton Library No. 57, [1955], 1972.

Wood, J. David, editor. *Perspectives on Landscape and Settlement in Nineteenth Century Ontario*. Toronto: McClelland and Stewart, Carleton Library No. 91, 1975.

Articles

Bond, C.C.J. "The Canadian Government Comes to Ottawa, 1865-1866." *Ontario History*, Vol. LV, no. 1 (1963), pp. 23-34.

Gentilcore, R.L. "Settlement." *Ontario*. Gentilcore, R.L. editor. Toronto: University of Toronto Press, Studies in Canadian Geography Series, 1972, pp. 23-44.

Gibson, James A. "Sir Edmund Head's Memorandum on the Choice of Ottawa as the Seat of Government of Canada." *Canadian Historical Review*, Vol. XVI, no. 4 (December, 1935), pp. 411-417.

———. "The Choosing of the Capital of Canada." *British Columbia Historical Quarterly*, Vol. XVII, nos. 1 and 2 (1953), pp. 78-85.

———. "How Ottawa Became the Capital of Canada." *Ontario History*, Vol. XLVI, no. 4 (1954), pp. 213-222.

Groulx, L. "Le choix de la capitale au Canada." *Revue d'histoire de l'Amerique Francaise*, (1951-1952), pp. 521-530.

Harris, R. Cole. "Historical Geography in Canada." *Canadian Geographer*, Vol. XI, no. 4 (1967), pp. 235-250.

Hodgetts, J.E. "The Civil Service When Kingston was the Capital of Canada." *Historic Kingston*, Vol. 5 (1956).

Knight, David B. "Impress of Authority and Ideology on Landscape: A Review of Some Unanswered Questions." *Tijdschrift voor Economische en Sociale Geografie*, Vol. LXII, no. 6 (November/December, 1971), pp. 383-387.

———. " 'Boosterism' and Locational Analysis, Or One Man's Swan is Another Man's Goose." *Urban History Review*, No. 3-73 (February, 1974), pp. 10-16. [Traces idea, from 1820's to 1840, to have Bytown (Ottawa) become capital.]

Knight, David B. and Burrows, Susan. "Centrality By Degrees: A 19th Century Canadian's Measurement for Central Location." *The Canadian Cartographer*, Vol. 12, no. 2 (December, 1975), pp. 109-120.

Marshall, John U. "Geography's Contribution to the Historical Study of Urban Canada." *Urban History Review*, No. 1-73 (May, 1973), pp. 15-24.

McLean, Mary. "Early Parliamentary Reporting in Upper Canada." *Canadian Historical Review*, Vol. XX, no. 4 (1939), pp. 378-391.

Pierce, D.J. and Pritchett, J.P. "The Choice of Kingston as the Capital of Canada." *Canadian Historical Association, Annual Report 1929*, pp. 57-63.

Spate, O.H.K. "Factors in the Development of Capital Cities." *Geographical Review*, Vol. XXXII, no. 4 (October, 1942), pp. 622-631.